The Conditioned Mind
Overcoming the Crippling Effects of Sin and Guilt

Michael J. Mannia

CROSSLINK
PUBLISHING

The Conditioned Mind

꒰ CrossLink Publishing
꒰ www.crosslinkpublishing.com

ISBN 978-1-936746-71-2
Library of Congress Control Number: 2013946422

Much gratitude and a heartfelt thank you to:
My Lord and Savior—Jesus Christ—You have blessed me beyond
measure; daughters Taylor and Alexis—for your inspiration; my
mother and siblings—for your love and support; Lois Hudson—for
editing and encouragement; along with the many brothers and sisters
in Christ, who, over the years, have welcomed me into the midst of
their brokenness and trusted my counsel as I leaned on the Lord for
understanding and guidance.

This book is dedicated to:
My bride, Jeannelle. Your love never ceases to amaze me!

Contents

Introduction *The Bottom Drops Out* vii

1. – *God's Intent for Humanity* 1

2. – *Two The Complexity of Sin* 21

3. – *Chapter Three Conditioned through Sin* 41

4. – *Chapter Four Breaking through Denial* 75

5. – *Chapter Five Matters of Repression* 121

6. – *Chapter Six Why We Rationalize* 161

7. – *Chapter Seven Resisting the Devil* 185

8. – *Chapter Eight Christ the Shepherd, Mediator,*
   High Priest, and King 229

9. – *Chapter Nine The Ministry of the Holy Spirit* 259

10. – *Chapter Ten Repentance* 289

Notes 303

Introduction

The Bottom Drops Out

For you, O God, tested us; you refined us like silver.
You brought us into prison and laid burdens on our
backs. You let men ride over our heads; we went
through fire and water, but you brought
us to a place of abundance.

Psalm 66:10 – 12

The year was 1969. Mankind first set foot on the moon. Richard Milhous Nixon succeeded Lyndon Baines Johnson as the thirty-seventh President of the United States during the turbulent times of the Vietnam War. The last issue of *The Saturday Evening Post* landed on magazine stands after 147 years of publishing. Sirhan Sirhan confessed to killing presidential candidate Robert F. Kennedy. Yes, there was much happening in 1969. From Yasser Arafat's election as leader of the Palestine Liberation Organization (PLO) to the death of former President Dwight D. Eisenhower, the world was plodding along on its tumultuous course. But of all the events that took place that year, there is one that has left an indelible mark upon my life. The date was April 28—a beautiful spring day in northern California, with a high in the upper seventies, blue skies, and a light breeze. At the edge of suburbia, a woman sat on the step of her front porch. She watched as her two-year-old son played with a tetherball while pork chops simmered on the stove in the waning hours of the afternoon.

The name given to her at birth was Bernice, but she never really cared for it. Everyone knew her as Bee. For sure, she had seen her share of hard times. As a child, Bee grew up during the Great Depression. Her father was a good provider and a loving man, but he was also an alcoholic. Her mother suffered from depression. During her teen years, Bee watched her classmates head off to fight a war in far-off lands. Some of them would not return alive. In early adulthood, she moved from a small town in Indiana to Chicago and attended nurses' training. It was there, at St. Anne's Hospital, where Bee witnessed both the beginning and end of life on several occasions. In 1969, at the threshold of midlife, she lived a busy but fulfilling life with her husband and eight children.

That April day, as Bee watched her son play with the tetherball, her husband returned home from a jog at the local high school track. He pulled the car halfway up into the driveway, and she got up to meet him.

"Gene, have you seen your son hit the ball?" The man looked over at the boy as his blond hair wisped in the breeze. "Hit the ball, son. Go ahead, hit it. You can do it," the father encouraged. Realizing he had his parents' undivided attention, the boy swung at the ball with all the vigor of a two-year-old. His parents smiled with pride, and both agreed that for such a young guy, he could really give it a good whack.

"Bee, I feel really dizzy," Gene said suddenly.

She looked at him alarmed.

"Hang on to me and I'll get you into the house!"

As they took the first step together, Gene collapsed, taking Bee down with him. She managed to hold his head and keep it from hitting the cement driveway. He was already unconscious. Gene began to convulse. Years of training as a nurse had prepared Bee to handle the most intense of situations, but nothing could have readied her for this day. This was different—this was *her* husband of nineteen years—the father of her children. In a state of shock and horror, she ran into the house and telephoned a neighbor.

"Joe, get down here quick! Gene's passed out on the driveway!"

She raced back outside with her heart pounding wildly in her chest, feeling as though it would burst. Time seemed to move in slow motion, like she was running against a current in waist-deep water.

When Bee returned to the scene, her mind took a double-take at the surreal sight of her son sitting by his father's head, laughing as he patted him on the face, trying to rouse him. It was like a living nightmare—one she desperately wanted to wake up from, but could not. She rushed to Gene's side and attempted to rouse him, as her neighbor sprinted up the driveway.

"Joe, help me get Gene into the house!"

But as they reached to lift him, she realized he was not breathing. Bee cried out to one of her daughters who was watching from the window as the horrific event unfolded. "Sandi, quick, call the Fire Department!" To Joe she said, "He has no pulse! We've got to do something!"

While CPR was a fairly new technique back in 1969, Bee had read about it in a nursing magazine and had actually practiced it using a pillow just months prior. Joe had watched firemen use it to resuscitate a young boy who had been found at the bottom of a neighbor's swimming pool. The two of them, although terrified, began CPR on Gene's limp body.

The sirens from the emergency vehicles announced their approach, but it seemed an eternity passed before they arrived—the fire truck first, followed by the ambulance. Neighbors rushed to the scene to assist with the children. Bee and her second oldest daughter, Suzanne, left with Gene in the ambulance. By the time they arrived at the hospital, his skin color had turned purple, and Bee knew he was dead. The ER team attempted to resuscitate him, but it was no use. At 6:15 p.m., Eugene Lawrence Mannia—*my father*—was pronounced dead, just fifty-six days after his forty-second birthday. I was the two-year-old who had been playing with the tetherball, the one who tried to rouse his father on the driveway. The next day, the words "arteriosclerotic heart disease" would be typed on my father's death certificate. A complete blockage of one of his arteries proved fatal. We laid him to rest on May 1, 1969. He was survived by his wife and eight children, his father and mother, an older brother and younger sister, as well as two nephews and nieces.

My father's death was like a bomb that shattered our sense of security; it blew our hopes and dreams apart. Our lives were forever changed; none of us would be the same. Following the aftermath of my father's untimely passing, we did what we could to pick up the broken pieces of our lives. It was about survival from that point forward. Each day melded into another, as if a thick fog had permeated our lives. My mother returned to her profession of nursing. Eventually, she found herself following in her own father's footsteps of alcoholism. As with many alcoholics, she was not entirely dysfunctional. She never drank on the job, was always the consummate professional while on duty, and eventually earned a promotion to director of nurses. But night after night, she came home and numbed her fears and anguish with booze. She did so for almost fifteen years, until my siblings and I sought professional help that culminated in an intervention. The outcome: twenty-eight years of sobriety at the time of this writing. Praise God!

Through the death of our father and alcoholism of our mother, my siblings and I learned well how to employ the self-deceptive practices of denial, repression, and rationalization. In doing so, each of us unwittingly became conditioned to think and behave in ways that were never a part of God's plan for our lives.

To one degree or another, every person has been (or will be) affected by life's tragedies, along with sin and guilt (their own, as well as that of others). The questions are: How have we learned to cope with the affects of such matters? Are our modes of coping functional that they will bring us closer to God? Or are they dysfunctional that they will drive us further away from our heavenly Father? The more we practice dysfunctional ways of coping, the more entrenched they become. We are then conditioned, and thus imprisoned, to a deceptive system of belief. To move off of our maladaptive modes of coping, we need to return to the core issues of our life from which the thought and behavior first developed. Doing so allows us to grieve. As we grieve, we develop awareness and acceptance of key factors; bringing healing and growth into our relationship with the Lord and others. In doing so, we are more apt to operate in the power, love, and soundness of mind afforded us through God's Spirit.

I have written this book to help readers overcome the crippling effects of sin and guilt. Part One is all about the power of sin, and the grip it can have on us. Part Two covers our self-deceptive practices where sin is concerned. Part Three aims to set the reader free from the crippling effects of sin and guilt. The biblical principles covered here are being utilized in our Christian counseling center at Kingdom

Community Ministries (www.kcmcounseling.com). It is my sincere prayer that you, too, will experience freedom from the crippling effects of sin and guilt, and that your life will be filled with an abundance of love, joy, and peace.

Chapter One

God's Intent for Humanity

And so we know and rely on the love God has for us.
God is love. Whoever lives in love lives in God, and God in him.

1 John 4:16

I t is hard to know where you are going if you do not know where you have been. This might sound like double-talk, but this statement actually makes sense. Perhaps another way to look at it is this: it is hard to get to where God wants you to be if you do not realize how your past is tied to your life today. For instance, I have made a conscious decision to practice sobriety in my life. What helped me make this decision is the fact that alcoholism can be traced back at least two generations in my family. Looking back on the generations helped me understand how generational sin has impacted my life. But this look back was not easy. The sin of others perpetrated upon me was a painful matter, and working through it was no walk in the park. Equally important was my assessment of my own sins and the pain I caused others. But with the help of the Lord, I was able to overcome. As a result, I have chosen not to continue these generational patterns of sin. So we see that looking back on the past can play an important role in better understanding how sin and guilt affects our life.

To further illustrate my point, consider the following: while your life here on earth may have started decades ago, God conceived of you before the beginning of time. Think about it: God knew of you before He formed the cosmos! God has always known you, and He has always loved you. Read what King David wrote:

> For you created my inmost being; you knit me together in my mother's womb. I praise you because I am fearfully and wonderfully made; your works are wonderful, I know that full well. My frame was not hidden from you when I was made in the secret place. When I was woven together in the depths of the earth, your eyes saw my unformed body. All the days ordained for me were written in your book before one of them came to be.[1]

The notion that our heavenly Father creates our inner being—our personality features, traits, and spiritual gifts—demonstrates just how unique we are. Nobody has ever existed with our exact combination of features, traits, and gifts—and nobody ever will. His forming of us in these ways also signifies an important timing to our life. Such specificity points to a wonderful purpose, one that involves a special role.

These are concepts the devil very much wants to thwart in the life of the Christian. Do you have a sense of your purpose and worth? If so, do you live your life in the *power* of this purpose and worth? If you answered no to either of these questions, or if you are unsure of what the answers are, then discovering what is stymieing you is vitally important to live an effective life for Christ. To do so, you are going to have to take a serious look back on your life. For some, this is likely to elicit painful emotions. But take heart, for God is with you. You can be rest assured our heavenly Father wants you to overcome the crippling effects of sin and guilt. Earlier in his life, King David wrote: "If the LORD delights in a man's way, he makes his steps firm."[2] This is not to say our Creator acts like a puppeteer. We do have free will. But without a doubt, God is always working things out for good.[3] I am confident He will do the same with any unresolved issue in your life.

God's Intent for the Human Race

Note the order of God's creative acts in the first chapter of Genesis. Verses 1 – 25 list all that our Creator put into place prior to the creation of Adam:

1. The "heavens and the earth," i.e., the cosmos from a singularity, resulting in the space-time continuum (v. 1)
2. The "formless" earth, i.e., when earth was covered with water (v. 2)

3. "Light," from our sun, was permitted to shine through thick atmospheric gasses, and thus began many key processes for the creation of life (v. 3 – 5)

4. The "expanse," i.e., earth's atmosphere, developed from the presence of water and other properties (v. 6 – 8)

5. Land masses were formed, which separate the seas and oceans (v. 9, 10)

6. Plant life created (v. 11 – 13)

7. Meteorological forces which make up earth's weather and seasons were set in motion (v. 14 – 19)

8. Biological life in the oceans and skies was formed (v. 20 – 23)

9. Biological life on land was created (v. 24, 25)

According to the Scripture all of this happened prior to creating Adam; humanity had nothing to do with the implementation of God's plan for creation. We are not so much the master of our own destiny as we like to believe; rather, we exist as part of a bigger plan—*God's plan.* And if we exist as part of God's plan, then our life is of great importance.

If we continue on with the chronology listed above, we will find a crucial shift in linguistics occurring at verse 26: "Then God said, 'Let us make man in our image, in our likeness, and let them rule over the fish of the sea and the birds of the air, over the livestock, over all the earth, and over all the creatures that move along the ground.'"[4] Here we have an intimate look into God's nature. Prior to this verse,

God said: "Let *there*..." or "Let *the*...;" but it was at this point that God revealed His triune nature by stating: "Let *us*..." It was no small matter that God first revealed His three-part nature when He was about to create Adam. It was there, at the creation of mankind, where God intimately consulted with Himself. In perfect unity and love, He infused His likeness into the human race. God's intent has always been to share with us the unity and love experienced within the Trinity. Regarding this point, theologian John Wesley wrote:

> He [Adam] had habitual conformity of all his natural powers to the whole will of God. His understanding saw divine things clearly; and there were no errors in his knowledge: his will complied readily and universally with the will of God; without [reluctance]: his affections were all regular, and he had no inordinate appetites or passions: his thoughts were easily fixed to the best subjects, and there was no vanity or ungovernableness in them. And all the inferior powers were subject to the dictates of the superior. Thus holy, thus happy, were our first parents, in having the image of God upon them.[5]

As Wesley noted, until sin entered the picture, Adam and Eve's will complied with God's. It might be hard to fathom such unification with our Creator, but I believe we humans hunger for this degree of connection with the Lord. Nonetheless, we struggle with willfulness;

our desire to strike out on our own and manage our life as we see fit. More specifically, we struggle with the notion that surrendering too much to God may result in our losing too much of our self.

The tie-in with our life is clear. The Creator of the cosmos saw fit to extend His love to all of humanity. This was not only true at the creation of Adam; it remains true today. I believe each of us, at some point, experience this truth through brief but significantly unifying episodes with the Lord.[6] It might be during a quiet time of prayer, or while gazing up at the night sky, sensing a brief, but profound connectedness to Him. Yes, His intent is the same today as it has always been—to enter into an intimate relationship with each and every one of us. But we must strive to be aware of how the devil has worked to hinder and pervert this relationship. Key events shape and influence our systems of belief. It is imperative that we determine if these systems of belief bring us closer to God, or if they drive us apart.

The Significance of Needs

In the second chapter of Genesis, we find God placing Adam in the Garden of Eden to manage it (v. 15). If we work from the premise that God's nature is one of love and order, we can then deduce Adam was brilliant. How so? Consider the fact that God would be neither loving nor orderly if He placed Adam in the Garden and gave him charge to manage its ecology, but did not ensure he had the knowledge and expertise to carry out the charge. Such an act would be mean-spirited and disorderly.

So we come to see that Adam was not some idiot bumbling through the Garden. To manage its ecology, he would have had been the first physicist, chemist, biologist, botanist, and more. There he was, communing with God, nothing hindering him in his relationship with his Creator; and there, too, was God, communing with Adam, imbuing him with the knowledge and expertise required to fulfill his purpose.

Given all of this, it is rather surprising to read in Genesis 2:18 that Adam was still in need of something. What could it have been? More specifically, where did this need come from? After all, Adam was fulfilling his God-given purpose. It is highly likely he would have experienced a great deal of satisfaction in his relationship with God, and from the work he performed within the Father's creation. So the question is begged again: where did the need for Eve come from? The answer is found in the understanding that it was God who placed this need in Adam; yet not just in Adam but in all of us as well. God hardwires us with essential needs; in doing so, He ensures that the motivations required for the fulfillment of our purpose are made available to us. For instance, God created us to be social beings; He knew that by wiring us with a need for relationship, we would be motivated to seek connection with Him and others. So, we come to understand that Adam needed Eve, because God placed the need there in the first place, setting in motion the means by which His love would multiply throughout humanity.

Clearly, each of us has needs. We need air, food, and water. We need purpose and vision.[7] But we also need to be nurtured through the love of others. Volumes have already been written on the topic of needs. For the purpose of this study, I will focus on what I believe to be two of our greatest needs and their significance in our life.

Our Need for Love

There is no greater extent to which we can relate with the Father and others than through love. It is by love that the Law is fulfilled. Love edifies. Within love, we find patience and kindness; but we do not find envy, boastfulness, or pride. There is no rudeness or self-seeking in love; but there is self-control, and no record is kept of wrongs. Through love, we rejoice in the truth, but do not delight in evil. Where there is love, there is protection, trust, hope, and perseverance. Indeed, the more we know the love of Christ, the more we are filled with the fullness of God.[8]

It is not a question of whether we *want* to be loved; rather, we *need* to be loved. Additionally, we need to reciprocate love. We need to feel loved as much as we need to love others. From this perspective, we can see that Adam not only needed to give and receive love with God, he also needed to experience reciprocal love with other humans. Thus, we find Eve entering the picture. Created from one of his own ribs, Adam stated when he first saw her that she was "bone of my bones and flesh of my flesh...."[9] Here he stressed the point of Eve's nature being more equal to his own than not. The relationship between Adam and Eve was very much representative of the unified and equitable relationship shared between the Father, Son, and Holy Spirit. Our first parents were unified with purpose. While each had their own unique qualities and position of authority, together they complemented one another. Until sin entered the picture, the love Adam and Eve shared was selfless. Within the confines of their relationship, they were to experience and represent God's nature for the next generation. Our Father has always desired godly offspring.[10] And so it was to be—each successive generation would initially come to know the loving nature of God through their parents' representation of that very love.

Our need to love and to be loved is so significant, so central in our life, that many of the ills faced in the world can be attributed to a lack of fulfillment of this all-important need. In his book, *Will and Spirit,* Dr. Gerald May, M.D. aptly observed:

> [R]egardless of how our parents actually did love us, as children we certainly felt more loved at some times than at others, the difference having been determined by our behavior and by the vicissitudes of our parents' moods. We were faced, then, with having to adjust to the disparity between an inner longing for unconditional love and an outer experience of conditional love. How we made this adjustment helped to determine our personality style....[11]

For example, let us say you are growing up in a home where your parents place a high value on a healthy degree of confidence in your God-given gifts. There are times when you turn to your father and mother for assistance and guidance. In these instances, your parents encourage you to first attempt to figure the matter out on your own. While your mom and dad are encouraging in this way, they are also reasonable. Both of them have a good sense of what challenges you can handle and are always found to be waiting in the wings (so to speak); ensuring that if you fail you can count on them to step in and provide support. Never do you get the sense that they love you any less because you attempted to find the answer but could not do so on your own. As you mature, a confidence grows within you, knowing that it is okay to tackle new challenges, and that, if you fall short, your parents will not withhold their love. Over the course of time, your personality traits of resourcefulness and sufficiency are strengthened. In this example, we would say there is minimal disparity between your inner longing for your parents' unconditional love and your outer experience of their conditional love. In other words, you sense that your parents' love for you is more unconditional than not. This dynamic is then likely to be present in your relationship with the Lord.

Let's look at this same scenario, only we will increase (to a moderate degree) the disparity between your inner longing for your parents' unconditional love and your outer experience of their conditional love. While supportive of your attempts to develop confidence, they are critical if you fail to find the answer on your own. During these times, your father and mother's criticalness stymies your sense of being loved unconditionally. Instead of strengthening your traits of resourcefulness and self-sufficiency, your parents' approach inhibits maturity in this area of your personality. As a result, you might tend to develop traits more akin to perfectionism, i.e., compulsive, controlling, with exacting will power. This is not to say anyone growing up in this type of scenario *will* develop perfectionistic personality traits; rather, it is one example of a myriad of dysfunctional traits we are apt to develop.

Finally, let us increase the disparity between your inner longing for your parents' unconditional love and your outer experience of their conditional love. Again, your father and mother place a high degree of importance on your being confident in your abilities, only, in this case, whether you succeed or not, your parents are condemning of your actions. In this scenario, you are damned if you do, damned if you do not. Rarely is love experienced, and, when it is, it is more conditional than not. In such an environment, you might be apt to develop a personality trait of dominance, i.e., forceful, aggressive, and stubborn. Then again, it could go the other way with the development of a trait of apprehension, i.e., self-doubt, anxiety, and being guilt prone.

So we come to see that the less conditional love is, the more positive love's impact on our life would be, and the greater is its propensity for the healthy development of our God-given personality traits. Conversely, the more conditional love is, the more we are driven toward traits that are not a part of God's plan for our life.

Our Need for Security

While love is the highest of emotional needs, I believe security runs a close second. To fulfill this need, three factors must be satisfied. The first is *routine,* which can be defined as a regular, unvarying procedure.[12] In our relationships, routine helps to bring order to our life. When we experience a healthy balance of order, we are able to trust to greater degrees. When we trust, we feel it is safer to be authentic—to be real. We need to sense that those we are in relationship with are being authentic with us as well. Routine helps to satisfy this need. For instance, if our actions remain consistent with our commitments, it will become routine for others to trust that we are genuine in our words. If I routinely arrive on time and prepared for meetings, my actions prove I am reliable and worthy of other people's trust. But if I routinely arrive late and unprepared, my actions prove I am unreliable. In the beginning, Adam and Eve were capable of complete authenticity. They not only knew their purpose within God's creation, but they were fully secure and satisfied in their roles. Selfless in their thoughts and actions, they lived out God's character by routinely being loving, joyous, and peaceful. Because these qualities were routine, they fully trusted the Father and one another.

The second factor associated with security is *familiarity*. The word *familiar* is derived from the Latin root *familia*, which means "family." Webster's defines *familiar* as "friendly" (informal), or "intimate"; "closely acquainted with."[13] In the context of relationships, familiarity enables us to become more intimate with others. Regardless of the type of relationship—husband/wife, parent/child, older/younger sibling, manager/subordinate—we need to sense we are familiar with the other person's modes of thinking and means of behavior. But if this dynamic cannot be achieved, then our sense of security will be hampered. Prior to the introduction of sin, Adam and Eve would have experienced the utmost in familiarity. Because they were not inhibited in their relationship with God, they felt completely secure in who they were. Adam and Eve were solid in their love relationship with the Father, as well as with each other. With such familiarity, they were capable of complete intimacy.

Within the context of relationships, routine and familiarity enable us to more accurately predict how people we relate with will behave. *Predictability*, then, is the third factor involved with our need for security. When we predict, we state what we believe will happen prior to it happening.[14] Predictability allows us to be more prepared for what is coming. The more routine our behavior, the more others will be able to accurately guess how we are likely to behave. The closer acquainted people are with our thoughts and feelings, the more effectively they can predict our next actions. In turn, this helps to satisfy our need for security. Adam and Eve were secure in their relationship with their Creator, as well as with each other, because they could accurately predict that love would be extended unconditionally.

Striving For Needs

In all of this, we come to see the significance of love and security. Regardless of the circumstances, to one degree or another, the motivations for our behaviors are primarily rooted in these two essential needs. This is not to say that these will be the only sources of motivation for our behaviors, but our need for love and security always factor in. When we sense a lack in our needs, we will strive to get them met. The question is: will we strive in functional or dysfunctional ways?

This striving is first and foremost undertaken in our key relationships. The less successful we are at fulfilling our needs, the greater is our propensity to develop dysfunctional personality traits. For example, the child who grows up in a home with an abusive parent experiences a lack of love and security. In such situations, some children will develop tendencies toward psychopathic behavior. Not that they will necessarily become psychopathic by definition, rather they will *tend* to cope with life through anger and defiance as a means to avoid feeling vulnerable. This is mainly true because love involves vulnerability. When the association is made that love equals pain, the tendency is to develop coping mechanisms aimed at avoiding the pain.

These types of children learn how to minimize vulnerability by keeping others at arm's length through anger and defiance.

In keeping with our example of the abused child, striving to get their needs met through performance and accomplishment is likely leaning them toward obsessive coping mechanisms. Here distorted ways of thinking can lead into entrenched modes of coping involving control. Overt forms might involve manipulation or coercion, while covert forms might involve caretaking, rescuing, and enabling.

Still further, children who develop the notion that their need for love might be won from their abusive parent are the children who lean more toward emotionalism. Such coping mechanisms can then develop into distorted ways of thinking, like perfectionism and unwarranted guilt. By attempting to be perfect, this overly emotional individual believes they might earn the love of others. But this line of thinking is a setup of the devil. It is a belief system doomed to fail because nobody, save Christ, is perfect. So this type of individual lives with a pervasive sense of guilt, because nothing they do turns out to be perfect.

God wired us with needs so that we would live out the purpose for which He designed us. Our Creator is not only a God of love and order; He is a God of multiplication as well. By creating us with needs like love and security, He knew we would then strive after relationships. It is only in relationship—first with God, and then with others—that these two particular needs are effectively met. As we pursue our needs for love and security, the possibility is then present for the multiplication of love. Thus, the love of God becomes multiplied through our life as we relate with others. In all of this, our needs will either drive us toward our Father, or they will drive us toward works of the flesh. The crux of the matter is determined by how we are conditioned to think, feel, and behave.

Summary

Our Creator has always known of us and has always loved us. He formed our innermost being—our personality for a very unique and important purpose. God fashioned us with a special set of characteristics so that we would fit perfectly into His plan. Our heavenly Father created the cosmos, because He wanted to fashion a space wherein He could extend His love. We call that space humanity. At the very point He chose to create Adam, His intimate, triune nature was revealed. With this revelation, we come to understand that God is relational and desires to have an intimate, loving relationship with you and me.

There is purpose in the way our Creator has fashioned each one of us. As a means to live out this purpose, God wires us with needs. Of all the needs we have, love is the most significant; it drives us toward fulfillment of our purpose like nothing else. Love motivates us to pursue relationship with God and others. When love is not extended in the ways God intended, significant issues can, and often do, arise. Feeling unloved can manifest into maladaptive tendencies, wherein self-affirmation is stifled. In such cases, self-hate begins to breed, and eventually this hate may become directed at society. When love is lacking, some are apt to develop a perfectionistic type of personality, where they hold fast to the belief that love can only be acquired through performance and accomplishment. The result is an attempt to willfully control people, places, and things. Others develop an apprehensive personality trait, bent toward self-doubt, worry, and guilt.

Our need for security runs a close second to our need for love. One of the factors associated with feeling secure is routine. We need a certain degree of regular, unvarying procedure in our life, or we will experience insecurity. In relationships, routine can enable trust because we can more accurately predict how others are going to behave and vice versa. When people routinely show their love for us, we come to trust their love is real. Again, the same is true of our loving actions toward others. Yet, when it comes to feeling secure, more than routine is required. We also need familiarity in our life, especially in our key relationships. When we are familiar with someone, we are more intimately acquainted with that person. This is why communication is vitally important in our relationships. Honest communication produces familiarity. The greater the degrees of routine and familiarity, the greater our ability to accurately predict how others are likely to behave. More predictability offers greater opportunities for security.

From all of this, we can better understand the significance of our needs, especially for love and security. When our needs are satisfactorily met, we are more successful in the fulfillment of our

God-given purpose. However, when we face challenges in getting our needs met, we also face challenges in the fulfillment of our purpose. If our needs go unmet to any significant degree, we become desperate. In our desperation, we are apt to behave in desperate ways. We might lash out in anger, seek to control others, or perhaps deny that our needs even matter in hopes of feeling loved by others.

God's intent for humanity is the same today as it has always been: to enter into a love relationship with us. To experience a close, intimate relationship with the Lord, we must first develop an awareness of what our needs are and the degree to which they are being met. Once we develop this awareness, we must then work to accept important truths. For instance, we might acknowledge our need for intimacy, but also have to accept that we fear such a thing because intimacy creates vulnerability. In this case, we can ask the Father to lead us into even greater awareness of why we fear intimacy. As we become more aware, we can then work to accept the truth, such as: we were abused, or perhaps someone we loved died, and now we fear getting close to others. As we work to accept the truth and process through our pain, we heal and grow. Such healing and growth enables us to live more for God's will. While this process of awareness, acceptance, and implementation of the Father's will sounds easy enough, more often than not, it proves to be one of our greatest challenges in life.

Opportunity for Reflection

1. Reflect on God's intent for the human race. What does this mean in your own relationship with the Lord?

   _____

   _____

2. How comfortable are you with the fact that God wired you with needs? Do you currently have needs that are not sufficiently being met in your key relationships?

   _____

   _____

3. In what ways have you striven to get your needs met that have proven to be:

   Successful:

   _____

   _____

   Unsuccessful:

   _____

   _____

Chapter Two

The Complexity of Sin

"Everyone who sins breaks the law; in fact, sin is lawlessness."

1 John 3:4

C hapter One helped us to see that God desires to have an intimate relationship with each one of us. The needs He wired us with drive us toward relationship. But our Creator is interested in more than a casual connection; there is a deeper purpose for the relationship He seeks. That purpose is love. Our Father in heaven loves us unconditionally. His desire is for us to love Him with all we have, as well as love our neighbors as we love ourselves.[1] As Christians, our love for Christ is the surest sign of faith we can display.[2] Indeed, Jesus said, "If you love me, keep my commands."[3] The challenge is that we are not always sure what God's will is in every moment of our lives. Even if we could know the Father's will moment by moment, none of us is perfect. Just like Adam and Eve, we, too, at times will choose our will over God's will. The apostle Peter informed us that love covers a multitude of sins.[4] As Christians, we praise Jesus Christ for His love, grace, and mercy. Yet we would do well to recognize that sin acts as a contaminant to our soul, and always carries with it the *potential* for us to become conditioned to think and behave in ways that fall outside the Father's will.

As noted in Chapter One, God imbued Adam and Eve with a brilliance of mind as a means to carry out His charge to manage the earth's ecology. But God also would have needed to give them something besides brilliant minds; they would need authority to manage His creation. We find evidence of this in the following passage:

> Then God said, "Let us make man in our image, in our
> likeness, and let them rule over the fish of the sea and the
> birds of the air, over the livestock, over all the earth, and
> over all the creatures that move along the ground." So
> God created man in his own image, in the image of God
> he created him; male and female he created them.[5]

The term "rule over" applies to dominion, which in Hebrew is known as *radaw* (raw-daw'), which means "to subjugate" or "bring under control."[6] Adam and Eve were given the right of dominion over God's creation here on earth. All that He had put in place ecologically was in subjection to their authority, which was affirmed through the Creator's spoken words: "let them rule over."

Not only were Adam and Eve brilliant and given authority to manage the earth's ecology, they were also created in God's image.

This is an exceedingly important point in relation to morality. The Hebrew word for image is *tselem* (tseh'-lem), which means "to shade."[7] Figuratively, *tselem* relates to illusion or resemblance. Adam and Eve—and therefore we, too—were created as representative figures of God, which begs the question: what characteristics were Adam and Eve *most* representative of? Perhaps we might come to a better understanding by examining what they were not representative of. First, they did not represent God in the *power* of their physical form. Our Creator is not bound by physics, i.e., matter, energy, motion, and force; rather, He is omnipotent. God created physics, and He is intimately involved with the forces found therein; however, He is not limited in any way by that which He has created. Certainly, Adam and Eve were given dominion over God's creation, but this did not make them omnipotent. Second, while Adam and Eve were brilliant, their intellect could never be compared to that of their Creator. God is omniscient; He is all-knowing. If Adam and Eve were omniscient, they would have already known everything about good and evil and thus would have had no need to eat of the fruit.[8] Even in their immortality, Adam and Eve were not fully representative of God. For unlike their Creator, they had a point of conception. Conversely, God is omnipresent; He exists both in and outside of time.

So in what way might we best understand Adam and Eve's representation of God? I believe the words of Solomon are helpful: "This only I have found: God made mankind upright, but men have gone in search of many schemes."[9] The Hebrew word for upright is *yashar* (yaw-shawr'), which means "to be straight or even."[10] Solomon was not referring to the way humans physically walk upright; rather, he was hitting upon our moral disposition. In all of this, we come to understand that Adam and Eve were most representative of God's moral character. Prior to sinning, they conformed to the righteous and just nature of our Creator. Both Adam and Eve were completely uninhibited in their capacities for love, joy, peace, patience, kindness, goodness, faithfulness, gentleness, and self-control—the qualities we recognize as the fruit of the Holy Spirit listed in Galatians 5:22, 23.

In theological terms, Adam and Eve's representation of God's image is known as *original righteousness.* Prior to the Fall, they were in right standing with their Creator, and a truly intimate relationship existed between Him and humanity. Adam and Eve were imbued with brilliance of mind, as well as an intimate knowledge of God's character. They understood the rudiments of His morality. Adam and Eve experienced these aspects of their Creator on the deepest of levels and in the most profound ways. This intimacy was part of the communion that not only took place in their relationship with God; it was very much a part of the relationship they shared with one another. In effect, their character was most like God's in this respect— righteous and just. In this setting, they knew total love and security.

However, sin ushered in a complexity to life that I believe God did not intend for us. The Scripture clearly supports this assertion. Paul wrote to the followers of Christ in Rome, stating:

> We know that the whole creation has been groaning as in the pains of childbirth right up to the present time. Not only so, but we ourselves, who have the firstfruits of the Spirit, groan inwardly as we wait eagerly for our adoption as sons, the redemption of our bodies.[11]

Solomon touched upon the complexity of sin when he wrote that God "has made everything beautiful in its time. He has also set eternity in the hearts of men; yet they cannot fathom what God has done from beginning to end."[12] In other words, what God has created is beautiful in every sense, and since the beginning, He has given humanity the ability to comprehend creation, specifically how it reflects His intent and glory.[13] However, after the Fall, humanity's ability to comprehend all of this was seriously inhibited.[14]

One example of our hampered ability for comprehension could be seen in the big bang theory. This term came to be coined out of the derisive words of astronomer Fred Hoyle in reference to the explosion that theoretically started the cosmos. Hoyle, as with many other scientists of his day, subscribed to the steady state theory—that the universe was neither expanding nor contracting. If this indeed were true, the biblical account of creation would have to be ruled false. The statement, "In the beginning God created the heavens and the earth"[15] would be erroneous, because a static universe would have no beginning or end; it would have always existed. However, through the work of individuals like Albert Einstein, Alexander Friedman, Edwin Hubble, Georges Lemaître, and others, it came to be widely accepted within cosmology that the universe is not static; rather, it is the expanding result from what was once a singularity. In other words, the universe has a beginning—just as the Genesis account states. Today, both theologians and cosmologists believe there was a beginning to the cosmos. What continues to confound scientists is how order resulted from chaos. Theologians understand that it is God who brings the order. This is one of the many examples of how humanity is capable of comprehending matters involving God and His creation; however, because we see these matters "dimly" as the apostle Paul stated,[16] it takes a considerable effort to regain a fraction of the understanding Adam and Eve possessed prior to sin.

What Was at Stake

As Adam and Eve stood before the tree of the knowledge of good and evil, all was still right within God's creation. But as each stretched out their hand and touched the fruit, gone in that very instant was humanity's unencumbered relationship with the Father. While His love continued to flow, no longer was the flow uninhibited. Adam and Eve's sin instantly began to clog the conduit through which the Father's love traveled, namely, their spirit. In that instant, the security of His plan was gone. A dark willfulness, unlike anything they had ever experienced, permeated their minds and immediately affected their relationship with one another. From the instant Adam and Eve violated the Father's will, their integrity began to erode.

Prior to the Fall, the uncoordinated, self-indulgent thoughts and behaviors which make up the "flesh" would have been subjugated by Adam and Eve's moral character. Clearly, they were capable of sin; however, before the Fall, they operated in a manner that was selfless as opposed to selfish—they loved unconditionally. There were no dysfunctional rudiments found in their personalities. The organized constructs involving reason and common sense were totally in line with God's will. This is not to say that Adam and Eve never had selfish tendencies, but until the Fall, they proved successful at subverting their will to the will of the Father.

From this perspective, Adam and Eve had no need to engage in the self-deceptive practices of denial, repression, or rationalization. Their ultimate need for love was met completely in their communion with God, as well as with one another. Perceptually, they did not view God's creation dimly as we now do; rather, they had an unobstructed view of God, themselves, and each other. They comprehended what their Creator had set in motion through a clear understanding of ecology. Cognitively, Adam and Eve were not inhibited in their perceptions prior to sin. Given the fact they held the representation of God's moral character, their ability to perceive would have been nothing like ours today. Prior to the Fall, their memory had not yet been stymied through complex self-deceptive defenses. Certainly, there would have been no need to sever their associations with God and His creation; there was no need to dissociate. Before the Fall, there was not a single reason for them to disconnect from:

- God's love and constant contact
- Their relationship with one another
- Their thoughts and feelings
- Their connection to anything within God's creation

Adam and Eve's judgment was based on a righteous and just character. They made decisions consistently in line with God's will.

With such communion, the opportunity for them to constantly subvert their will to that of their Creator was ever present, the key word here being *opportunity*. As long as Adam and Eve subverted their own will to the Father's will, they would have continued in their holy dispositions. But each had the freedom to act deliberately. Contained within that freedom was the power to choose something other than God's will.

The Fall

In a very real moment in time, Adam and Eve faced the serpent and demonstrated their capacity to be willful, to choose their own way versus that of their Creator.

Now the serpent was more crafty than any of the wild animals the Lord God had made. He said to the woman, "Did God really say, 'You must not eat from any tree in the garden'?" The woman said to the serpent, "We may eat fruit from the trees of the garden, but God did say, 'You must not eat fruit from the tree in the middle of the garden, and you must not touch it, or you will die.'" "You will not surely die," the serpent said to the woman. "For God knows that when you eat of it your eyes will be opened, and you will be like God, knowing good and evil." When the woman saw that the fruit of the tree was good for food and pleasing to the eye, and also desirable for gaining wisdom, she took some and ate it. She also gave some to her husband, who was with her, and he ate it. Then the eyes of both of them were opened, and they realized they were naked; so they sewed fig leaves together and made coverings for themselves.[17]

Gone in an instant! No longer would Adam and Eve enjoy an uninhibited relationship with their Creator; the free flow of knowledge and authority from God to humanity was now encumbered. Certainly, nothing of their willful act lessened the Father's love for them; God's love has and always will exist. Yet the instant sin entered into creation, its vile nature began to pervert what God previously declared was good.[18] In that exact moment of temptation, Adam and Eve still possessed the freedom to choose. They could have chosen God's will, but they chose to follow their own desire for wisdom and power.

What must have it been like in the first moments after the Fall? Consider living a life with no presence of evil—not even having the knowledge of such a thing. You know only that which God had created—all is good. Then, in the blink of an eye, your mind becomes filled with the knowledge of evil. In one moment, all your thoughts are pure and good, and then the next moment ushers in the most horrific and terrifying of thoughts. In that instant, Adam and Eve began to view each other in perverse ways. Never before had they lusted for one another. This is not to say they were not sexual beings; clearly, God was not only intent on them procreating,[19] He wanted them to experience the joys of sex together.[20] But once Adam and Eve had fallen outside of the Father's will, they began to view each other in ways He never intended. They sewed fig leafs together as a means to dissociate from the distress of their perverse thoughts. Gone was the unwavering sense of love without conditions. Gone was their sense of security.

In that very moment of reaching out and touching the forbidden fruit, God had to separate Himself from Adam and Eve. Certainly, not with respect to His love; rather, He needed to separate from their unholy nature. This was not an act of anger on His part. As an all-loving God desiring to share His triune nature with humanity, our heavenly Father did what was necessary. Because His holiness is absolutely pure, only the purely holy can exist when His presence is unencumbered. Without separation, our Creator's holiness would have vaporized Adam and Eve in their fallen state. But look at the love of the Father, working to meet His children right where they were in a manner they could tolerate; *walking* toward them, not running in haste and anger.[21] We get the sense Adam and Eve understood this Being to be God. We see God utilizing this shielding technique throughout the Scripture: Abraham met his Creator through Melchizedek;[22] Moses encountered God in a burning bush;[23] the apostles came to truly know their heavenly Father through the God-man, Christ Jesus.[24] An all-loving God would not have left Adam and Eve alone in the garden. Indeed, He did not.

How shocked and frightened they must have been! Adam and Eve were unsettled in their minds for the first time, yet their loving Creator came to them in the midst of their self-induced crisis. He called to them, "Where are you?"[25] Certainly, being omniscient, He already knew where they were. Perhaps He spoke as a means to present a familiar voice to them. After the Fall, this would have been a very real need they had; their world was turned upside down through their willfulness. Instantly, they would have sensed the pain and fear of spiritual separation from their Father as their sin became a wedge. Then, again, maybe the question was posed as a means for Adam and Eve to step back and consider: "Yes, where am I? What is it I've done?" Regardless, there was God, making His way to them when it would have been impossible for Adam and Eve to make their way back to Him. Such is the nature of our Father; no matter what we do to subvert His will, He continues in His loving ways. God will not excuse away our sin, but His desire for connection remains ever present.

The complexity of sin is witnessed in the perverse actions of Adam and Eve. Not just in their willfulness to eat the forbidden fruit, but very much so in their attempts to lie and cast blame afterward. Adam's response to God's question was: "I heard you in the garden, and I was afraid because I was naked; so I hid."[26] Here we find evidence that Adam's holy disposition had changed. Prior to the Fall, he experienced a relationship with the Father that involved constant communion; there was nothing inhibiting him from relating with God.

But after the Fall, Adam stated he "was afraid." The Hebrew word rendered here is *yare'* (yaw-ray'), which means "to fear"; however, the implication can also pertain to moral reverence.[27] This point is significant, because it signals humanity's shift away from an ability to effectively represent the attributes of God's moral character. Adam's admission to being afraid could be viewed as another indicator of his falling away from the Father's original intent. Prior to the Fall, Adam feared nothing. Adam and Eve not only lost their ability to fully identify with their Creator, they lost their place of authority within creation as well. In much the same manner, we, too, slip away from our identity and God-given authority when we engage in sin. Just like Adam and Eve, we, too, can become lost in depravity when we choose our will over God's will.

Our loving Father gives us opportunities for repentance, so we can get right with Him again and best fulfill our purpose in life. The questions posed to Adam and Eve were opportunities to get real with their Father. In His omniscience, God knew their every thought, whether or not they were telling the truth. But He did not ask these questions to trick them. God was providing the opportunity to surrender their will back to His. Adam could have answered honestly in the first place and admitted he sinned, moving toward contrition and repentance, but he chose to continue in his willfulness. Consider the immense degree of love God displayed in that moment. Not only did He meet Adam and Eve in the midst of their crisis, but He also approached them in a patient manner with opportunities to repent. What grace!

God asked Adam directly about eating the fruit: "Have you eaten from the tree that I commanded you not to eat from?"[28] Astoundingly, not only did Adam continue to hold on to his own will, he actually placed the blame upon both Eve and God by saying: "The woman you put here with me—she gave me some fruit from the tree, and I ate it."[29] No longer was Adam capable of maintaining the balanced state of mind he was originally created to possess. Immediately, following the Fall, we find Adam practicing self-deceptive acts by denying the truth and rationalizing his behavior. Eve was found to be no better in her fallen state; she also cast blame. "The serpent deceived me, and I ate."[30] Observe just how complex this situation became in the very early stages after sin entered this world.

Adam and Eve went from being the authoritative representatives of God's righteous and just character, as well as managers of the world's ecology, to being lost, lonely souls in the middle of a world that had quickly become foreign to them.

Following their fall, we witness the complicating effects sin has on the mind. Adam and Eve sought to deceive themselves and God through denial, repression, and rationalization. Fallen and broken, their logic was overtaken by their own will. In their selfish state, the will of the Father was no longer acceptable. They were singularly focused on their own selfish aim and gratification. As God addresses Adam and Eve after the Fall, we see an imbalance in their minds; willingness has given way to willfulness. The organized constructs of their psyche sought to satisfy their impulsive desires in a way that would minimize the painful consequences. Their defensiveness is proof of this point. For how reasonable is it to attempt to hide and deceive an all-knowing, all-powerful, ever-present Creator? Adam and Eve's morality was completely altered at this time. Their sin was like a powerful wedge that drove them away from the perfect relationship with their Creator. While the love of God continued to flow, Adam and Eve's ability to receive and reciprocate love was significantly inhibited. Enter the root constructs of such personality traits as psychopathic, perfectionistic, and apprehensive.

Where This Leaves Us

Overall, as Christians, we seem to struggle more with our fallen nature rather than experience the power of holy dispositions contained within us. Why is this so? The answer is found in the imputation of sin. When we impute, we attribute responsibility for a specific outcome to someone or something else.[31] As we talk about someone's attributes, we are generally speaking about specific characteristics of that individual. To say sin is imputed into us is the same as saying it is very much a part of our being. This is precisely what the apostle Paul was touching upon when he stated, "sin entered the world through one man, and death through sin, and in this way death came to all men."[32] Adam and Eve were not only spiritually affected by sin; it literally became a part of their nature. Their nature was then genetically passed along to the generations that followed.

The mutation resulting from sin is understood to be true from what God spoke into being after the Fall. To Eve He said: "I will greatly increase your pains in childbearing; with pain you will give birth to children. Your desire will be for your husband and he will rule over you."[33] Sin changed Eve in every sense. Going forward, as a mother, she would experience pain and sorrow in her mind and body—something our Creator never intended for her. This would prove to be the case because her children would be born into a sin nature. They, too, would choose their own will, and their choices would bring grief. In the Hebrew language, the word for desire is *tshuwqah* (tesh-oo-kaw'), which means "stretching out after," or "a longing."[34] In other words, God was signifying to Eve that she would long for Adam to function in his former character. She was going to desire Adam's unconditional love and the security she once felt in her relationship with him prior to the Fall. To this day, we can still see this dynamic playing out in marriage. The less a husband meets his wife's desire for godly leadership, the more she is apt to attempt fulfillment of the desire by taking control. I have counseled many couples where the wife was "stretching out after" her husband's love in the most desperate of ways. Understand that this was not God's punishment of Eve; rather, it was His declaration of the consequence as a result of her own actions. No doubt, an all-loving God would be grieved. Just as a loving parent does not want to see their child experiencing the painful consequences of their misdeeds, an all-loving God likewise does not desire for these matters to come to pass. In an act of compassion, the Father addressed Eve as a means to help prepare her mind for the changes which had already begun to take place.

To Adam God said: "Cursed is the ground because of you; through painful toil you will eat of it all the days of your life. It will produce thorns and thistles for you, and you will eat the plants of the field. By the sweat of your brow you will eat your food. Until you return to the ground, since from it you were taken; for dust you are and to dust you will return."[35]

As with Eve, Adam would also experience pain that was not a part of God's original plan. In some manner, the ecological structure of the world was changed, i.e., "cursed" through sin. The result: Adam would "toil" for sustenance. What God had previously made provision for would now be performed at the hand of man. As with Eve, God worked to prepare Adam for the consequences of his actions by letting him know the changes coming his way. And just as God had stated when He first commanded Adam and Eve not to eat of the tree of the knowledge of good and evil, eventually they would experience a physical death. Just as it went for our first parents, it goes for all humanity.

Summary

God's original intent for humanity was to maintain our holy disposition by abiding in His will. Mankind was to be most representative of our Creator's moral character, so that we could best extend love. Prior to the Fall, God's love flowed unencumbered into the lives of Adam and Eve. But the free flow of His love hung in the balance as they reached out for the forbidden fruit. Both of them gave in to the indulgence of self. We can see the organized constructs of Eve's own will beginning to rationalize why it would be all right to eat the fruit—it looked good and pleasing; it was desirable for gaining wisdom. In that very moment, Eve's will won out over the Father's will. She had the freedom to choose, and she made her choice.

Standing right there beside her was Adam, who could have intervened or refused to participate in Eve's sin, but instead he followed suit.

Gone in an instant was the uninhibited communion Adam and Eve shared with their Father. From the moment they touched the fruit, their ability to receive and extend God's love was hampered. Adam and Eve were now infected with sin. Life was significantly dimmer on the other side of the Fall. Their view of God, as well as one another, was obstructed by their own willfulness. Enter the self-deceptive practices of denial, repression, and rationalization. Adam blamed God and Eve, while Eve blamed the serpent. In a moving act of compassion, God met them in the midst of their crisis with love, grace, and mercy; both had opportunities to repent, but neither chose to.

The sin of our first parents has been imputed into each of our lives. It is now very much a part of who we are as human beings; thus, we come to see that sin perverted everything God had originally created to be beautiful. As Charles Hodge observed, sin carries two significant characteristics: the first relates to guilt; the second to the pollution of our being.[36] In all of this, we witness the complexities of our dichotomous nature. The implications of sin and guilt are staggering.

Opportunity for Reflection

1. With respect to God's will, what significance does immorality have on your life?

   _____

   _____

2. Do you relate to Adam and Eve's desire to do their will over the will of the Father?

   _____

   _____

3. In what ways can you see:

   The providence of God playing out in your life?

   _____

   _____

   Free will playing out in your life?

   _____

   _____

4. The devil used doubt as a means to entice Adam and Eve to eat the forbidden fruit. In what ways do you see Satan using this same technique in your own life?

   _____

   _____

Chapter Three
Conditioned through Sin

*"So I find this law at work: When I want to do good,
evil is right there with me. For in my inner being I
delight in God's law; but I see another law at work in
the members of my body, waging war against the law of
my mind and making me a prisoner of the law of sin at
work within my members."*

Romans 7:21–23

While God is working His plan of restoration, we must come to terms with the fact that sin is not just something we do—*it is something we are*. But this does not mean we have to operate in it. Just because we have the capacity to hate does not mean we have to live in hatred. We cannot solve a problem we are unaware of, nor can we solve a problem if we are unwilling to accept the need for change. Chapters One and Two helped us develop a greater awareness of God's intent for humanity and the immense complexity of sin. Here, in Chapter Three, we will continue our efforts to build awareness by assessing the ways we become conditioned by sin.

Whenever we sense a lack of love and security in our key relationships, we face a quandary—we feel uncertain and perplexed. Intrinsically, we know we have these needs; yet the quandary arises because we are oftentimes unsure of how to get them met. The more we lack love and security, the greater our distress will be. All too often, we learn to cope with distress in maladaptive ways involving self-deceptive modes of thinking. For example, a particular wife feels a painful lack of love in her marriage, so she focuses a significant amount of time and energy on caring for her children and work-related activities to keep her mind preoccupied. By doing so, she limits the amount of time spent feeling the pain associated with the lack of love. At the same time, her husband also feels the sting of love's lack, so he dulls his distress by viewing pornography. Through this behavior, he experiences brief euphoric episodes that alter his mood. Until emotions of guilt and shame take over, he feels free from the distress of the marriage. These behaviors are the result of this husband and wife's denial and repression of their painful emotions. They then rationalize why it is okay for them to behave in these manners. But it is plain to see they are only deceiving themselves. In reality, they are distressed over their relationship, and their attempts to avoid the truth only add to the distress.

Distressing Ramifications of Sin

Any type of strain produces stress, no matter if the strain originates from a spiritual, mental, emotional, or physical source.

Depending upon the factors involved, stress can have positive or negative consequences in one's life. Basically, there are two types of stress, *eustress* and *distress.* The first type is healthful, such as when we go to the gym and exercise. The second type, *distress,* is a state that occurs when we experience persistent strain that cannot effectively be coped with or adapted to. Through repeated experiences with distress, we can be led into maladaptive states, where modes of thinking and manners of behavior fall outside of God's will—which is precisely the aim of our enemy, the devil. To better understand how this is so, let us study a theory known as General Adaptation Syndrome (GAS).

Alarm

Endocrinologist Hans Selye served as a pioneer in the study of distress and developed the GAS theory involving a three-stage process. The first was identified as *alarm.* The moment we sense a threat, a complex physiological response is generated. During alarm, our body rapidly increases production of certain neurochemicals like adrenaline and norepinephrine, resulting in changes to our cardiovascular, respiratory, gastrointestinal, renal, and endocrine systems. In this state, we focus our mental energies on what is alarming us; the greater the perceived threat, the more intense our focus. Emotionally, we might feel fear, dread, anger, etc. Physically, we experience such changes as an increase in heart rate and breathing, muscle tension, a surge of energy, dilated pupils, and more. In effect, our mind and body are preparing to fight or flee.

Resistance and Adaptation

If our state of alarm persists, we will experience the second stage of GAS—*resistance/adaptation.* Because our body could not tolerate the strain of continuous alarm without eventually exhausting its energy stores, it first attempts to cope with the distress through resistance. For example: if you were being chased by someone who meant to do you harm, and you managed to get a safe enough distance away, you might slow your pace down from a sprint to a jog. In other words, your body would resist the constant exertion of running at full force once you perceived the threat was no longer immediately upon you.

Dr. Selye observed that if resistance does not prove effective in coping with persistent distress, we will then attempt to adapt. For instance, several years ago, my wife, daughter, and I relocated to Texas. The apartment we moved into was close to a railroad track. Of course, the train came by at night, blaring its horn for a nearby intersection. You can imagine our surprise the first evening this occurred. But just weeks later, we had adapted to the sound and slept right through the noise. This is one form of adaptation. Learning to cope with the distress of a loved one's drug addiction by attempting to rescue them from the consequences of their behavior is yet another form of adaptation to distress. Albeit an unhealthy form, but nonetheless, it is another example of the way we might attempt to cope with prolonged distress. So it can be seen that we do not just adapt physically, we do so mentally, emotionally, as well as spiritually.

Exhaustion

If we are unsuccessful at reducing our distress through resistance or adaptation, we'll experience the third stage of GAS, known as *exhaustion.* In this state, we suffer the effects of physiological breakdown. The more frequently we experience this third stage, the greater the likelihood for development of an illness, such as heart disease, mental disorder, overwhelmingly powerful emotions, spiritual apathy, and more. While we might not want to accept the fact there will be distressing times in our life, like it or not; it is a reality we all must face. Yet many of us were not taught how to cope effectively with distress. Furthermore, we tend to overlook the conditioning factors associated with the distress of sin. This is not to say all distress is the result of sin; however, where there is sin, there is distress.

As a means to delve deeper into the complexity of sin's conditioning elements, let us take a look at the lives of two individuals—Tyra and Carol. These ladies experienced similarities in their family life while growing up. Both had been raised in homes with a good deal of distress resulting from their parents' sin, yet there are distinct differences in the way each became conditioned to cope.

Meet Tyra

When I first met Tyra, she was fifteen years old and growing up in a Christian home; however, her mom and dad argued frequently with a good deal of intensity. As a result of her parents' strife, she often experienced distress. Sometimes she woke in the middle of the night to their yelling. Other times, when Tyra and her mother were shopping together, her father would call on the phone and the result was an argument. When the family went on vacation, her parents fought; on and on went the arguing. It was a constant source of distress in Tyra's life, where her needs for love and security were insufficiently met. At one point, Tyra attempted to deal with the argument by letting her parents know just how much it affected her. Unfortunately, instead of taking her concerns to heart, they told her to stay out of it. So she took to withdrawing as a means of coping. But no matter how much she attempted to resist by diverting her thoughts and feelings, the stress associated with her parents' behavior continued. The cycle of alarm and resistance/adaptation played out frequently in her young life. By the time, Tyra came in for counseling, she was thoroughly exhausted and significantly depressed.

Her repeated attempts to resist the distress developed into maladaptive coping mechanisms involving denial and repression. When her parents' fought, she retreated to her bedroom to escape her painful thoughts and emotions by listening to music, or calling friends on the phone to talk about anything other than what was really going on. These behaviors, incrementally but cumulatively, conditioned Tyra to cope with sin in ways God did not intend.

Some might ask what sin her parents actually committed. Consider the following passage:

> Wives, in the same way be submissive to your husbands so that, if any of them do not believe the word, they may be won over without words by the behavior of their wives, when they see the purity and reverence of your lives....Husbands, in the same way be considerate as you live with your wives, and treat them with respect as the weaker partner and as heirs with you of the gracious gift of life, so that nothing will hinder your prayers.[1]

Note that in each directive given to the wife and husband, God's word says: "In the same way." This begs the question: in what way? The answer is found in the following passage: "To this you were called, because Christ suffered for you, leaving you an example, that you should follow in his steps."[2] Consider how different Tyra's home life would have been had her father honored his wife's needs, and if her mother had been more respectful toward her husband. I am not suggesting they should have never disagreed with one another. However, I do assert they needed to die in their willfulness and produce fruit of the Spirit much more frequently.[3] In order to better understand this point, let us delve deeper into the words of the apostle Paul:

The acts of the sinful nature are obvious: sexual immorality, impurity and debauchery; idolatry and witchcraft; hatred, discord, jealousy, fits of rage, selfish ambition, dissensions, factions and envy; drunkenness, orgies, and the like.[4]

Through this passage we can more clearly see the sin of Tyra's parents, which involved:

- *Sexual immorality:* in this case, adultery
- *Hatred:* intense animosity or hostility
- *Discord:* lack of agreement
- *Rage:* violent, explosive anger
- *Selfish ambition:* concerned chiefly with one's desire to achieve something
- *Dissension:* strong disagreement; a contention or quarrel
- *Factions:* a group representing strife

Animosity is understood to be active hatred, or our acting out of hate toward others. When we live in constant discord with someone, we tend to develop animosity, oftentimes directing it at that individual, especially when our needs for love and security go unmet. Left unchecked, these feelings can turn into rage, and would involve explosive outbursts. In relationships, selfish ambition stifles love and security. In attempting to get our needs met, we might seek to control others through contention and quarreling. As a means to justify our position, we tend to develop factions by getting other people involved whom we believe will side with us. This is precisely what had occurred with Tyra's parents, which, in turn, inhibited their ability to produce fruits of the Spirit.

In all of this, I am not suggesting we should live our lives with a victim's mentality. While it is undeniable that Tyra had been victimized by her parents' sin, she ultimately is responsible for her own thoughts, feelings, and behaviors. As she grows and matures into adulthood, Tyra will come into the fullness of that responsibility. Additionally, I am not asserting that her parents should be perfect. The fact is, no matter how much we are in touch with God's will, no matter the degree to which we are able to die to our own willfulness, in this lifetime, we will struggle with our dichotomous nature of flesh and spirit. Nonetheless, for a number of years, Tyra's parents engaged in behaviors that clearly fell outside of God's will.[5] The harsh reality is that their sin had significantly impacted their lives, as well as the life of their daughter.

Meet Carol

Carol was an educated, astute woman in her late thirties when she came in for counseling. She recalled that, when she was yet a child, her parents argued frequently, which led into more intense altercations. Mean words were exchanged, objects were thrown, and, at times, they would get physical with each other. Not only was there a lack of love in the home, Carol's sense of security was sorely inhibited as well. So when her parents began to argue, Carol busied herself with cleaning around the house. She wiped the counters in the kitchen, swept the floor, tidied the bathroom, and more. This behavior served her in three key ways. First, cleaning was a repressive act that took her mind off painful thoughts and feelings. Second, she learned she could gain her parents' approval through this type of behavior, which increased her feeling of being loved. Third, sensing her actions had this effect, she came to believe she could partially control her parents' behavior by cleaning; in turn, this perception increased her sense of security.

Over time, Carol became entrenched in her maladaptive ways of thinking and behaving. She developed a compulsion toward cleaning. Decades later, she continued to engage in this same type of behavior whenever she faced conflict. Without realizing it, she utilized this maladaptive coping mechanism thousands of times in her life. Eventually, the mechanism became so procedural that she defaulted to it anytime she experienced distress.

The Connection of Spirit, Soul, Mind, and Body

We humans are an amalgamation of spirit, soul/mind, and body. There is a real connection between these elements that must be attended to. Sin affects our whole being, not just our soul. To delve deeper into the impact sin has on us as humans, we must be willing to assess matters from a metapsychological perspective. Such an

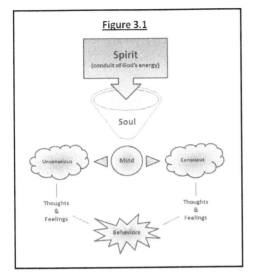

Figure 3.1

approach involves systematic analysis of concepts relating to our humanness that move beyond the limits of empirical psychology—an approach that places God central.

Such analysis might be illustrated as in Figure 3.1, wherein the *spirit* is viewed as the conduit through which God's energies flow.[6] The *soul* is the animating and vital principle of who we are, as it acts like a funnel, channeling God's energies into our mind.[7] The *mind* acts as a component of the soul and is made up of our collective conscious and unconscious processes, which further mediate, i.e., direct and influence our mental and emotional states, as well as our physical behaviors.[8] The *body* can then be considered the intersection of spirit, soul, and mind, serving as the animated component of the amalgamation. In other words, we are spiritual beings intersecting with a fallen world through our physiological states. In this illustration, it can be seen that God gives us free will— the freedom to think, feel, and behave as we choose. But as was covered in the previous two chapters, our heavenly Father has a will of His own, and His desire is for us to choose His will over ours. To be effective at living out God's will, we must develop an awareness and acceptance of how He wants us to cope with distress.

The Systems of Learned Behavior

Given all of this, what are the observable and quantifiable aspects of behavior affected by sin? Let's begin with a working definition of behavior. The actions and reactions of a person or animal in response to external or internal stimuli is perhaps the most succinct definition of *behavior* to work from.[9] Our actions and reactions are the results of how we mentally mediate energy involved with the stimuli. The ways by which we have learned to cope with any given stimuli will determine the outcome of our behavior. For instance, if we learned to mediate the energy associated with a perceived threat by avoidance, then our actions will likely involve repressive types of behaviors. If we have learned to mediate the energy associated with anger in covert ways, then our behavior will typically involve actions geared toward passive-aggressiveness. If we learned to cope with the distress associated with sin through self-deception, then our behaviors are likely to involve acts of compulsivity.

To better understand the significance of learned behavior, let us take a closer look at the acquisition of knowledge. Specifically, knowledge is gained through complex cognitive processes involving perception, association, reasoning, development of skills, and communication. Through *perception* we gain awareness directly via our physical senses. When we make *associations,* we are establishing mental connections between thoughts, emotions, and sensations. *Reasoning* involves the motive for an action, decision, or conviction. The *development of a skill* is typically accomplished through repeated experiences. *Communication* allows for the receipt and conveyance of information tied to perceptions, associations, reasoning, and skills.

Tyra gained knowledge of her parents' struggles in marriage through what she saw and heard. Their sin, coupled with her perceptions, produced distressing stimuli. The energy associated with her distress was mediated into thoughts and emotions, resulting in specific types of behaviors. As a child, Tyra would not be able to effectively deduce the reality of this situation—specifically, her parents' fighting, which was not her fault. Yet she unwittingly reasoned that somehow she was the cause of their unhappiness. While faulty, this line of reasoning motivated her to attempt to solve this problem, so her needs for love and security could be satisfied. For years, Tyra attempted to appease her parents by getting good grades, doing extra chores around the house, and repressing her own thoughts and feelings so as not to make waves. But her attempts to cope with her parents' sin in these manners proved ineffective, which intensified her efforts to suppress the distressing thoughts and emotions through behaviors geared toward withdrawal. From this perspective, the tricks and schemes of the devil are clear to see. In much the same way he divided and conquered Adam and Eve, he was doing the same with

Tyra's parents: playing on their willfulness and ultimately perverting God's purpose for their lives, as well as their daughter's life.

Modes of Learning

To further understand the ways we are conditioned by sin, let us look at three specific modes of learning: *associative, nonassociative,* and *deductive.*

Associative Learning

Essentially, this mode of learning is based on the assumption that ideas and experiences reinforce one another.[10] Observed within this mode is the operant conditioning pattern involving a process of behavior modification in which the likelihood of a specific behavior is increased or decreased through positive or negative reinforcement each time the behavior is performed. Through this pattern of conditioning, we come to associate the pleasure or displeasure of the reinforcement with the behavior.[11]

In Carol's case, her behavior associated with cleaning intensified through positive reinforcement. As a young girl, she observed that her father would come home at night, take his shoes and socks off, and leave them near the front door. Her mother felt embarrassed when family or friends dropped in to visit and there would be her husband's socks and shoes lying on the floor for all to see. In her mother's mind, the fact that her husband behaved this way elicited thoughts that he did not care about what was important to her. As a result, she felt less loved and was angry. On the other hand, Carol's father viewed this matter as an attempt by his wife to criticize and control him. In turn, he, too, felt frustrated and less loved.

Her parents typically fought over this issue at least once a week. Observing this, Carol would wait a couple of minutes after her father removed his shoes and socks. Then she would sneak up to the front door, grab them and run, placing them in her father's closet. Carol's behavior was strengthened due to the positive effect of the consequence, i.e., her parents stopped arguing about the issue. While the immediate outcome of her behavior yielded a positive effect, in the long run it only served to reinforce maladaptive codependent coping mechanisms like caretaking, rescuing, and enabling. These modes of coping are generally unhealthy, because they tend to be rooted in fear and guilt as opposed to love. Left unchecked, codependent behavior can develop into a compulsion, where we feel compelled to behave in ways God never intended. Compulsive states of mind significantly inhibit the flow of love in our life. There is little joy in such behaviors, and, at best, peace is found to be fleeting, if there is any peace to be found at all.

Nonassociative Learning

Another mode of learning is known as *nonassociative,* which involves two different response patterns: *habituation* and *sensitization.*

The term *habituation* can be misleading, because it does not mean forming a habit. Rather, it relates to the decline of a conditioned response following repeated exposure to a stimulus.[12] Think of habituation as becoming desensitized. It is the result of nerve cells becoming less sensitive and responsive to repeated stimuli. For instance, let us say you had a terrible fall and broke your arm. After the bone was set and your arm casted, your doctor prescribed a strong medication for pain. While the pills work well for the first few days, over the course of time cells in your brain begin to habituate, becoming less responsive to the medications's effects. After a while, you notice that the prescribed amount does not work as effectively as when first taken.

When it comes to the way we cope with distress, habituation plays a key role. For instance, recall that Carol originally experienced a heightened state of alarm when her parents fought. But over time, the degree to which she felt this way declined because she came to believe she had some control over her parents' behavior by cleaning. Through repeated exposure to her parents' fighting (the stimulus), coupled with repeated behaviors of cleaning (the conditioned response), Carol experienced less alarm.

In effect, her parents' sin served as a cause-agent for Carol's development of habitual coping mechanisms that eventually became compulsive. Herein, we find another example of how we can become conditioned to cope in maladaptive ways as a result of other people's sin being perpetrated upon us. Of course, the goal in acknowledging such matters is not to foster a victim's mentality; rather, the goal is to bring the unfruitful works of darkness out into the light, so we can heal and grow, as well as address the conditioning factors associated with the sin.[13] In part, this is how we move from living life as a victim to living life as a victor.

The second response pattern involved with nonassociative learning is *sensitization,* which is the process of becoming susceptible to a given stimulus that previously had no or little effect.[14] Suppose, as a child, you observed a particular bully on the playground picking on other children. While you felt sorry for these kids, this bully's actions affected you in no significant way. But one day, the bully turns his sights on you. He demands you give him your lunch money, but you refuse. All of a sudden, you find yourself pushed down hard to the ground. The bully threatens that you better give your money to him tomorrow or matters will get worse. Previous to this encounter, you experienced little in the way of sensitivity to the bully's actions. But now, you are on the lookout for this mean kid. You are less apt to play carefree as before, and you find yourself watching the bully from far away.

In Tyra's case, prior to the age of eight, her parents argued very little. When they did, it was more of a disagreement of sorts as opposed to an intense fight. The stimulus associated with their disagreements had no significant effect on her. However, shortly after Tyra turned eight, unbeknownst to her, her father discovered that her mother was having an affair. The intensity and frequency of her parents' disagreements increased, escalating into intense arguments. As the intensity of distress increased, so too did her sensitivity to their arguments. Greater sensitivity resulted in more frequent use of avoidant types of behaviors.

When Tyra sensed her parents were about to argue, she began to experience distress. As noted earlier, in her distress, she engaged in a distorted mode of thinking—believing she was to blame for her parents' behavior. The result was an intense feeling of guilt. An interesting dynamic tends to result in such cases. If we believe we are to blame for the actions of others, then maybe we can change *our* behaviors and therefore change the outcome of other people's behavior. This line of thinking proves maladaptive, because it is self-defeating. In reality, we typically have little control over the behaviors of others. This is especially true in cases of child to adult, wherein the child is attempting to control the adult. The more Tyra attempted to control her parents' behaviors, the more defeat she experienced, which she then internalized. In the case of children, this line of thinking and behaving tends to be less of a conscious act, wherein the child is driven at a deeper level by their needs and emotions. Nonetheless, we can see how the devil uses these circumstances in a child's life to perpetuate a pervasive sense of guilt, potentially stymieing fulfillment of their God-given purpose in life.

Deductive Learning

The third form of learning we will look at is *deductive*. When we deduce, we actually make conclusions based on premises we believe to be true. Premises are rooted in propositions—statements that affirm or deny something.[15] When we believe a premise to be true, we then believe the conclusion to be true as well. This mode of learning factors into our entire life, especially where childhood deductions are concerned. In terms of the acquisition of knowledge, children tend to view their world concretely and not so much abstractly. For example, many young children believe Santa Claus is real, that he lives at the North Pole, with an army of elves in his employ to make toys. On Christmas Eve, he boards his sleigh, which happens to be propelled by flying reindeer, and delivers toys to all the well-behaved boys and girls around the world. Children very much believe these things to be real; in their mind, all of this is concrete. However, as children grow older, their ability to perform abstract thought develops further. Typically, somewhere between the ages of eight and ten, children begin to question if Santa is actually real. This has to do with their ability to more effectively deduce matters. As children mature, Santa represents a growing dilemma. They want to hold on to the wonder represented in the story, yet newly developed premises begin to contradict their earlier conclusions about Santa's existence. Children come to understand that reindeers cannot fly, elves do not exist, and even boys and girls who misbehave tend to get presents on Christmas. Based on these newer premises, they eventually conclude that Santa is not real.

If there is no cause for us to revisit our premises, we simply maintain our line of thought and behavior. For instance, children are apt to internalize what is happening in their environment because they view themselves as the center of their world. This being so, the tendency is for children to believe they are the cause of what occurs in their life, good or bad. In Tyra's case, she incorrectly perceived herself as the cause of her parents' fighting. Because of this faulty premise, she attempted to resolve matters through her behavior. But as time passed, she became angry with herself because she actually lacked the power to change her parents' behavior. Unable to express her emotions outwardly, Tyra turned them inwardly, which eventually developed into self-contempt. In effect, she came to believe there was something inherently wrong with her, that she was unlovable. Once again, we find evidence of the enemy's schemes to thwart God's purpose for Tyra's life—working to convince her through the sins of her parents that she was to blame and was ultimately unlovable.

Tyra's misperceptions led to erroneous conclusions through which she came to associate disagreements with guilt. Anytime one of her parents or friends saw things differently than she did, Tyra instantly believed she was wrong for thinking that way. Through her associations, she unwittingly conditioned herself to react by withdrawing from family and friends at any time she felt guilt.

Carol also made associations when it came to disagreements. Whenever she encountered differing opinions, she experienced fear and anxiety. Immediately, she would begin looking around for things to clean. In those moments, she busied herself so much with cleaning that she had no time to interact with others.

Tyra's and Carol's approaches to cope with the distress of sin involved conditioned modes of thinking, feeling, and behaving. It was never God's plan for them to live their lives conditioned to deny their needs or repress their thoughts and emotions. Rather, He desires that we live a life overflowing with love, joy, and peace. To do so, we must learn to be aware of (1) what we are thinking and feeling, (2) why we think and feel that way, and (3) ascertain God's will in any given situation where our thoughts and feelings are concerned. It is important to note that our motivation for why we think and feel as we do is rooted in our needs. When assessing the *why* in point number two, it would be good to ask ourselves what needs are not being met. Not just our own needs, but the needs of others. Point number three brings God central into our thoughts, feelings, and needs. Ultimately, our Creator's will is for us to live our lives in the full context of our thoughts and emotions, while at the same time producing fruits of the Spirit through our behavior.

The Neurological Ramifications of Sin

Our brain is comprised of billions of interconnected nerve cells otherwise known as neurons.[16] While they are not the only type of cell found in the brain, they make up the greatest number therein. The essential purpose of the neuron is to receive, decipher, and send information in the form of a signal to other nerve, muscle, or gland cells. This exchange of information is accomplished through a process known as electrochemical signaling. The result of this signaling is called an action potential, which is a pulse-like wave of voltage traveling from one neuron to another.[17]

Neurons are interconnected via a system of branching cellular extensions called axons and dendrites (see figure 3.2).[18] Through these extensions, one neuron might make thousands of connections with other neurons.

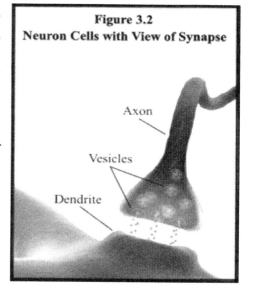

Figure 3.2
Neuron Cells with View of Synapse

For the most part, axons send signals while dendrites receive them. At the end of each axon, vesicles—i.e., small sacs—produce neurotransmitters, which transmit nerve impulses. When a signal needs to be sent from one cell to another, neurotransmitters produced within the vesicles of the axon are released and received by neuroreceptors in the dendrite of the other cells. In effect, this transference enables the exchange of information from one neuron to others, which ultimately culminates in larger bodily action.

How might have this neurological signaling played out in Tyra's case? The consistency in which she experienced distress pushed her beyond resistance/adaptation to exhaustion, resulting in disorder.

Eventually, Tyra withdrew every time she experienced distress in her life. Her grades suffered, she quit the volleyball team, and interacted less with family and friends. In addition, her appetite waned and she lost weight. Tyra found it increasingly difficult to sleep at night; her mind raced with worrisome thoughts. The lack of sleep and proper nutrition exasperated her state of exhaustion. Over a period of time, she became severely depressed and suicidal. Tyra's depressed state was very much tied to a spiritual battle, but with neurological implications. At first, her parents' arguments produced a state of alarm, wherein millions of neurons received and sent signals. As the distress of her parents' fighting continued over time, neurons in Tyra's central nervous system began to send out signals to resist the distress, which resulted in avoidant types of behaviors as a means to further reduce stimulation.

However, as the distress in Tyra's life persisted, she began to experience exhaustion; neurochemical signaling could not maintain the constant exertion of energy needed to resist the distress of her parent's arguing. Ultimately, she needed to find a new state of being. Adaptation kicked in as systems of neurons and other cells adjusted to the frequency of distress in a process known as neuroadaptation.

In Carol's case, she, too, experienced neuroadaptation due to the distress she endured while growing up. However, she did not experience these changes in quite the same way as Tyra. Instead of depression, she developed an adaptation toward hypervigilance, an elevated state of sensory sensitivity. One result of this change was the increased transmission of norepinephrine, which is both a neurotransmitter and hormone. In part, it serves in our fight-or-flight response through a process known as vasoconstriction, which increases heart rate and blood pressure, triggering the release of glucose from energy stores in our body.[19] These stores of energy then give us the means by which we can effectively fight or flee from a threat. Because of her hypervigilance, Carol often perceived nonissues and minor issues to be more of a threat than they actually were. In effect, her alarm response had kicked into hyperdrive, so much so that she experienced a perpetual state of anxiousness.

The Ramifications of Sin on the Soul

From a theological perspective, the soul is not only the eternal part of our being, it is considered to be where the mind resides. From this perspective, we can begin to see the significance of sin's conditioning elements upon the soul. Consider the following passage:

> For though we live in the world, we do not wage war as the world does. The weapons we fight with are not the weapons of the world. On the contrary, they have divine power to demolish strongholds. We demolish arguments and every pretension that sets itself up against the knowledge of God, and we take captive every thought to make it obedient to Christ.[20]

Essentially, we are to deconstruct modes of thought not in line with the knowledge God makes available to us. Through this knowledge, we can actually avoid sinning. The key is to put this knowledge to use. In Tyra's and Carol's repressed states, each had become conditioned to avoid painful thoughts and feelings; thus, they were sorely inhibited when it came to examining or taking captive of their own thoughts and making them obedient to Christ. Both were caught in vicious cycles of maladaptive thinking and dysfunctional behavior. In such conditioned modes, neither Tyra nor Carol could experience the abundant life of love, joy, and peace. Each submitted to unhealthy coping mechanisms, which were like yokes of slavery. In all of this, their purpose in life was stifled.

Our Personality and Sin

The suffix *ity* is used to form nouns which express a state or condition. So when we talk about *personality,* we are referring to the state or condition of being a person—the total qualities and traits involved with one's behavior, temperament, emotions, and mental proclivities.[21] The term *proclivity* means: inclination, i.e., a tendency toward a certain condition or character.[22] While genetics and environment factor into the formation of our personality, it is God who originally gives us our proclivity or inclination toward our uniqueness as a person. God dials in the specific coordinates of our personality traits, while genetics and environment affect these coordinates.

From this perspective, we can better understand sin's impact on our mind. Each of us is born in a unique time, with a special set of qualities and traits for a specific purpose that fits perfectly into the plan of our Creator. Tyra and Carol were inhibited through sin. Neither of them was remotely close to living their life in accordance with God's will and purpose. They had not experienced freedom in Christ, nor were they able to stand firm and stop their submission to the enemy's yoke of slavery. In all of this, we come to see that unless we develop awareness of the ways we are conditioned by sin, our propensity will be to continue in these enslaving modes of thinking and manners of behavior. But once we become aware of these matters and accept our need to change, we can then surrender in greater degree to God's will. The apostle Paul put it this way: "It is for freedom that Christ has set us free. Stand firm, then, and do not let yourselves be burdened again by a yoke of slavery."[23]

Sin greatly distorted Adam and Eve's sense of who God had created them to be, and sin has the same effect on each of us as well. Because our identity is comprised of the distinct and persistent traits of our personality, the manner in which we behave, the type of temperament we tend toward, the emotions we are likely to feel, the means by which we cope with our emotions, and the inclination to think in certain ways all factor into the makeup of our identity. While sin erodes God's original intent of our personality—stifling the flow of love, we can allow God's Spirit to work in our minds and recondition us to live out God's purpose. In Christian counseling, we call this *repentance*, which involves a change of mind and heart.

Let's study this point further. Consider the following answer Jesus gave to the question, "Which commandment is the first of all?"

> "The most important one," answered Jesus, "is this: 'Hear, O Israel, the Lord our God, the Lord is one. Love the Lord your God with all your heart and with all your soul and with all your mind and with all your strength.' The second is this: 'Love your neighbor as yourself.' There is no commandment greater than these."[24]

With love being the greatest force ever, think of how different this world would be if we were less conditioned by sin. What if we were able to keep sin from eroding our God-given identity? Consider that which would be loosed in heaven and on earth. For sure, there would be more frequent acts of love. With love in abundant supply, there would be less anger and hatred in the world. People would feel more secure in their relationships. We would struggle less with tendencies toward dysfunctional personality traits. With more love, we would fear less. Would not our heavenly Father's kingdom come that much sooner as His will was done on earth as it is in heaven?

Tyra and Carol—Good News

While it was a sad state of affairs for these two ladies, God proved to be much bigger than their conditioned states. Tyra mentioned to a friend that she did not think life was worth living anymore. Her friend told her mom, who then called Tyra's mother. The result was that she came in for Christian counseling and began receiving help. Her parents, too, came in for marital counseling, which proved successful in helping them resolve the issue of infidelity. As the three of them laid down their own wills, each was able to manifest Christ-like character to greater degrees. Today, Tyra and her parents have a healthy, functional relationship filled with an abundance of love, joy, and peace.

As for Carol, she, too, came in for Christian counseling. Over time, she gained a deeper understanding of the ways she was conditioned to think, feel, and behave. She was strengthened by our Lord to implement more functional coping skills, effectively breaking her old maladaptive ways. Now, she lives the abundant life. These two ladies serve as good examples of what happens when we work to overcome self-deceptive ways of coping and submit to the ways of our Father. Whenever we do so, He is faithful to transform our mind.

Summary

God created us with the ability to sense danger and respond with alarm. In this state, our entire being works to resist the distress by coping with the threat via fighting, fleeing, or adapting. In our attempts to resist, we sometimes develop modes of self-deceptive thinking involving denial, repression, and rationalization. Once conditioned into these modes, we are then hampered in our ability to "take captive every thought to make it obedient to Christ."[25] Maladaptive approaches to resist distress can bring us to the point of exhaustion, where breakdown occurs and disease can develop.

The things we learn in life affect the relationship between spirit, soul, mind, and body. As we experience spirituality, we grow more aware, and therefore more familiar, with aspects of God's creation. Awareness and familiarity enable knowledge, which provides understanding. All of this sounds simple enough; however, the processes by which we ascertain knowledge are complex and involve perception, association, reasoning, acquisition of skills, and communication. Each of these processes contains its own set of variables. For instance, we do not always perceive things as they truly are. Sometimes we make associations based on faulty premises. There are instances when we choose irrationality over reason.

Through the factors of habituation, sensitization, and operant conditioning, we might learn to think and behave in ways that fall outside of God's will. But when God is invited into these processes, we can better ascertain His will in every aspect of our life. Our loving heavenly Father always has our best interest at heart. God knows what works for us. His aim is not to control; otherwise, why would He give us the freedom to choose? He wants the best for us. As we become more aware of the ways we are conditioned to think and behave, we can choose to follow God's will. Doing so opens us to more fully receive the Father's love, grace, and mercy, which transforms our mind and best enables us to fulfill the purpose He wove into our being.

We are much more than the sum total of our thoughts, emotions, and behaviors; we are spiritual beings intersecting with a physical world that is broken. But our Creator has given us the capacities of cognition and emotion for good reason; it is through these capacities that we ultimately live out His plan and purpose. Recall that sin is thinking and behaving outside of God's will. When we repress our thoughts and feelings, we are committing a sin. There are legitimate reasons why God does not want us to repress; for one, it affects homeostasis. From a neurological perspective, prolonged repression can inhibit the synthesis of serotonin, affecting cognition, mood, appetite, and more. In such a conditioned state, our ability to fulfill God's purpose is literally depressed. Bottom line: our attempts to cope with reality by leaning on our own understanding and minimal power results in sin. But when we lean on our Father for understanding, we gain insight and perspective; spiritually, we are strengthened, which edifies our mind and body.

Each of us was created with purpose. God fashioned us with a unique set of characteristics that fit perfectively into His plan. There has never been a person matching our exact combination of characteristics—

and there never will be. Such uniqueness points to tremendous purpose and value. But sin perverts all of this. It tweaks our identity. Through sin, we lose sight of God's intent for our life and adopt a distorted view of who we were created to be. In such a state, we sometimes become prideful; at other times, we might degrade our value. Either way, through sin, we lose sight of our true identity and unwittingly thwart God's purpose for our life. But I encourage you to keep on reading. We really can gain awareness of sin's complexities and be empowered to leave our self-deceptive modes of thought and behavior behind.

With this chapter, we end part one, in which we looked at God's intent for humanity; His desire to have a personal relationship with each one of us; and the complexities of sin and how God's plan for our life is perverted when we choose willfulness over willingness. Next, we move on to part two, with an in-depth look at the self-deceptive practices of denial, repression, and rationalization.

Opportunity for Reflection

1. What have been the major sources of distress in your life?

   _____

   _____

2. Complete the following sentence: My tendency is to resist distress by:

   _____

   _____

3. With what frequency do you experience exhaustion as a result of distress in your life? (check one)

☐ Infrequent   ☐ Somewhat Frequent

☐ Frequent   ☐ Very Frequent

4. What associations have you developed that affect your relationship with the Lord and others?

_____

_____

5. After reading this chapter, I now see habituation and/or sensitization play out in my life in the following ways:

_____

_____

6. Are there conclusions you have made in life based on faulty premises that need to be changed?

_____

_____

7. I have been conditioned by sin in the following ways:
My own sin:

_____

_____

The sin of others:

_____

_____

8. Sin has affected my God-given personality in the following ways:

_____

_____

Chapter Four

Breaking through Denial

"Do not conform any longer to the pattern of this world, but be transformed by the renewing of your mind. Then you will be able to test and approve what God's will is—his good, pleasing and perfect will."

Romans 12:2

We now begin part two where we will focus on the matter of self-deception, namely, denial, repression, and rationalization, and how these modes of thought and behavior impact our ability to live in accord with our Father's will. Self-deception is like a table with three legs—each is vital for support of the system; remove one and a collapse occurs. So, too, is the case with our self-deceptive practices. If we stop denying that issues of sin exist in our life, our system of deception will fall. When we move away from our acts to avoid dealing with our sin, denial and rationalization come crashing down. Ceasing to justify our sin topples denial, which allows us to stop repressing and to focus on God's will, as opposed to our own.

It is a fact that we cannot solve a problem unless we are (1) aware that it exists, and (2) willing to accept that changes are in order. But all too often, our acts of denial stifle awareness and inhibit acceptance. In effect, by denying the presence of an issue, we are saying, "I'm not going to deal with this." When we live in this state, we operate more in survival mode and less in the capacity of a victor. This is a significant point. Jesus said: "In this world you will have trouble. But take heart! I have overcome the world."[1] As Christians, we are joint heirs with Christ, which means, we can operate in His authority. Much like a police officer operates under the authority of the law, we, too, can learn to live life under the authority of God. But denial of our sinful behaviors leads us into conformity with the patterns of this world, which involve covetousness, immorality, rebellion, idolatry, and other acts of folly.[2] More often than not, denial proves to be a maladaptive mode of coping, opposite to what Paul directed us to do in the opening passage of this chapter. So we must learn to *anakainosis* (an-ak-ah'-ee-no-sis) our mind—renew or renovate the way we think, cope with feelings, and behave.[3] When we renovate something, we restore it to an earlier condition; however, *anakainosis* also means to impart new vigor or revive.[4] By conforming less to the ways of this world, we can more aptly allow our mind to be transformed through the grace of Christ and the redeeming work of the Holy Spirit. Transforming our mind in this way enables us to produce more fruits of the Spirit. Matthew Henry put it this way:

The work of the Holy Ghost first begins in the understanding, and is carried on to the will, affections, and conversation, till there is a change of the whole [person] into the likeness of God, in knowledge, righteousness, and true holiness. Thus, to be godly, is to give up ourselves to God.[5]

But when we live in denial, we cannot fully give ourselves up to the Lord. In effect, we stifle the process of sanctification; we stunt our growth in holiness.

Meet Cedric

Cedric first came to counseling feeling a significant lack of worth. He recounted how, as a young man, he felt responsible for much of the trouble his family experienced. He stated, "I'm to blame for our problems. Things would have been better had I achieved more." While growing up, Cedric indicated that his father was gone for days at a time. "I really didn't understand it then," he said, "but as I got older, I began to see that my dad drank a lot and spent time with other women. He would work hard for a week or two, but on payday, he headed to the bar, where he partied away the family's money."

As a child, Cedric came to believe he was at fault for his father's behavior, recalling: "I thought if I could get good grades and do well in sports, my dad would want to be home more. So I worked my tail off, pretty much got A's and B's in school, and was always one of the top athletes in the sports I played. I made state finals, but was never able to bring home the championship. My dad would have been so proud to see me get that." Cedric's parents divorced when he turned eighteen. "Mom told me she never wanted to leave dad while I was living at home," he recounted. "But when I left for college, she threw in the towel. I was angry when I found out. How could she just leave him after being married all those years? Where was he going to go?"

In adulthood, Cedric continued his attempts to gain his father's love and approval. During one session, he said, "I call him all the time and try to see him as often as possible. Most times, if I want to be with him, I've got to meet him at the bar. I worry about my dad. I'm afraid something bad is going to happen to him one day. If it ever did, I'd feel ashamed. I really believe it's my job to watch out for him." In the beginning of counseling, it was hard for Cedric to see the error of his father's ways. "Everybody wants to see him fail. He's got nobody else but me," he asserted. But over time, Cedric came to better understand it was his father who failed him. He had important needs, too, but his dad fell short of meeting those needs. At one point, he said, "I never really gave much thought to how I felt about my father's drinking and womanizing. I'd just focus on what I could do to earn his love."

Cedric came to see that he had actually turned his anger with his father inward and developed self-contempt. "I remember feeling so angry with myself," he said. "I hated the fact that I'd try hard and nothing seemed to change with my dad. At times, it seemed like the harder I worked to get him to love me, the less he'd show it. I really thought I was some kind of idiot." With the understanding that his father's behavior was never really about what Cedric did or did not do, he began to overcome his self-contempt. He grieved the loss associated with decades of unmet needs and eventually came to a point of acceptance and forgiveness. As a means to set healthy boundaries, as well as present an opportunity for his father to get help, Cedric participated in an intervention. At that meeting, Cedric's father made the decision to get help for his compulsive behaviors. Three years later, his father continues to work an active program of sobriety and abstinence. He has also worked hard to repent of his ways and made amends with those he has hurt. Cedric and his father are closer than ever.

Denial Defined

Cedric's case provides a good example of how denial can factor into our life. Formally, *denial* can be defined as both a conscious and unconscious defense mechanism characterized by refusal to acknowledge painful

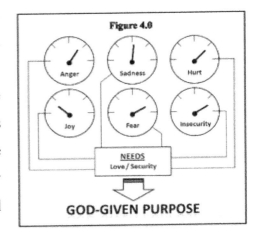

realities, thoughts, or feelings.[6] In such instances, the issue at hand is too distressing, so we refuse to accept it as reality. The significance of denial is illustrated in Figure 4.0. God created us with the capacity to feel emotions for good reason; they act as gauges tied to our beliefs and needs. For example, when our needs for love and security are not sufficiently met, several key emotions will indicate this lack. We might feel moderate degrees of anger and sadness. The level at which we experience hurt feelings could register on the high side as well. Our sense of joy might be in serious decline. Fear and confusion could very well be on their way to peak in the high range. Each of these emotions signals something important about our needs for love and security. The ability to assess *what* we feel and *why* we feel that way is vitally important in taking action to get our God-given needs met. The greater degree to which our needs are satisfied, the more effective we will be at fulfilling our purpose. However, when we deny thoughts and emotions, we become less effective at satisfying our needs, and the net result is sin.

But it also should be noted that denial is not always a bad thing. In fact, there are times when it serves as an important component in coping. For instance, as we first encounter crisis or trauma, we tend to experience shock and deny what has happened. When someone important to us dies, we experience loss and engage in denial. In effect, the pain and anguish associated with the loss is too great for our mind to fully comprehend and process in that moment, so we deny reality. The same holds true when we are victims of abuse. It is not uncommon for those in the midst of a traumatic situation to experience numbness and deny what is truly happening. If we had to completely come to terms with such matters all at once, our mind would become overwhelmed with distress and pathology—disease would most likely set in rather quickly. So God, in His infinite wisdom, allows for a space of grace, a period of time when we disconnect from what is greatly distressing us. In this respect, denial can prove to be healthy, as it helps us to incrementally come to terms with an issue that is otherwise too overwhelming. However, it has never been God's intent that we would remain in denial.

When Denial Becomes Dysfunctional

When it comes to denial, where does the line lie between function and dysfunction? To answer this question, we will need to assess three types of denial, and the ways they prove to be maladaptive.

Simple Denial

The term *simple denial* relates to the manner by which we are able to so thoroughly deny reality in certain situations. We practice this form of denial when the unpleasant facts of an issue are denied altogether.[7] It is typically the mechanism we employ when someone close to us dies, or when we suffer a traumatic event. The greater the intimacy and dependency on the person who was lost, or the more severe the trauma, the greater the likelihood of denial. But if we remain too long in this state, we become delayed in processing through our grief, which in turn stymies healing and recovery. In such instances, pathology tends to breed, which can manifest into complicating factors like persistent and deep depression, excessive hostility, moodiness, guilt, substance abuse, hyperactivity, suicidal thoughts, and more.[8]

You might recall that it was noted in Chapter One that our need for security is tied to the factors of routine, familiarity, and predictability. Too much uncertainty about people, places, or things produces distress, because it tends to negatively impact our sense of security. Take the apostle Thomas for example. Here was a man who left everything behind to follow Christ. This was no small sacrifice. He might not have understood early on that Jesus was the Messiah, but at the very least, he knew there was something extraordinary about this Man; enough to make him leave his old life behind. As a disciple, he witnessed the miracles of Christ. He was privy to the teachings of the Lord and given power and authority by Him to perform miraculous works.[9] But, just like each of the disciples, Thomas was perplexed about the ways of Christ. On one hand, Jesus had cured the sick, healed the disabled, raised the dead, fed multitudes from practically no food at all; He even walked on water and more![10] But on the other hand, the Lord spoke of things Thomas could not wrap his mind around, like His talk about leaving, His role as a servant, and how some among the group would deny and betray Him.[11] We can sense his angst when he asked Jesus: "Lord, we don't know where you are going, so how can we know the way?"[12] As Thomas's uncertainty grew, so too would his insecurity. It is likely there would have been times when it was overwhelming for him. But then the worst of circumstances occurred. Not only was Jesus arrested, He was beaten mercilessly, flogged to the point of grotesque disfigurement, and crucified among criminals—even though He was guilty of no crime.[13] Where was the heavenly power Christ could have called upon to stop all of it? Why would He allow such a thing to happen?

These events were more than a crisis for His disciples; they were traumatic. The difference is that, in a *crisis,* we are not completely powerless to change the course of events. While a crisis might prove to be tumultuous, we generally have a sense that somehow we are going to make it through, that we will one day rise above our circumstances. But when facing *trauma,* we experience actual or threatened death or serious injury, or a threat to the physical integrity of oneself or others. A crisis might scare us, producing fright or alarm. But trauma involves intense, sharp, and all-encompassing fear. Thomas witnessed the brutal act of Christ's scourging and crucifixion, a horrific event he had no control over. For the disciples, the trauma did not end with Christ's burial; they were very much aware that those who persecuted Jesus would likely inflict their brutality upon them as well. All of this would have been exceedingly distressing for Thomas and his friends to the extent they would have likely experienced the numbing effects of simple denial.

Following the death and burial of his beloved Lord, Thomas found himself holed up in an attic of sorts with his fellow disciples, fearing for his life. Days later, after stepping out for a bit, he returned to an unimaginable scene. What must it have been like to be Thomas that day? Perhaps, as he walked up the steps, he heard his compadres speaking loudly and joyously. But how was he to comprehend the event they were all clamoring about? Jesus had returned! Not only that, He appeared right out of thin air! He even spoke, saying, "Peace be with you!"[14] Then He showed His wounds—the places in His wrists where the nails had been ruthlessly driven, the side where the spear entered and pieced the pericardium of His heart, and the evident disfigurements caused by the scourging.[15] It must have been a grotesque yet fantastically wonderful sight to see. Christ had also said something about the Holy Spirit and forgiving sins. The next thing they knew, He was gone![16] No exiting out the doors, He simply just disappeared. Understandably so, Thomas's reaction to all of this was disbelief, saying, "Unless I see the nail marks in his hands and put my finger where the nails were, and put my hand into his side, I will not believe it."[17] Even though he had walked closely with Christ for some three years, this was too much for the disciple to accept.

After a week passed, Thomas and his fellow disciples were still hold up in the attic. The others maintained their stories. They seemed confident in what they saw and eagerly awaited the return of the Lord. It would be reasonable for Thomas to feel some degree of irritation with his friends. Perhaps he thought, *Why don't they just be quiet? Can't they accept He's dead? He's not coming back! But what was it that really happened last week? How could they all have imagined the same thing?* Then, suddenly, with the doors securely locked, Jesus appeared once again! Not only does Thomas see Him, but he hears Him say, "Peace be with you!"[18]

Jesus turned to Thomas with an offer to inspect His wounds—to actually touch Him! In utter awe, the following words come out of the disciple's mouth: "My Lord and my God!"[19] No longer does he doubt. Now, he knows for sure he is truly in the presence of Immanuel—God with us!

The case of Thomas provides us with a good example of how simple denial tends to play out when faced with a distressing issue we cannot find a solution for. But over time, this form of denial proves to be ineffective, because reality cannot be avoided altogether. We might deny our house is burning down, but sooner or later, we will have to accept reality as we look over the charred remains of our belongings. In like fashion, we might deny that the abuse we suffered in childhood was any big deal; yet we continue to harbor great pain and live in a spirit of fear. God graciously allows us to practice denial for a period of time during distressing events, but then He calls us to begin the painful but important process of working through the hurt and fear, so that we can live in a spirit of power, love, and sound mind.

Minimization

When the facts of an issue are accepted but the significance or impact is denied, it could be said we are minimizing.[20] For example, a woman might admit that her husband has an "issue" with anger, but it is the *impact* of his abuse that she cannot accept. We tend to minimize in such cases because we are afraid and feel powerless. This is especially true where the threat of further abuse is present. In these situations, the survivor attempts to minimize the impact of the abuse, because she is terrified of reprisal and generally feels powerless in the cycle of abuse. Yet something must be done to resist or adapt to the distress. In cases where simple denial is no longer effective, survivors are likely to cope with the ongoing distress by acknowledging that a problem exists, but accepting the impact of the abuse will prove to be a whole other challenge.

Conversely, in cases where *we* have perpetrated sin upon others, we might admit to the facts but minimize the damage caused by our actions. Consider the account of King David. In his day, it was commonplace for armies to go off to battle in the springtime. But one year, David chose to stay home while his soldiers went off to war.[21] Now, it was also customary for Hebrews to rest during the hottest part of the day, which was what David had done one particular afternoon. When he awoke from his nap, he went up to the rooftop and saw a beautiful woman bathing across the way. Here is what happened next:

> David sent someone to find out about her. The man said, "Isn't this Bathsheba, the daughter of Eliam and the wife of Uriah the Hittite?" Then David sent messengers to get her. She came to him, and he slept with her. (She had purified herself from her uncleanness.) Then she went back home. The woman conceived and sent word to David, saying, "I am pregnant."[22]

This was not the first time the king found himself morally compromised. While he spent much of his reign in Jerusalem, David ruled for some seven years in Hebron, where he had six sons by six different wives.[23] After his move to Jerusalem, he had several more children with other wives and mistresses.[24] It appears as though David struggled with a sexual compulsion. Yet Bathsheba was not without sin in this matter either. She proved to be as cunning as she was beautiful. Perhaps she took notice of the king's daily regime and planned to bathe when he went up to the rooftop following his afternoon nap. Regardless, Bathsheba demonstrated her cunningness when she later worked a deal that ensured her position of royalty, along with the ascendency of their second son, Solomon, to the throne.[25]

But this time around, David found himself in deep over his head. In cases where a man committed adultery with another man's wife, the Law called for the death of both the adulterer and adulteress.[26] To cover up his sin, David conspired to keep the unfruitful works of darkness in the dark. He sent word to his commander, Joab—who was off leading a battle the king himself should have been overseeing, ordering Bathsheba's husband, Uriah, to report back to him in Jerusalem. For two days, David attempted to entice Uriah to go home and be with his wife. This way, the king could cover up his actions. If anyone were to ask Bathsheba about her pregnancy, she could claim it was her husband's child. But Uriah was unwilling to do this on account of his devotion to his fellow soldiers who were still at battle. Realizing his plan had failed, David sent Uriah back to the front lines with a letter for Joab, instructing his commander to position Uriah at the forefront of the battle, and then retreat so that he would be struck down. The command was carried out, and Uriah was killed.[27] David had innocent blood on his hands.

Simple denial itself would not suffice in coping with such a complex problem. David could not ignore the fact that he impregnated another man's wife and arranged to have that man murdered; nor could he do anything to change the Law. He could have chosen to repent of his ways before the Lord, as well as those affected by his sin, in hopes of receiving mercy. But David was already steeped in self-deception; the odds of him coming clean on his own volition were slim to none.

Without a doubt, all of this would have been distressing for the king. David was a man who, at one time, sought the heart of God.[28] Yet, there he was, buried deep in his own sinful compulsions with a woman bent on gaining power and control. What was he to do? The facts in this case could not be ignored. Bathsheba was pregnant with his child. If Uriah was to ever find out, he most likely would not stop until the Law was satisfied. So David *minimized* the impact of his adulterous and murderous actions to cope with the distress. It was not until the prophet Nathan confronted the king with his sin that he repented. But as a result of his sinful ways, David's household faced much adversity.[29]

I gave this example of King David to illustrate how minimization tends to play out when we become enslaved to sin. Make no mistake about it. David was a man after God's own heart,[30] a great warrior for the Lord, and an even greater worshiper of the Most High God. But it could be said that David fought against two Goliaths—the first was as a fifteen-year-old boy in the valley of Elah; the second was as a grown man installed by God as king over His chosen people, yet battling addiction to sex. Both battles were spiritual in nature.

Each of us would do well to pray for revelation. If we ask the Lord to reveal areas in our own life where we are minimizing the impact of sin, I am confident He will reveal the truth. Doing so is never an easy endeavor. But, as Christians, we must always remember that we are to live as children of light.[31] When we bring the unfruitful works of darkness out into the light, we can, through Christ, overcome such works, no matter if they are our sins or the sins of others perpetrated upon us.[32]

Transference

This type of denial occurs when we redirect the feelings we have for one person onto another. One clear example of transference is found in the case of Cain and Abel. Cain is understood to be Adam and Eve's firstborn son.[33] In the Hebrew language, his name means: lance, as in striking fast with a spear. But the word also carries a connotation of having an affinity toward someone.[34] Because of this, biblical commentators have suggested that perhaps Adam and Eve thought Cain was the "promised seed."[35] Recall that after the Fall, God addressed the serpent saying, "I will put enmity between you and the woman, and between your offspring and hers; he will crush your head, and you will strike his heel."[36] It is possible that Adam and Eve put their firstborn son on a pedestal, so to speak, thinking that he was going to be the one to right *their* wrongs and strike the fatal blow to the enemy. Further support for this assertion comes from the name of their second son, Abel, which means "emptiness" or "vanity."[37] The implication is that, in some way, he did not or could not produce the desired outcome his parents hoped for. Perhaps they believed he lacked the substance required to be the redeeming offspring God had mentioned. Such a notion could have simply come from the misguided belief that first was best. In this case, Cain was the firstborn. If this notion were indeed true, then Adam and Eve might have believed their firstborn son was the one best positioned and equipped to deal with the devil. But what they misunderstood was that it would be a distant offspring, namely, Jesus who would be the one to crush the head of the devil.

The result of these misperceptions would, more likely than not, produce dysfunctional dynamics within the family. As was noted in Chapter Two, when excessive conditions are placed on love, the result can be the development of psychopathology. If Cain sensed his parents' love was conditional upon him meeting unrealistic expectations, it is probable that he grew to resent them. Abel would not have been emotionally unscathed from these dynamics either. With his older brother viewed as the one to be desired, he might have felt the sting of favoritism in the relationship with his parents. Certainly, it is possible that Abel took to appeasing his parents as a means of getting his needs satisfied, while Cain coped with these distressing dynamics by defying the unrealistic expectations his parents placed on him.

The Scripture reveals there was something different about Abel's character. Evidence of this is found in how each man chose to relate with God. The biblical account states that it occurred in the course of time, or, more specifically, at a designated time the brothers brought their offerings before the Lord.[38] It appears this was to be an event dedicated to search one's heart and assess what sins had been committed against their heavenly Father. Abel's offering was an atoning act in which he demonstrated a true desire to repent of his ways, as well as his sense of God's grace and mercy at work in it all. The fact that time for such atonement was appointed meant that both men likely understood what their Father was asking of them. Our Lord has always sought relationship with humanity. Even after the Fall, we can see that God's will is to meet each person, Cain and Abel included, at a place where their heart is softened and open to His love. Yet each brother came with a different state of mind. Abel arrived filled with contrition, and obediently offered up to the Lord that which was acceptable for an act of atonement. His sacrificial offering was chosen from among the best of his flock. The shedding of blood indicated Abel understood that the price to be paid for his sin was death, but it was the Father's mercy that sustained his life. Conversely, Cain arrived with a sacrifice unsuitable for a sin offering, which signifies a hardened heart and a mind set on disobedience. But the most blatant difference in Cain's offering from that of his brother's was a lack of faith. The great biblical commentator, Matthew Henry, saw it this way:

> Abel offered with an eye to God's will as his rule, and God's glory as his end, and in dependence upon the promise of a Redeemer; but Cain did what he did only for company's sake, or to save his credit, not in faith, and so it turned into sin to him. Abel was a penitent believer, like the publican that went away justified:

> Cain was unhumbled; his confidence was within
> himself; he was like the Pharisee who glorified himself,
> but was not so much as justified before God.[39]

Cain's anger boiled at the rejection of his offering. Years of pent up frustration over the conditionality of his parents' love may very well have hardened his heart. But it is important to understand that God was not rejecting Cain; rather, He was addressing the unfruitfulness of his maladaptive coping mechanisms. Listen to the words of a loving Father addressing His son's counterproductive ways of dealing with life: "Then the LORD said to Cain, 'Why are you angry? Why is your face downcast? If you do what is right, will you not be accepted? But if you do not do what is right, sin is crouching at your door; it desires to have you, but you must master it.'"[40] Note that God was not asking Cain to do the impossible; He was looking for him to do what was right. Functional relationships require times of self-reflection. While we cannot be fully objective with ourselves, we can ask God to search our hearts and reveal the thoughts and behaviors that stifle the flow of love. If we discover unmet needs, we can then ask the Lord to guide us in healthy ways of getting them met. Then again, perhaps we will have to come to terms with how our own actions fall short in meeting the needs of others. This kind of contemplation is not easy to do, but we must accept the importance of doing so and turn from our denial. As we become more aware of the state of our needs and those of others, we then have the opportunity to choose healthier means of coping.

This was precisely the point God was addressing with Cain. Doing what was right meant being angry but still following the will of the Lord. Our Father's desire is for us to work to maintain a balanced approach when it comes to this powerful emotion. There really is a way to experience anger but still produce love, joy, peace, patience, kindness, goodness, faithfulness, gentleness, and self-control.[41] Les Carter and Frank Minirth did a masterful job addressing this point in *The Anger Workbook,* in which they define anger as the intent to (1) preserve personal worth, (2) get essential needs met, and (3) maintain basic convictions.[42] So what kind of worth did Cain have? First, he was part of God's creation, knit into his mother's womb and fashioned together in personality, because the Lord had wonderful plans and a definite purpose for him. Those plans included hope for a bright future even though he lived in a fallen world. Just as your life matters greatly to God, so too did Cain's life. But when we tie our worth up in anyone other than the Lord, we are subject to that person's moods and behaviors. As their moods fluctuate up and down, so too does our sense of worth. If Cain was viewed by his parents to be the promised seed, the pressure to meet their expectations would have been enormous at times. Storing his worth up in his parents but then falling short of their unrealistic desires would have negatively affected his sense of value. The more he felt it diminish, the angrier he became.

As was established in Chapter One, God created us in love, for love. Not only do we need to feel loved, but there must be opportunity for us to reciprocate love as well. Acceptance of this reality means coming to terms with the fact that outside of God's love, all other forms of love are conditional to one degree or another. How we learn to cope with this reality makes all the difference. If Cain's parents had placed him on a pedestal, then he would have gotten the message, loud and clear, that they wanted him be someone other than who God created him to be. Such dynamics can impact one's needs in significant ways. Cain might have sensed that his parents loved him. But with so many conditions, he would most likely question the degree to which they cared about meeting his needs and thus how much they truly loved him. For Cain, the vexation in all of this would have stemmed from a self-defeating cycle. He needed to sense his parents' love, but to gain it, he had to meet their conditions, which were unrealistic. It is likely that, over the years, Cain developed contempt for himself and others. He could have very well come to hate himself for having needs at all. But one cannot love others unless they love themselves.[43]

Inherently, he would have sensed an injustice was being done, that it was wrong for his parents to place such unrealistic expectations on their love. Perhaps, at times, there might have been a feeling they were mean about the way they held their love just out of arms' reach. No matter how hard he tried, regardless of the height of his jumps, there may have been times when Cain simply could not grasp that which he so desperately needed. The more he encountered these dynamics, the stronger his convictions would have grown—and so, too, would his anger. Thus, the Lord saw fit to address the situation. In effect, He was asking Cain to do the right thing, to check his state of mind and the condition of his heart. It was a call for him to pause and reflect, to contemplate what he was feeling, why he was feeling that way, and how his heavenly Father willed for him to cope with it all.

God said to Cain, "[I]f you do not do what is right, sin is crouching at your door; it desires to have you, but you must master it." The Hebrew word used here for sin is *chatta'ah* (khat-taw-aw'), which means "an offense and the penalty it carries."[44] But this word also relates to *expiation,* specifically the way one atones or makes amends for an offense.[45] It is likely God was addressing both of these points with Cain. First, that he would come to see how he had fallen into sin by developing contempt, as well as transferring his hatred for others onto his Creator. The Lord did not make Adam and Eve behave as they did. But He graciously provided Cain's parents with a hope for the future, that one day their wrongdoings would be made right. Yet it was his parents who took that hope and mistakenly transferred it onto their firstborn son. God wanted Cain to search his mind and heart so he would come to that realization. In doing so, he might also see that the issue was not about his worth but about his parents' misperceptions. Perhaps if he had taken the time to contemplate these truths, Cain would have also come to see that his heavenly Father loved and greatly valued him. While he needed to sense his parents' love, the fact was his real worth was not to be tied up in his relationship with his parents; rather, it was to abound in the Lord. Just because someone might be inhibited in displaying their love for us does not mean our worth is diminished.

The Lord also addressed Cain from the perspective that his growing hatred was significantly affecting his ability to relate in loving ways. Not only was he rejecting his parents; he was now rejecting his Creator. God was warning Cain that his contempt was welling up like an enormous wave, and if he did not change course, the wave would come crashing down on him. Just look at the grace and mercy of the Lord! How patient our heavenly Father is! He lovingly sought to assist Cain, offering him the help needed to break through his denial of the real issues and work toward a healthy resolution. He could have chosen to listen to his heavenly Father. If he had done so, the Lord would have guided him, step-by-step, into righteousness where he would have found an abundance of love, joy, and peace. Instead, Cain chose to follow his own will, and the results were devastating. What ensued was the ultimate act of transference: "Cain said to his brother Abel, 'Let's go out to the field.'" Cain then attacked and killed his brother."[46]

God pronounced Cain to be full of hate, and he was too unstable to remain in relationship with his family due to the hardening of his own heart.[47] In his hatred for himself and others, the firstborn son of humanity had lost his identity. No longer would he be a member of the first family nor would he continue in his profession as a farmer. In effect, it was Cain's maladaptive choices of coping with unmet needs that resulted in a form of psychopathology that made him unsafe to be in relationship with. As in many cases of psychosis, his personality was deranged; that is, out of order from what God had originally intended. While we can see Adam and Eve's contribution to the dysfunction of the family unit, it was Cain who was culpable for his own actions. Amazingly, we continue to see God's love, grace, and mercy play out as He attends to Cain's fear of being murdered, too, one day. And the Lord provided him with some sort of mark, signifying to others that he was not to be harmed.[48]

Cognitive Dissonance

No matter whether it is an outright refusal to accept the truth, minimize, or transfer, denial breeds dissonance, which equates to a lack of agreement, consistency, or harmony.[49] Cognitive dissonance is then understood to be a condition of conflict or anxiety resulting from inconsistency between one's beliefs and one's actions.[50] God created us for a state of balance called homeostasis—a balanced mind and body. But when there is dissonance between the way we think and the way we behave, we feel conflicted and automatically seek a resolution. For instance, if I consider it wrong to steal but then take a candy bar from a store without paying for it, I will experience some degree of dissonance. I believe it is wrong for me to take what I have not paid for, but in this example my actions would be contrary to my belief, resulting in distress. The question is: what will I do about this dissonance? Will I go back to the store, apologize, and pay for what I took, or will I attempt to put the theft out of my mind altogether, i.e., simple denial? Will I tell myself it is no big deal, i.e., minimization, or will I shift the frustration of my inner conflict onto someone else, i.e., transference?

Let's say a woman finds herself in an abusive marriage. Prior to meeting her husband, she heard stories about women being abused by their spouse and would think it is wrong for those women to stay in the marriage. At that time in her life, these convictions were strong. Now, she finds herself embroiled in such a relationship. While she still believes the right thing to do is to get out, her fear is paralyzing. The inconsistency between her convictions and behaviors adds more distress to her situation. Overwhelmed in it all, she minimizes the impact of the abuse as a means of coping. At times, she considers the stories she has heard about other wives being abused and thinks, *Some of those women have it much worse than I do.* Sadly, she is only fooling herself. Odds are, the cycle of abuse will not only continue, but it will intensify over time as she practices denial through minimization.

In this situation, both the husband and wife are sinning. The man's sin is obvious. It was never God's will that he should abuse his wife.[51] His behaviors thwart God's plan for both his and his wife's life, as well as stifles the flow of love. But where in any of this is the woman's sin to be found? Our Father's will is for us to not keep unfruitful works of darkness in the dark. Rather, He calls us to expose such works.[52] God directs us to examine ourselves,[53] to search our mind and heart for issues that inhibit us from fulfilling our purpose of love. When we allow fear to overtake us, we become demoralized. Recall that, in Chapter Two, the issue of morality was addressed, wherein it was established that God has a moral code, a right way of thinking, and wills for us to live in accord with Him. When we do so, we are best positioned to fulfill our purpose in life. Thus, our Creator has given us a spirit of power, love, and sound mind to carry out a courageous self-inventory.[54] But when we allow fear to demoralize us, the result is disorder and confusion.[55] Ultimately, we end up living less effectively for the Lord. While it is understandable that this woman lives in fear of her husband, it is God's will that she not deceive herself by denying the gravity of her situation. Until there is freedom from the cycle of abuse, she will continue to live an inhibited life—one where love, joy, and peace are significantly stifled.

Let's revisit Cedric's case for a moment. Recall that he unwittingly shouldered much of the responsibility for his father's drinking. In effect, he was practicing denial through minimization, trying to convince himself that his father's behaviors were not as problematic as they actually were. Cedric did not so much deny the facts, but he minimized the impact by shifting the blame onto himself, a process otherwise known as *internalizing.* Just like Carol in Chapter Three, Cedric also believed he could covertly control his father by behaving in ways he thought would gain his approval. At a less conscious level, he believed his father's behavior was wrong. But whenever this realization entered his consciousness, he began to feel distressed due to cognitive dissonance. If he was to accept the reality of his father's sinful behavior, then Cedric would have to acknowledge he was powerless to change him. As a young man, accepting this truth would have proven to be very challenging. It was not until he was able to break through his denial that he began to accept reality and change his codependent ways.

Self-Assessment

It is one thing to cover these points when they relate to someone else, but applying them to our own life often proves to be a whole other matter. But unless we are willing to do just that, we will continue in our modes of self-deception. Now, we begin the process of self-assessment where we take time to apply these truths to our own life. Bear in mind that you are not alone in this endeavor. Christ mediates on your behalf, and the Holy Spirit has already been at work to bring to light the issues God wants resolved in your life.

> Take time to review the following lists, checking items you believe are applicable to your life. While these lists are not all-inclusive, they can assist in identifying common causes for living in denial. We will first begin with sins we have *suffered,* followed by sins we have *perpetrated.*

Sins (suffered)

Addiction/Substance Abuse:

I grew up in a family where my parent(s)/caregiver(s) were addicted to:

_____ Alcohol

_____ Prescription and/or illicit drugs

_____ Shopping

_____ Gambling

_____ Sex (e.g., sleeping with prostitutes, affairs, pornography, etc.)

_____ Eating

_____ Other behaviors that I now see were compulsive to the point where their life was unmanageable. List the behavior(s):

_____

Criminal Abuse:

_____ I have been robbed at gunpoint/knifepoint or turned over my possessions at the direct or implied threat of physical harm.

_____ My home was robbed.

_____ My car was stolen.

_____ Besides what is listed above, someone stole a possession of mine that was of great importance.

_____ There was a time in my life when someone intentionally conned me.

Mental/Emotional Abuse:

_____ As a child, my parent(s)/caregivers(s) often humiliated, criticized, and/or ridiculed me.

_____ Growing up, my parent(s)/caregiver(s) were frequently cold and distant toward me.

_____ I remember being called names or made fun of by others on a regular basis during childhood.

_____ My spouse/partner humiliates and criticizes me any chance he/she gets.

_____ My spouse/partner works to keep me isolated from family and friends.

_____ In my marriage/relationship, my spouse/partner limits my access to work, money, or other important resources.

_____ If I were to express my true thoughts and feelings, I know my spouse/partner would ridicule me.

_____ Someone significant in my life uses sarcasm as a way of punishing me when they are angry (e.g., they tease in mean-spirited ways).

Neglect:

As a child, or now as an adult dependent on others, my basic needs were/are neglected in one or more of the following ways:

_____ I had/have to beg or steal for food as a result of my parent(s)/caregiver(s) lack of provision.

_____ Food or other essentials were/are withheld for unreasonable periods of time as a means to punish me. (Note: Being asked to leave the dinner table *on occasion* would not apply.)

_____ My parent(s)/caregiver(s) did/do not take the necessary means to *reasonably* ensure my safety.

_____ As a result of my parent(s)/caregiver(s) actions, I was/am frequently absent from school.

_____ Little or no attempt was/is made for me to receive the medical care I needed/need.

_____ I was/am consistently dirty and at times had/have severe body odor.

_____ I lacked/lack sufficient clothing for the weather.

_____ There was/is seldom anyone home to provide the care I needed/need.

_____ As an adult, my parent(s)/family members care very little for my well-being.

_____ I believe my spouse purposely withholds his/her love and support of my/our family.

Physical Abuse:

_____ I was raised in a home where I suffered physical beatings that left welts, bruises, scratches, fractured or broken bones, burns, etc., at the hands of my parent(s)/caregiver(s), sibling(s) or other individuals I lived with.

_____ As a child, I was physically picked on, pushed around, and/or beaten up by other kids.

_____ As an adult, I have experienced physical beatings that left welts, bruises, scratches, fractured or broken bones, burns, etc., at the hands of my spouse, sibling(s), adolescent or adult children, caregiver(s), etc.

Sexual Abuse:

When I was a child, an older individual (i.e., adolescent or adult) did one or more of the following to me:

_____ Talked about my body or their body in sexual manners that now seem to me were sexually gratifying to that individual.

_____ Showed me pornography.

_____ Showed me private parts of their body.

_____ Asked or forced me to show private parts of my body.

_____ Asked to touch or actually did touch the private parts of my body in a way that now seem to me were sexually gratifying to that individual.

_____ Asked or forced me to touch the private parts of their body.

_____ Asked or forced me to view and/or touch the private parts of someone else's body.

_____ Asked or forced others to view and/or touch the private parts of my body.

_____ Any other physical, visual, verbal, or psychological contact/interaction with me that I now see was sexually gratifying for that individual.

_____ As an adolescent or adult, I was raped.

_____ I was coerced/forced into prostitution.

Spiritual Abuse:

_____ I have suffered under the spiritual leadership of others as they abused their authority by shaming, coercing, and/or manipulating me in ways that inhibited my experience with God's love, grace, and mercy.

_____ There was/is a spiritual leader in my life who did/does not tolerate questions or inquiry about their teachings or God's word.

_____ A spiritual leader in my congregation made it clear they believe they are the only source for knowing the truth about God.

_____ There was a time in my life when I was involved with a cult or the occult either because my parent(s)/caregiver(s) were involved or because I joined unaware.

This completes the list of sins that might have been perpetrated upon you. As you worked through each category, did you find yourself struggling to come to terms with any of the points? If so, it is possible you might be in denial. Ask yourself the following questions:

1. Could it be that I really did suffer this type of sin but am struggling to accept the truth?

    _____ Yes _____ No

2. What is the likelihood that I am in denial about this issue?

    _____ Highly Unlikely _____ Somewhat Likely

    _____ Likely _____ Highly Likely

3. Do I acknowledge the sin but minimize the effect it has on my life?

    _____ Yes _____ No

4. Have I transferred the pain associated with the sin onto other people?

    _____ Yes _____ No

If you are struggling to accept the sin you have suffered, understand you are not alone. To one degree or another, we all participate in acts of denial over some issue in our life. However, God has brought you to this point for a reason. Now is the time to acknowledge that the sin was real, that it did occur and has impacted your life. In the past, your denial served in allowing you to survive sinful situations. But now, God wants you to be free from the pain and the ways you have been conditioned as a result. Remember: "It is for freedom that Christ has set us free. Stand firm, then, and do not let yourselves be burdened again by a yoke of slavery."[56] Also, understand we are not called to bear the burden of these types of sin on our own.[57] Coming to terms with such matters is likely to require assistance. I encourage you to seek godly counsel. If you believe you are in need of professional counseling, visit with your pastor/minister, or go to the American Association of Christian Counselors (AACC) website (www.aacc.net), and click on the link titled, FIND A CHRISTIAN COUNSELOR.

The next list pertains to your perpetration of sin upon others. Sin tends to have a generational component; those who have been sinned against have the propensity to continue that sin through transference to the next generation. You might find yourself checking items from both the previous and following lists.

Sin (perpetrated)

Addiction/Substance Abuse:

> After looking back on my life, I now see I am battling an addition to:
>
> _____ Alcohol
>
> _____ Prescription and/or illicit drugs
>
> _____ Shopping
>
> _____ Gambling
>
> _____ Sex (e.g., sleeping with prostitutes, marital affairs, pornography, etc.).
>
> _____ Eating

_____ Other behaviors that I now see are compulsions that result in unmanageability in my life. List the behavior(s): _____

Criminal Abuse:

_____ I have robbed people at gunpoint/knifepoint or forced individuals to turn over their possessions at the direct or implied threat of physical harm.

_____ I have robbed another person's home.

_____ I have stolen a car.

_____ I intentionally conned someone.

Mental/Emotional Abuse:

_____ As a parent/caregiver, I have humiliated, criticized, and/or ridiculed my child/children/adults in my care with frequency.

_____ I have consistently been cold and distant toward my child/children/adults in my care.

_____ I called names or made fun of others on a regular basis when I was growing up.

_____ I humiliate and criticize my spouse/partner any chance I get.

_____ I see now that I work to keep my spouse/partner isolated from family and friends.

_____ In my marriage/relationship, I limit my spouse/partner's access to work, money, or other important resources.

_____ I would most likely ridicule my spouse/partner if he/she were to express his/her true thoughts and feelings.

_____ I have practiced infidelity in my marriage.

Neglect:

As a parent/caregiver, I see now that I am (or did) neglect my child's/children's/adult's basic needs in one or more of the following ways:

_____ They had to beg or steal for food as a result of my lack of provision.

_____ Food or other essentials have been withheld for unreasonable periods of time as a means to punish my child/children/adults in my care. (Note: Asking your child to leave the dinner table *on occasion* would not apply.)

_____ I did not take the necessary means to *reasonably* ensure my child's/children's/adult's safety.

_____ As a result of my actions, my child/children is/are/were frequently absent from school.

_____ I made little or no attempt for my child/children/adult(s) in my care to receive the medical care they needed.

_____ My child/children/adult(s) in my care was/were consistently dirty and at times had severe body odor, and I neglected to do anything about it.

_____ I see that I failed to provide my child/children/adult(s) in my care with sufficient clothing for the weather.

_____ As a parent, I see now that I have spent too much time away from home. As a result, I failed to provide the care my child/children needed.

_____ I find myself caring little about the well-being of my adult child/children.

_____ I purposely withhold love and support for my spouse/family.

Physical Abuse:

_____ I have given my child/children/adult(s) in my care physical beatings that left welts, bruises, scratches, fractured or broken bones, burns, etc., or allowed others to abuse my child in such ways.

_____ I physically picked on, pushed around, and/or beat up other kids when I was growing up.

_____ I have physically beaten my spouse/partner in such a way that left welts, bruises, scratches, fractured or broken bones, burns, etc.

Sexual Abuse:

As an adolescent or adult, I have done one or more of the following to a child:

_____ Talked about my body or their body in manners that were sexually gratifying to me.

_____ Showed them pornography.

_____ Revealed private parts of my body.

_____ Asked or forced them to show private parts of their body.

_____ Asked to touch, or actually did touch, private parts of their body in a way that was sexually gratifying to me.

_____ Asked or forced them to touch the private parts of my body.

_____ Asked or forced them to view and/or touch the private parts of someone else's body.

_____ Asked or forced others to view and/or touch the private parts of that child's body.

_____ Any other physical, visual, verbal, or psychological contact or interaction with them that was sexually gratifying to me.

_____ I have raped someone.

_____ I have coerced/forced someone into prostitution.

Spiritual Abuse:

_____ As a spiritual leader, I see now that I abused my authority by shaming, coercing, and/or manipulating people in ways that inhibited their experience with God's love, grace, and mercy.

_____ As a spiritual leader, I find it difficult to tolerate questions or inquiry.

_____ As the spiritual leader of my congregation, I believe I am the only source for knowing the truth about God.

_____ I have been a leader in a cult or the occult, or I have purposely led others into a cult or the occult.

As with the first list, it may also prove challenging to acknowledge the truth about sins you have perpetrated. Keep in mind you would not be the first to struggle in this way. To one degree or another, we all perpetrate sin. If you find yourself challenged to accept any of the points on this second list, ask yourself the following questions:

1. Did I experience moderate to intense guilt when reading through any of the points?

    _____ Yes   _____ No

2. What is the likelihood that I am in denial about the issue?

    _____ Highly Unlikely   _____ Somewhat Likely

    _____ Likely   _____ Highly Likely

3. Do I acknowledge the sin but minimize the effect it has on those I perpetrated?

    _____ Yes   _____ No

4. Have I transferred the pain and anger caused by someone in my life to another person through any of the acts on this list?

    _____ Yes   _____ No

Understand that God has brought you to this point. In effect, He has utilized several factors (this book included) to break down your denial and begin the soul work that will ultimately set you free. But to experience this freedom, you need to stop participating in the unfruitful works of darkness.[58] You need to stay vigilant; the devil does not want the truth revealed. He knows that if you bring your sin out into the light of

God, His love, grace, and mercy will break the yoke of slavery around your neck. You will then more aptly follow after the ways of the Lord, reflecting His glory into this dark world. As you work to face the reality of your sins, and the toll they have taken on those you have perpetrated, you will find yourself asking for, and receiving, forgiveness from the Father. Remember: "If we confess our sins, he is faithful and just and will forgive us our sins and purify us from all unrighteousness"[59]

Confessing our sin is an important step, but it is just that—*a step* in the process of sanctification. Once we confess, God will then work to purify us from unrighteousness. A significant part of this purification process involves contrition. When we are contrite, we feel regret and sorrow for our sins.[60] Such a state involves a heartfelt ache, a profound sense that our actions brought harm upon another. True contrition produces the motivation to change our thought and behavior so as not to offend again. It can also motivate us to make amends for our actions. From this perspective, we can better understand how confessing our sin brings about greater degrees of purity and righteousness.

Summary

The apostle Paul exhorted us not to be conformed to the patterns of this world, but to experience transformation through the renewing of our mind.[61] Living in denial about unresolved issues inhibits our ability to change and stifles the flow of God's love in our life. This is not to say our heavenly Father withholds His love; rather, our denial clogs the flow. When denial is broken, the love of God flows more freely in and through us.

In this chapter, we met Cedric, a man who had learned to minimize the pain and anguish of his father's compulsive behaviors. He longed to receive the love of his father but was denied fulfillment of this need for decades while his dad practiced his addictions. As a means to cope, Cedric learned to deny the truth and accept a lie, believing he could perform for his father and get his needs met. Failed attempts resulted in Cedric turning his anger inward, which led him into self-contempt. But in counseling, he effectively broke through his denial; he came to accept that his father was an alcoholic and womanizer, and that he was powerless over his father's addictions. As he released himself from the distorted premise that he was responsible for his father's behaviors, Cedric experienced a series of breakthroughs. More and more, he opened himself up to the love of God and was able to stop taking responsibility for his father's actions. In doing so, Cedric managed to establish healthier boundaries, with the end result that both he and his father were able to break through their denial and experience the healing flow of God's grace.

Denial was defined as an unconscious defense mechanism characterized by refusal to acknowledge painful realities, thoughts, or feelings. We learned that God has given us the capacity to feel emotions because they serve as gauges for our needs. The more in touch we are with what we are feeling and why we are feeling that way, the more in tune we can be with our God-given needs. When our needs are effectively met, we can then best live out our purpose. We also learned that denial is not always a bad thing. God created us with the capacity to think and behave in such a way as a means of coping with life when it overwhelms us, like when someone important to us dies or something of significance is lost. Our heavenly Father allows for a time of denial so we can incrementally, but thoroughly, process through the pain of our loss and maintain a healthy balance of mind. But we also came to see that denial becomes maladaptive when we refuse to ever cope with the issue at hand. It is at this point that denial becomes sin. God knows that such a state of mind not only inhibits His flow of love into our life, but it stifles the flow of love from us out into this world.

Faced with overwhelming situations in life, we tend to experience powerful emotions, such as fear, guilt, and helplessness. Unless we are vigilant, the intensity of these emotions can, and often does, keep us in a state of denial to the point where we simply do not want to think about the issue. This type of denial was illustrated in the life of the apostle Thomas. Yet there are other times when we find ourselves more readily accepting a particular matter, but we minimize the effects as a means of coping. Whenever we feel powerless to resolve an issue, we may find ourselves practicing this form of denial, just as King David did. When we minimize, we deny the significance of the sin. It is never the will of God that we live for an extended period of time in denial. Doing so inhibits our relationship with Him and others, as well as opens the door for the enemy to further perpetrate evil.

We also covered the issue of transference. How we take the unresolved feelings toward one person and transfer them onto another. As we saw in the case of Cain, when we engage in transference, we are operating in the flesh rather than the Spirit of God. The apostle Paul wrote that in such a state of mind, our behaviors end up involving acts of sexual immorality, impurity, and debauchery; idolatry and witchcraft; hatred, discord, jealousy, fits of rage, selfish ambition, dissensions, factions and envy; drunkenness, orgies, and the like.[62] An interesting side note here is the word rendered *witchcraft*. The Greek word Paul used here is *pharmakeia*,[63] which is where we derived the word *pharmacy*, the underlying implication being *self-medicating*. In effect, these types of denial result in discord, wherein our behaviors fail to line up with our awareness, perception, reasoning, or judgment. Whenever this occurs, we experience conflict in the form of dissonance. In such cases, we must either change the way we think or change the way we behave. In the end, our thoughts and behaviors must line up, or else we will live in distress. If we find our behavior to be problematic but choose not to change it, we must then practice some form of denial as a means to cope with the cognitive dissonance. The net result is all too often a cycle of defeat.

Now that you have completed the self-awareness section of this chapter, you may very well find yourself conflicted. If you checked some of the items on the lists but minimized the impact of the sin, you will find yourself experiencing dissonance and thus distress. You may have acknowledged the sin occurred, only to convince yourself the impact was minimal. But now, the Spirit of God is pressing upon you the truth of the matter. Yes, the sin occurred, and there is significance in it all. Will you maintain your self-deceptive practices and continue to deny the effects of sin? Or will you accept the truth of this matter and allow God's Spirit to transform you?

Because we are generally conditioned to think and behave as we do, change does not come easily. It would be unrealistic to ask you to *readily* accept an issue of sin all at once—one that perhaps you have spent a considerable amount of time denying. Coming to terms with a deeply-rooted issue is a *process*. It will take time to resolve such matters. The first step is to begin breaking through your self-deceptive practices involving denial and accepting that sin is an issue in your life. Regardless, if it is our own sin or the sin of others perpetrated upon us, the fact remains—sin is always polluting and corrosive. For those of you struggling to come to terms with this reality, I sincerely pray that the catalysis for healing and transformation has been sparked. In the next chapter, we will cover another leg of self-deception—repression.

Chapter Five

Matters of Repression

Therefore each of you must put off falsehood and speak
truthfully to his neighbor, for we are all members of
one body. "In your anger do not sin": Do not let the
sun go down while you are still angry, and
do not give the devil a foothold.

Ephesians 4:25–27

n the previous chapter, I likened the system of self-deception to a three-legged table—one leg represents denial, the second repression, and the third leg involves rationalization. If one of the legs of this system is removed, our self-deceptive practices tumble down. Chapter Four covered denial. We are now going to look at a second leg in this system of deception—*repression*. In effect, repression involves the *avoidance* of painful thoughts and feelings. It is different from denial, in which we choose not to *accept* an issue. When we repress, we tend to acknowledge a problem is present but seek to avoid the associated distress. Does God want us to live repressed lives as followers of Jesus? I assert the answer is no. Recall that God fashions us with needs so that we might best fulfill the purpose He created us with. In effect, when we choose not to cope with sin, we are avoiding certain thoughts and feelings. This not only stifles fulfillment of our needs, but we tend to become entrenched in the sin.

Repression Defined

The American Heritage Dictionary defines repression as the unconscious exclusion of painful impulses, desires, or fears from the conscious mind.[1] When it comes to the motives as to why we engage in repression, there are differing schools of thought. I believe The Unified Theory of Repression (TUTOR) offered by Matthew H. Erdelyi, Ph.D., has strong merit. Dr. Erdelyi hypothesized that repression is "a consciousness-lowering process," wherein a class of operations, i.e., thought processes and behaviors, reduce accessibility to consciousness of a particular issue.[2]

Subclasses of Repression

Essentially, there are two subclasses of repression involving *inhibitory* and *elaborative* processes. Inhibitory processes seek to achieve the goal of decreasing or stopping distress through acts of avoidance. For example, Stevie is in the fifth grade and is continually harassed by his teacher. He frequently is the butt of her jokes and the recipient of her criticism in front of other students. His teacher's sarcasm and judgmental behavior is mentally distressing and emotionally painful. Stevie wishes there was an adult he could speak with, but his father left home when he was an infant, and his mother is an alcoholic who would most likely make a scene. In addition, he fears reprisal from his teacher if he were to speak up. So Stevie engages in an inhibitory type of repression by busying himself with various activities.

Before school starts, he can be found in a flurry of action— making his bed, fixing breakfast, doing the dishes, finishing his homework, all of which help reduce his anxiety about going to school. On his way, Stevie fantasizes about being a spy on an important undercover mission, making sure to be on the lookout for the remotest signs of danger. In effect, this is an unconscious attempt to resist the distress of going to school by refocusing his energies on behaviors that preoccupy his mind. Lately, when his teacher starts in on him, he finds himself looking down at the ground, counting the number of tiles on the floor. As his teacher rants, he counts.

Just as Tyra escaped to her bedroom to listen to music, and Carol repressed her distress through cleaning, or how Cedric coped with his anguish by staying busy in school and sports, Stevie has also found a way to resist the distress he experiences. While each individual is successful in their efforts, in that their distress is initially lowered, the inherent challenge comes in the form of being conditioned into a repressed state of mind. Such a state keeps us in a survivor's mentality as opposed to living life as a victor, which is what Jesus said He came for.[3]

Whenever we experience distress, we generally attempt to cope in ways that will inhibit it from continuing. But when our attempts prove unsuccessful, we are then forced to adapt. This is where we attempt elaborative acts of repression. One such attempt is understood to involve the method of *reaction formation*. In this method, we transpose, i.e., reverse our desires associated with a particular person or thing.[4] For example, let us say Juan really wants to be included with a certain group of kids at school, only this particular group does not seem all that welcoming. In the beginning, he thinks to himself, *I really want to be a part of what they're doing.* But as time passes, only a couple of members seem interested in allowing him in; the others are more standoffish. As a means to cope with the distress of rejection, Juan begins to transpose his desires, telling himself, *I'm not so sure I want to join now.* In reality, his desire has not changed, Juan still wants to be a part of the group; however, if they do not accept him, he can cope with the distress by convincing himself otherwise. So Juan represses his desires, along with the pain of rejection, by working to convince himself that he is the one rejecting the group—not the other way around.

A second method of coping found in elaborative repression is known as *displacement*. In this mode, we are not so much attempting to avoid our feelings as much as we are looking for a more secure way to experience them. For instance, Kaylee is a teenage girl who finds herself crushing on a boy at church, only she senses the boy does not share the same feelings for her. Yet her attraction does not stop just because his feelings are not mutual. So she works to reduce her distress by focusing her energies on befriending this young man's girlfriend, and, of course, she does not disclose her true feelings. He is often the topic of conversation between these two girls. By maintaining the front, Kaylee vicariously experiences a form of relationship with the boy by practicing displacement with her friend.

A third coping mechanism found in elaborative repression is termed *symbolization.* This occurs when an object or idea takes on a new meaning in which emotional energies related to some other matter are transferred onto the symbol. We actually engage in symbolism more than you might think, such as the way a wedding ring symbolizes a lifelong commitment and a love without end, or how the flag of the United States represents freedom to many Americans. However, when it comes to matters of repression, symbolization tends to distort our view of reality. For example, when Lizette was twelve, her uncle began to molest her. He threatened that if she ever told anyone, he would likely go to jail, and his brother (Lizette's father) would be so angry with her that he would never forgive her. Because Lizette knew her father and uncle were close, she believed his lie and kept the abuse secret. As an adult, she practices symbolization by being tough; wherein she is highly oriented toward getting tasks done by taking charge in a direct, no nonsense manner. She is out to conquer her emotions, and holds others at bay through her impatience and anger. By doing so, Lizette succeeds in showing others (especially men) that *she* is in charge, which helps her to feel safer and less distressed. Yet her act of avoidance via this form of repression keeps Lizette stuck in the pain and anguish of her past abuse. Her ability to receive and reciprocate love is stifled, thwarting her purpose in life.

Our tendency toward a certain type of repressive behavior (inhibitive or elaborative) appears to be predicated, in large part, on operant conditioning (positive or negative reinforcement). Of the cases listed thus far, it can be seen that each person's repressive coping mechanisms were successful enough at resisting or adapting to the distress to qualify as positive reinforcement, because, to one degree or another, their behaviors were effective at lowering their level of distress. However, we must not lose sight of the fact that both healthy and unhealthy means of coping can be positively reinforced. For example, let us say I am stressed because I am late for a meeting, and happen to get away with driving fast and running a red light or two. My distress is lowered as I walk into the meeting less late than what I would have had I not driven this way. Thus, the effect of my behaviors could be considered positive because they lowered my overall level of distress. But my driving fast and running red lights would never be considered positive behavior.

As was discussed in Chapter Four, in terms of developing coping mechanisms, the more positively a particular behavior is reinforced, the greater the likelihood the behavior will be repeated as a means of coping. While repression is mostly viewed as being negative, as it is maladaptive and can produce pathology, our inclination to engage in it can be attributed to the fact that repression often proves successful at lowering our level of distress. However, the success of repression is short-lived. Even when negative behavior proves successful at reducing our distress, the net results are always negative. For instance, getting drunk as a means to cope with distress will most likely prove successful. Alcohol numbs our painful emotions for a time, which lowers our distress; thus, the behavior will be positively reinforced. However, getting drunk has negative consequences; therefore, it is considered to be a negative mode of coping. Alcohol is a poison, and drinking poison is generally not found to be a positive thing. Drinking alcohol impairs perception and judgment, which all too often results in serious consequences. Depending upon the degree and frequency of reinforcement, getting drunk as a means to resist distress can lead to attachment, which opens the door to addiction. So, in the short run, getting drunk might very well prove effective at numbing painful feelings and lowering distress. But, in the long run, this method of coping only serves to avoid dealing with issues. The more we do so, the less we are likely to find healthy resolutions. Therefore, repression could never be considered a viable solution. Rather, it complicates our life, which inevitably increases our distress.

Memory and Repression

Encoding, Storage, and Retrieval

Now that we have defined what repression is and studied its subclasses, let us look at how it impacts *memory*, a working definition of which could be: the mental faculty of retaining and recalling past experience.[5] Essentially, the means by which we retain and recall can be broken down into three stages. The first is understood to be *encoding*. At this stage, we receive stimuli through one or more of our senses and modify it into information.[6] This information is then kept in a permanent record during the second stage of memory known as *storage*. In part, our ability to store memory is why problems do not improve through repression. Because the mind seeks to resolve what is unresolved, we cannot count on our efforts to avoid as a reasonable solution. While we might not be conscious of a particular memory, the unconscious mind not only knows it is there, but it recognizes that the accompanying distress is unresolved. In such cases, the unconscious mind will seek to raise the memory up to a conscious level so resolution can be achieved. This process is otherwise known as recall. The means by which the mind accomplishes this function is through *retrieval*—the third stage of memory. Retrieval involves mental processes that bring stored information back into consciousness.[7] This typically occurs in response to a cue. For example, you are walking down the hall at work and see a new employee you met two days ago. Instantly, your mind mediates, i.e., directs energy in the form of electrical impulses to neurons in the temporal portion of your brain, and recognition of this person's face occurs. This recognition then acts as a cue to neurons in the hippocampus, where the individual's name is retrieved from storage. As you pass each other in the hall, you say, "Hello, Dwayne. How's it going?"

Another example might be the way a man tends to recall his father's abusive behavior whenever he smells freshly cut grass. As a boy, his dad would wake him early on Saturday mornings and make him cut the lawn. Afterward, his father would inspect his work, invariably finding it was not performed to his unrealistic expectations. So, he would take his son inside and beat him with a belt. Now, as a grown man, the smell of freshly cut grass serves as a cue, triggering what is known as an olfactory memory, i.e., a memory associated with a particular smell. Not only is smell associated with this memory, but the unresolved painful emotions are as well. As recall of the memories is triggered, this man unwittingly conditions himself to cope with the resulting distress by bingeing on alcohol.

Declarative and Procedural

Once the process of memory has taken place, it then can be broken down into two classifications known as *declarative* and *procedural*. Declarative memory pertains to intentional, i.e., conscious recall of past experiences. Two facets of conscious recall are *semantic* and *episodic*. Semantic memory involves simple meanings and impersonal facts,[8] such as recalling that Mt. Everest is the tallest mountain in the world (on land), or who won the Super Bowl last year. On the other hand, episodic memory pertains to personal experiences in our past involving time, location, emotion, and other contextual knowledge.[9] If you actually climbed Mt. Everest, in addition to semantic memory, you would have all sorts of episodic memory as well. Recalling who won the Super Bowl last year is semantic; remembering the fun you had at the Super Bowl party you attended is episodic.

A key point to note is this: *when an episodic memory is triggered, so too are the associated emotions.* If we cope with emotional pain through repressive modes, then the issue never really gets resolved, just avoided. Each time we cope with these painful memories through repression, we end up positively reinforcing what is otherwise a dysfunctional coping mechanism. This can lead us into habitually maladaptive methods of coping, which is precisely what Paul was addressing in Romans 7:14–25. We can proclaim we are new creations in Christ all we want; however, we must also be willing to address the ways we have learned to repress our thoughts and feelings.

The second classification of memory is *procedural,* which allows us to recall functions like combing our hair, pouring a cup of coffee, or throwing a baseball without having to consciously think

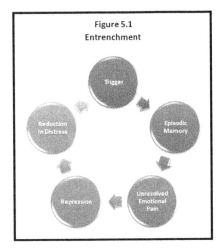

Figure 5.1
Entrenchment

about every step in the process. This is not to say we are unaware of the fact we are doing these things; rather, we can perform functions such as these and not have to fully concentrate.

Figure 5.1 illustrates the typical process by which we become entrenched in self-deceptive behaviors like repression. Something acts as a trigger and retrieval of an episodic memory occurs, and we reexperience painful emotions. If our act of repression proves successful at lowering the distress, then our methods of thinking and behaving in this regard will be reinforced. As the cycle recurs, this mode of coping becomes entrenched. Over time, repression becomes procedural; thus,

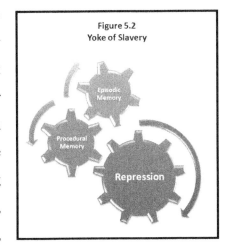

Figure 5.2
Yoke of Slavery

we submit to this yoke of slavery without being aware of it (see Figure 5.2). Such conditioning equates to imprisonment. We want to experience freedom in Christ and live the abundant life, but our conditioned modes of coping keep us in survival mode where there is little in the way of love, joy, and peace.

When it comes to procedural memory, there is a rather interesting wrinkle that occurs. It has to do with an effect known as the *illusion-of-truth,* in which we are more likely to believe a familiar statement than an unfamiliar one.[10] We tend to perceive repeated statements as having greater validity than those less frequently repeated. The challenge of such an effect is that it can lead to an inaccurate premise about a statement's truthfulness. Recall in Chapter Three that I touched upon the matter of deduction and the importance a premise plays in drawing conclusions. In effect, we base our beliefs on our conclusions. Because we live our lives in accord with our beliefs, it is important we base them as much as possible on Christ-centered premises. Deduction enables us to assess God's truth in any given matter, which affords us the opportunity to draw accurate conclusions and live in accord with His will.

I have counseled many people who lived their lives believing certain statements they heard repeatedly during childhood. Statements like: "You are no good." "What an idiot you are." "You'll never amount to anything." Hearing these statements repeatedly brought them to a point where they unconsciously accepted them as truth. In effect, these statements became a part of their procedural memory. Decades later, these individuals automatically tell themselves: *I am no good. What an idiot I am. I will never amount to anything.* In most cases, these people are not even aware they make these statements aloud. When we are conditioned to think in such ways, we become guilt-ridden and shame-based. Ultimately, our ability to fulfill God's purpose is stifled.

Schemas

It is important to understand that we typically do not retrieve stored memory in rote fashion. In other words, we do not recall in specific, sequential detail; rather, we mostly do so through the use of meaning.[11] As retrieval of memory occurs, elements of what transpired are combined with knowledge from existing organized thought structures called *schemas. Intellectual schemas* reflect biases, logical expectations, and cultural habits, while *emotive schemas* involve wishes, attitudes, and defenses. Regardless of the type, schemas distort memory. The means by which these distortions occur are complex; however, in a simplified explanation, the memory tends to degrade over time, causing gaps. When retrieval of a degraded memory occurs, the gaps are filled in through a process known as *schematic augmentation.*[12] What do they get filled in with? The answer is existing biases, expectations, habits, wishes, attitudes, and defenses.

There is an inherent challenge in such instances as both true and false recalls can occur.[13] For instance, let us return to the example of the wife in chapter four, who has suffered from her husband's physical, mental, and emotional abuse for a number of years. The accuracy of her childhood memories involving males may very well be augmented through her schemas. In such a case, she might develop this bias: men are not trustworthy. Her expectation is that men will always hurt her in one way or another. The result is a distorted memory of her father, wherein she views him as being less trustworthy than he actually is. The same might be the case for a husband who has lived with a critical wife for a number of years. He, too, could end up augmenting his childhood memories involving his mother. Here we find yet another way sin can pollute our life. Just as sin experienced in childhood can condition us to think and behave in maladaptive ways, so too can sin experienced in adulthood pollute our memories of childhood. This is precisely why we must work to break down the stronghold of denial and take painful memories captive for Christ as opposed to avoiding them through repression. In this respect, we approach the Lord with our emotional wounds and ask Him to assist us in resolving the matter so we can leave our conditioned modes of maladaptive thought and behavior behind.

The Word of God and Repression

Does God's word have anything to say about the issue of repression? Consider the following passage: "A simple man believes anything, but a prudent man gives thought to his steps."[14] When we are prudent, it could be said we are wise in handling practical matters, that we exercise good judgment or common sense.[15] Think of the impact repression has on our thoughts and behaviors, how it stifles our ability to exercise good judgment. We cannot make a wise decision if we are unwilling to look at all the factors associated with an issue. Recall the opening passage of this chapter: "Therefore each of you must put off falsehood and speak truthfully to his neighbor, for we are all members of one body. 'In your anger do not sin': Do not let the sun go down while you are still angry, and do not give the devil a foothold."[16] Repression is a falsehood because it prevents conformity to what is true. In effect, it constitutes an act of avoiding reality. How can we speak truthfully to our neighbor if we are unwilling to accept what is real? Allowing the sun to set on our anger is the same as avoiding an issue. As was illustrated in Chapter Four, our emotions serve as gauges, providing us with important information about our needs, which are tied to our God-given purpose. Yet repression inhibits this vital connection between emotions and needs.

Dokimazo pas katecho kalos (dok-im-ad'-zo • pas • kat-ekh'-o • kal-os').[17] These are the words the apostle Paul wrote in his first letter to the church at Thessalonica. The English translation is rendered as: *Test everything. Hold on to the good.* When we test someone or something, we subject them/it to a procedure for critical evaluation as means of determining presence, quality, or truth.[18] God has given us the ability to think and feel so that we would critically evaluate what is and what is not good. Unmet needs are not good, because such a state thwarts our purpose. So we must take time to contemplate what we are thinking and feeling, especially in our relationships. Once this is done, we can better assess the state of our needs. The manners by which we cope with unmet needs are of great importance, not only for our own well-being but for the well-being of others. In all of this, we come to see that repressing thoughts and feelings has a negative impact on our state of wellness.

The psalmist wrote: "Test me, O LORD, and try me, examine my heart and my mind."[19] But given that repression involves the lowering of consciousness, we unwittingly disconnect ourselves from this critical process of examination. While our heavenly Father always has our best interest at heart, He will not violate our freedom to think and behave as we see fit. So He allows us to make choices, even if they are not in our best interest. Understand that this is a painful process for the Lord. The more we practice avoidance as a coping mechanism, the less apt we are to lean on Him for understanding. Ultimately, this proves to be detrimental all the way around: physically, mentally, emotionally, and spiritually. But it is not as though we are without guidance. As Christians, we have the Scripture and the Holy Spirit, along with the healthiest, most functional model for coping with sin—Christ Jesus. Consider these words:

> [L]et us throw off everything that hinders and the sin
> that so easily entangles, and let us run with

perseverance the race marked out for us. Let us fix our eyes on Jesus, the author and perfecter of our faith, who for the joy set before him endured the cross, scorning its shame, and sat down at the right hand of the throne of God. Consider him who endured such opposition from sinful men, so that you will not grow weary and lose heart.[20]

Note that there was joy set before the Lord. Jesus knew that His victory over sin and death was at hand. He had already surrendered His will to the Father while in the garden of Gethsemane.[21] It is fitting that the word Gethsemane relates to a place of crushing, i.e., olive presses, for this is where the locals of Jerusalem brought their olives to be pressed into oil, and it is the place where Christ allowed His own will to be crushed. It was there in the garden that Jesus truly gave up His life. Not to minimize the significance of His sufferings while on trial and during His crucifixion, but those acts involved the *formalities* of Christ bearing the punishment of our sins. The actual act of surrendering His life to the Father had already occurred. Jesus suffered unimaginable grief during His time in Gethsemane. But ultimately, He experienced joy in the end, because He could see how His act of pure love was the very thing that conquered the grave and made way for humanity and heaven to reunite once again.[22] Regardless of our circumstances, this same kind of joy is set before us as well. All we need to do is surrender to the Father's will.

In no way did Christ avoid the issue of propitiating for our sins. Not only did He go into the garden, He clearly communicated His thoughts, feelings, and needs to His disciples. Once they arrived, Jesus expressed His need for them to pray. He then took Peter, James, and John, His inner circle of friends, a bit farther into the garden, where He expressed feeling overwhelmed with sorrow even to the point of death. Christ next asserted His need for them to pray while He went off on His own to be with the Father. When He returned, He found His disciples asleep. Again, Jesus asserted His needs by waking them and petitioning them to pray.[23] Total surrender does not come easy; it did not for Jesus, and it does not for us. Two more times He returned to His place of prayer, petitioning the Father, but in the end, He freely gave up His own will. Jesus had the freedom to avoid this issue, but instead He chose to face what was before Him. We can take great comfort in knowing that our Savior understands the challenges involved with facing troubles. We can also choose to follow His lead and face what lies before us.

Mystery and Repression

God wants us to relate with His triune nature: Father, Son, and Holy Spirit. All of this sounds good and well, but it is much easier said than done. Always at play is the issue of our willfulness, especially when it comes to the mysteries of our Creator. How is it that an omniscient God who looks ahead in time and sees the way we willfully disobey Him still chooses to love us? This is a great mystery indeed, one which we willfully attempt to solve. We ask ourselves, *Why is it that God loves me so; what are His motives?* When it comes to mystery, we tend to want to define it. We are troubled by the notion that some mysteries are anything but temporary, and would rather consider a mystery something that it is not yet solved.[24] We are more comfortable with this perspective. When we consider a mystery to be temporary, we can then relax a bit with the notion that perhaps, one day, we might solve it. In willfulness, we seek to be the master of our destiny. Indeed, the very thought that we have little, if any, control over the mysteries of life provokes distress. As Dr. Gerald May aptly wrote:

> Mystery can be experienced, sensed, felt, appreciated, even loved, without being understood. This may not be easy; it requires a surrender of all willfulness, a risking of self-image, and a nurturing of intuition....Such encounters with mystery can be very beautiful, but often they are also associated with considerable anxiety.[25]

The notion that we need not always attempt to solve mystery but rather learn to live with it is not one we readily accept. We tend to reject mystery because it reminds us that we are not God. It spotlights our vulnerabilities and points to the fact that we lack control of the world we live in. Experiencing this lack can be downright terrifying at times. We are then inclined to repress such distressing thoughts and feelings. After all, if there is little we can do to gain more control over our life, then we are faced with one of two options: (1) accept reality and learn to live with the uneasiness of it all, or (2) deny reality and repress the associated thoughts and feelings. What we choose in this respect will impact our relationship with God. At some point, we must come to terms with the fact that entering into an intimate relationship with our Creator means entering into mystery. Are we willing to live with the mysteries of God without willfully trying to control Him? Can we overcome our urge to repress the fear, anxiety, anger, etc., that comes with letting go of the illusion of control? Any such attempt requires preparation of our mind to accept the reality of the unknown and surrender our willfulness to solve it. We cannot be God, but we can be in relationship with Him. Coming to terms with the mystery surrounding our Lord—especially His love, grace, and mercy—is vitally important if we are to experience an intimate relationship with Him.

Cognition and Repression

The Lord has fashioned us with a capacity for *cognition*, the mental processes by which we develop knowledge. The impact repression has on our cognition can be significant. Let's work to put off falsehood by delving deeper into these processes.

Awareness

God designed us with the ability to be aware, to perceive of Him and His creation through the senses He has given us. While awareness does not always equate directly to knowledge, it does provide us with the ability to be conscious of such things as events, objects, and patterns.[26] Without awareness, we could not know events were taking place in our life, and objects such as things, people, and goals would be meaningless. The patterns of life consisting of forms, styles, traits, and features would be senseless as well. Through awareness, we have the ability to be open to the sensations and experiences of life—to watch a sunrise on a spring morning, and at the same time be aware of the crispness in the air, as well as take note that God has set all of this in motion. We are cognizant of such things because our Creator saw fit to fashion us with awareness.

Another key point is that each of us has been given the capacity for a *subjective* quality of conscious experience. How one person is aware of and perceives a sunrise is not necessarily how another person might be aware of and perceive the same sunrise. While there are many commonalities we share as humans, each of us experiences life in our own subjective way. We might understand what it is like to feel grief, but none of us knows exactly what it is like for another person who is grieving. Yet it is our God-given ability to be aware that enables us to *empathize*, to identify with, and understand another person's situation, feelings, and motives.[27] Through awareness, we can experience mutual understanding and affection with others—it is what we call being *sympathetic.*[28] Because we are aware, we have the capacity to relate to our Creator, as well as with one another, on deep and meaningful levels. *A significant point to all of this is that repression stifles awareness.* When painful thoughts and emotions are associated with certain events, objects, or patterns, our tendency is to shift energies away from these associations in an attempt to avoid distress.

Reason

Our basis or motives for actions, decisions, and convictions are rooted in our ability to reason. God provides us with the capacity for logical, rational, and analytical thought.[29] He does so because He is relational. He thinks about us constantly, and He wants us to contemplate our relationship with Him as well. The Father desires that we search for Him, that we come to better understand His characteristics, so that our relationship will deepen.[30] Through reason, we can better understand the Lord's will by examining the following points of His word:

- *Content:* The meaningful parts of His assertions as they apply to our life.
- *Method:* The means by which He deals with a particular matter in our life.

· *Validity:* The degree to which His assertions are ultimately found to be true in our life.

Through the application of reason, we develop greater intimacy with our Creator as we come into a deeper understanding of His character and will. To further illustrate these points, let us look at a assertion Jesus made:

> [E]veryone who hears these words of mine and puts
> them into practice is like a wise man who built his house
> on the rock. The rain came down, the streams rose, and
> the winds blew and beat against that house; yet it did not
> fall, because it had its foundation on the rock.[31]

With respect to *content,* Jesus' assertion is meaningful, because we can learn to stand firm on the word of God—not being swept away by life's challenges. The *methods* by which God deals with challenges in our life are numerous. For instance, Philippians 4:13 communicates that He strengthens us, while Psalm 23:2, 3 assures us that He guides in ways that are right. The *validity* of God's assertions are found in repeated observations of the following points: (1) if we build our life upon Him, we will find strength beyond our own in times of trouble, and (2) when we follow Christ, He leads us on the path of righteousness.

But when we repress, we are less conscious of the motives involved with our actions, decisions, and convictions—we become stuck. We repeat the same behaviors, but expect different results. This cycle can produce a good deal of distress and lead us into hopelessness. In a repressed state, we lower our consciousness to the point where we cannot effectively reason the solution. The net result is that we unwittingly give the devil a foothold.

Judgment

Our capacity for cognition also includes the ability to make judgments, which are the formations of opinions after we have given consideration to a particular matter.[32] Being able to perform such a function is vitally important in our relationship with God and others. Through judgments, we perceive and distinguish relationships. Being able to judge soundly is key to effective discernment. Without the ability to distinguish, we could not form opinions, nor would we have the capacity to evaluate situations, understand circumstances, and draw reliable conclusions. Every waking moment, our behavior is based on the judgments we make. Given this fact, maintaining the highest level of consciousness becomes vitally important to ensure we are making the kind of judgments that align with our heavenly Father's will. But when we live a repressed life, our awareness is lowered, which in turn stifles our ability to reason. The net result is our hampered judgments. This was never God's will for us. It pains Him to see us in such a state. His desire is for us to operate in the full capacity of our cognitive and emotive abilities; this way, we are best positioned to fulfill the purpose He wove into our life.

Emotions and Repression

In addition to cognition, God has fashioned us with the capacity for emotion. According to The American Heritage Dictionary, *emotion* is defined as "a mental state that arises spontaneously rather than through conscious effort, and is often accompanied by physiological changes."[33] Such a view is more in line with neurobiological theory, which is predicated on the assertion that emotion is strongly tied to neural mapping in the limbic system of the brain. This portion of the brain forms the inner border of the cortex and includes the:

· *Hippocampus*, for long-term memory
· *Amygdale*, involved with emotional learning
· *Anterior thalamic nuclei*, which moderates alertness and serves with learning and memory
· *Limbic cortex*, tied to support of emotion, behavior, and long-term memory.[34]

While empirical data clearly demonstrates that the limbic system is *involved* with emotion, neurobiological theories have yet to conclusively prove emotions *originate* from this system within the brain.

Another school of thought stems from cognitive theories, wherein the assertion is made that cognitive constructs—like evaluations and judgments—need to be present for an emotion to form. For example, you return home from work to a dark house. You turn on the light and see someone stealing your possessions. The moment you become aware of this situation, you begin to make key evaluations: *Am I in danger? Do I stay and fight...or run?* From these evaluations, you quickly form judgments: *I will stay and fight. Or, I will flee.* As a result of these evaluations and judgments, you feel emotions, e.g., fear, anger, etc. Your body responds in a number of key ways, which almost instantaneously prepares you for fight or flight. Certainly, emotion can influence judgment. While it might be wiser to flee the scene, anger can override your fear, and you make the judgment to stay and fight. This cognitive perspective suggests we think these thoughts first, and then we feel the emotions, which culminate in behavior.

Both schools agree on the point that some form of psychic energy enables our thoughts and emotions to exist. They also support the notion that this energy originates, and is self-contained, within the human body. To view this source of energy as originating from outside our body would inject a good deal of mystery. As was touched upon earlier, mystery is something we generally are not comfortable with. Nonetheless, from a theological perspective, all energy originates from God because He is the Creator of the cosmos.

The Scripture reveals that His energy is beyond natural law.[35] His word also supports the notion that His energy is the creative force found in all things.[36] The Bible further reveals that God's energy maintains matter.[37] The fact that psychic energy exists, and is the basis of development for thoughts and emotions, is not in dispute here. What is in dispute is the *origin* of psychic energy. Undoubtedly, science will continue working on the "how" of this energy; yet the more profound question is "why." Why has our Creator chosen to utilize His energy in these manners? Perhaps His ultimate aim is to empower us to love, because He Himself is love.

While the cause of our psychic energies remain mysterious, it is clear that the Lord desires for us to live our life in such a way His energy flows through us. This means we are not to avoid our emotions by repressing their associated energy. Our Creator gave us the capacity for emotion; He intends for us to live our life in the context of our feelings. This is not to say we are to allow our emotions to lead us around. We are not the sum total of our feelings; however, they do make up a vitally important facet of who we are. The questions in this matter are: (1) Will we submit to the Father's will and allow His energy to manifest in our life as He intends? Or (2), will we subvert His will for our own selfish interests? The way we choose to think determine the directional flow of our emotional energy. When we choose our own will, the flow of that energy manifests itself in one kind of negative form or another.[38] But when we choose to follow the will of God, the flow is always positive.[39] So we come to see in all of this that repression not only lowers our consciousness, but it also involves a redirect of our emotive energies. This generally results in shifting our thoughts and feelings away from God, and attaching them to someone or something else. In such actions are found the rudiments of idolatry.

The Will of God and Repression

Kelly was raised in a home where she was forced to eat everything on her plate. When she was ten years old, she contracted the flu. Two days later, she rejoined her family at the dinner table but could not stomach much. Her father became enraged when he saw she did not eat all of her food. Grabbing a handful off her plate, he viciously crammed the food into her mouth. He repeated this action until her plate was empty. Kelly ran to the bathroom and vomited. Afterward, her father beat her with a belt for throwing up. For much of her adult life, she repressed this and several other abusive acts at the hands of her father.

Now in her mid-twenties, Kelly struggles with anorexia for what she says are "seemingly unknown reasons." In counseling, she fights against a deeply rooted bias, namely, people who leave food on their plate are selfish and do not care that others in the world are starving. This was what she heard her father say repeatedly while she was growing up. This statement, coupled with the traumatic experience of what would happen if she could not eat all the food on her plate, developed into an illusion of truth. So Kelly ensures she will not become one of those "selfish people" by eating very little throughout the day. In her hypervigilance, she makes sure she can finish her entire meal by severely limiting the portions. In effect, her anorexia provides a sense of power and control. By minimizing her intake, Kelly guarantees that everything on her plate will be eaten, which helps her to think and feel nothing bad will happen. Yet, because she is repressed, Kelly's God-given ability for awareness, reason, and sound judgment are significantly hampered. Unwittingly, she internalized her father's contempt, resulting in anorexic behavior. As Kelly continues in her entrenched modes of dysfunction, she does not live in the abundance Jesus came for her to have, and the God-given purpose for her life is stifled.

What is God's will for Kelly's life? Certainly, His desire is to share an intimate relationship with her in which she connects with His love, grace, and mercy. The Lord wills for her to grow in holiness, whereby she would experience a lightness of spirit and the abundant life of joy and peace. But her conditioned modes of thinking and manners of behaving keep her from experiencing these things. As a result of her father's sin, Kelly is conditioned into a state of self-deception. Occasionally, an episodic memory involved with the abuse is triggered. Unresolved in it all, she is quickly overwhelmed with painful thoughts and feelings. In these instances, her procedural memory serves as an automatic default for coping, and she unconsciously intensifies her anorexic behavior. Unless this cycle is changed, Kelly will most likely continue in this maladaptive pattern, her condition will worsen, and she will likely die from complications associated with her disorder. To this extent, the devil will have achieved his despicable aim of stealing Kelly's peace of mind and effectively killing her hope. Without hope, Kelly will be utterly destroyed.

While others might not struggle with repression to the degree Kelly does, God's will is for us to not engage in this self-deceptive practice. Rather, the Father desires to see us live our lives with a high degree of awareness. In this way, we can reason as to which of our needs are not being effectively tended to. With this degree of awareness, we can then position ourselves well to make sound judgments as to how the Lord wants us to get our needs met.

Self-Assessment

Like the previous chapter, we again come to the point of self-assessment. How is repression manifesting in your own life? With what kind of frequency and intensity are you engaging in this maladaptive behavior? Below is a list of questions intended to help assess the degree to which you struggle with repression. Answer each question by circling the number that best indicates how you agree or disagree at this time in your life. Circle only one number per question.

	Strongly Disagree	Disagree	Unsure	Agree	Strongly Agree
1. I avoid conflict.	1	2	3	4	5
2. I store up my emotions.	1	2	3	4	5
3. I was raised in a home where I was abused, or have witnessed abuse.	1	2	3	4	5
4. I am not sure why I feel the way I do.	1	2	3	4	5
5. I am in touch with my thoughts and feelings, but do not openly express them.	1	2	3	4	5
6. I shut down certain memories whenever they come up.	1	2	3	4	5
7. I am not comfortable in my own skin.	1	2	3	4	5
8. I lack a sense of humor.	1	2	3	4	5
9. I do not trust people.	1	2	3	4	5
10. There is a significant block of time in my past that I seem to have no or little memory of.	1	2	3	4	5
11. I have hurt people but avoid thinking about it.	1	2	3	4	5
12. As a child, it was not okay for me to express my thoughts and feelings.	1	2	3	4	5
13. I keep busy so I do not have time to think about certain painful issues.	1	2	3	4	5
14. It is okay for others to have their thoughts and feelings, but it is not okay for me.	1	2	3	4	5
15. I am out of touch with my feelings.	1	2	3	4	5

Add up your total score and list it below:

Total: _____

Scoring:

> 15 – 35: Overall, you are not inhibited when it comes to accepting and working through your thoughts and feelings. If there are painful events that occur in your life, you are able face reality and resolve matters.

> 36 – 45: A score in this range denotes a degree of ambivalence; you are torn between conflicting thoughts and emotions. You might accept that painful events occurred in the past, but are unsure what impact they have on your life today. This could equate to minimization, for which it is likely that you mildly to moderately repress distressing thoughts and feelings.

> 46 – 60: A score toward the lower end of this range indicates there is a strong probability that repressive coping mechanisms are at work in your life. A score toward the higher end of this range indicates frequent use of repression as a coping mechanism.

61 – 75: A score in this range indicates significant use of repression as a coping mechanism. One or more of the following are highly probable:

- You suffered some type of abuse or traumatic experience that remains unresolved.
- You struggle with compulsive behavior, such as eating, drinking, drug use, shopping, gambling, sex/pornography, etc.
- You have brought harm to others and are overwhelmed with intense feelings of shame when you think about it.

If you scored in the 15 – 35 range, then praise the Lord. You are living a life unencumbered by repression. If you scored in any of the other ranges, then today you are given the opportunity to look further into the unresolved matters of your life. Here are suggestions in light of this opportunity:

1. In the assessment you just took, look at the statements where you answered with scores of fours or fives. Pray on these statements. Ask God to assist you with revelation as to why you answered to these degrees. For example: Statement seven –

"I am not comfortable in my own skin." Let's say you indicated strong agreement by circling the number five. Bring this matter before the Lord; ask Him to reveal what it is that causes you such discomfort in your own skin. Irrespective of the revelation you receive—no matter how uncomfortable the answer might be—stand firm. Do not repress your thoughts and feelings. Stick with it long enough to receive the Lord's revelation as to what He wills you to do. Accept that this situation might require help from a member of the clergy or a professional Christian counselor. If need be, visit the American Association of Christian Counselors website, www.aacc.net; click on the link titled, FIND A CHRISTIAN COUNSELOR.

2. Anticipate a possible flood of memories and emotions as you stand firm and no longer submit to the yoke of slavery called repression. Tell yourself the emotions might be intense, but they are just emotions, and God has given you the strength so they will not overtake you.

3. Read Ephesians 5:11. Next, petition the Lord as to whom He desires for you to confide in about these issues of sin. If you have been abused, I would *not* advise confronting your perpetrator until you have first worked with a reputable Christian counselor and are being advised to do so.

4. Read Philippians 3:13–15. As the Spirit of God impresses upon your spirit, pray for strength that you would press forward and

not repress the issues of sin any longer. It would be important to note that the Greek word the apostle Paul used here for forgetting is *epilanthanomai* (ep-ee-lan-than'-om-ahee), which means "to lose out of mind."[40] To loosen that which is distressing you, you are going to need to stop repressing.

5. Read Romans 12:19. Watch for the pendulum effect. Ceasing to repress a particular matter does not give you license to seek vengeance on those who have hurt you. God wills for you to be free from the pain and anguish that has bound you. Bitterness and resentment will only keep you enslaved. Forgiveness is a *process*—one that typically involves grieving whatever the painful matter entails and effectively working through the unresolved pain and anguish. Most people in such cases will need support and guidance. Pray that God would direct you to the right professional who can assist. Again, the American Association of Christian Counselors might be able to help you locate a Christian counselor in your area: www.aacc.net; click on the link titled: FIND A CHRISTIAN COUNSELOR.

6. Read 1 John 5:4. Prepare your mind for victory! Proclaim that you will one day experience an abundance of love, joy, and peace as you overcome your repressive modes of coping.

Summary

Now that we have worked through the ins and outs of repression, there is better understanding of what it means to not let the sun go down on our anger. God never intended for us to live a repressed life; when we do so, it impacts our relationship with Him and others. His will is for us to prepare our mind for a deep, meaningful relationship with Him. The Lord wills that we be sanctified, that we grow in holiness and draw ever closer to Him. An intimate relationship with the Father is the best assurance for living an overflowing life with love, joy, and peace.

Through Dr. Erdelyi's work on The Unified Theory of Repression (TUTOR), along with the work of many others, the conscious and unconscious ways we practice repression are better understood. Our attempts to resist distress by avoiding issues reduces accessibility to consciousness. While our inhibitory and elaborative efforts might prove effective at lowering our immediate distress, the Lord wants us to solve issues in life, not avoid them. "For God did not give us a spirit of timidity, but a spirit of power, of love and of self-discipline."[41] Avoiding issues rather than leaning on the Lord for wisdom and strength serves only to reinforce our misconception that we are powerless. In such a state, we submit to a yoke of slavery and thwart fulfillment of our God-given purpose.

Repression stifles us in taking thoughts captive for Christ.[42] For many people, the lies repeatedly spoken into their life are hard to overcome, but through Jesus we can find the strength to rise above. Grieving the festering anguish left in the wake of sin is no easy task, yet it is not impossible either—not where God is concerned. We really can overcome. We need only to receive His Spirit to be strengthened to cope with our unresolved issues in life. This is why self-deceptive practices, such as denial and repression, can be so devastating. When we practice these maladaptive modes of coping, we deceive ourselves with the notion that if we just do not think about our painful issues, they will go away. Recall: God created us for a state of balance; our mind will seek resolution of any issue that remains unresolved, no matter how much we might attempt to avoid it.

We can learn to accept this reality, to turn and face our unresolved issues. We can experience victory as we receive the spirit of power, love, and sound mind that our heavenly Father has always made available to us. It is not hopeless; it is full of hope. You might say, *"Yes, all of this sounds good and well for others, but you do not know what's buried in my past."* I, too, said these words at one time. Many of my counselees have spoken them as well. In effect, this line of thinking equates to more avoidance. Be encouraged; God is faithful. He will see you through so that you can more freely relate with Him and others. The abundant life of love, joy, and peace is there for you to receive.

At times, each of us will struggle with repression. It is a mystery in many respects. We ask ourselves: *Where was God when…? Why did He allow…?* Consider that God is ever-present, He is right there with us when sin is perpetrated upon us, as well as when we are perpetrating sin. While it might be hard to fathom, as offended and hurt as we are, the offense is always greatest against God. Nowhere is this more apparent than when we look to the cross. This is a great mystery, indeed, but as we work through our unresolved anguish, we come to a place of acceptance and appreciation of the mystery.

Our Creator has given us the capacities for cognition and emotion through which we have the ability to be aware of and to feel. We can reason by employing logical, rational, and analytical thought. Repression need not inhibit us any longer. Throughout this book, you have been formulating judgments. For those struggling in this area of self-deception, it is my sincere prayer that you will allow awareness to percolate in your conscious mind. I pray you will employ reason to the information presented here.

The emotions contained within unresolved issues can be exceedingly intense and overwhelming. At Kingdom Community Ministries (www.kcmcounseling.com), we work with people who have been abused in the most horrific of ways. The amount of pain and anguish these individuals have carried around in their life can be downright staggering. In the face of such suffering, it is amazing to consider how they survived at all. When we are conditioned into a mode of survival, love, joy, and peace become significantly inhibited. Not only have I witnessed this as a Minister of Christian Counseling, I too have personally experienced what life is like in survival mode. But there was a time in my life when my denial was broken enough for me to become aware of my self-deceptive practices. This awareness did not come all at once but gradually, by working through the layers. As I applied reason, I came to understand that while my emotions were very intense at times, they were not going to kill me. This was not any easy reality to accept; there were times when I honestly felt as though my emotions might do just that. But with the strength afforded me through the Lord, alongside the guidance of my counselors and support of others, I began to overcome. As I developed more functional coping skills, I practiced self-deception to a lesser degree. Eventually, I stopped submitting to the enemy's yoke of slavery. I experienced freedom in Christ and now live the abundant life. This is not to say I no longer face challenges—I do every day. But just like Paul, I too have found the means by which to be content in all things.[43] Through the strength of Christ, I was able to overcome my conditioned modes of self-deception. I am fully confident He will do the same for you. All you need to do is ask Him to help. Now, as we work to no longer conform to the pattern of this world but rather be transformed by the renewing of our mind, we next look at the final leg that supports the practice of self-deception—*rationalization.*

Chapter Six
Why We Rationalize

There is a way that seems right to a man,

but in the end it leads to death.

Proverbs 14:12

I n this chapter, we will shift our focus to the third leg of self-deception: *rationalization.* Recall that in the previous chapter, it was asserted that reason is the basis, or motive, for our actions, decisions, and convictions. When our premises make logical sense, it is because we have employed reason, that we are sound in our thinking and within the bounds of common sense.[1] Based on this, the term *rationalization* can cause confusion as it is the opposite of being reasonable. By rationalizing, we seek to devise self-satisfying yet false reasons for our behavior, especially as a defense mechanism through which irrational acts or feelings are made to appear rational.[2] Through denial, we seek to refuse certain realities. In the course of repression, our goal is to avoid those realities. But it is through rationalization that we attempt to alter reality, to justify untrue or disharmonious reasons for certain behaviors. In effect, we create a fallacy—a false reality that does not align with God's truth.

The ABC's of Rationalization

Recall that in General Adaptation Syndrome, prolonged bouts of distress must be either resisted or adapted to, lest we exhaust ourselves. Denial and repression tend to be stronger forms of resistance, while rationalization is geared more toward adaptation. When we rationalize, we are not so much denying or avoiding reality; rather, we are attempting to alter reality. Along these lines, Albert Ellis, Ph.D., developed an approach known today as Rational Emotive Behavior Therapy (REBT). Ellis built the REBT model on the hypothesis that emotional states are a derivative of thought processes predicated on what he termed the ABC's, wherein *A* stands for *adverse* event; *B* for *beliefs* associated with that event; and *C* for emotional and behavioral *consequences* resulting from our beliefs. According to Dr. Ellis, irrational beliefs about life events cause irrational emotions and behaviors. Conversely, rational beliefs result in rational emotions and behaviors.[3]

Within REBT, adversity involves internal and external events that could have occurred in the past or might occur in the present or future.[4] Our beliefs about adverse events stem from our premises. Ellis asserted that when our beliefs intersect with adverse events, the result is an emotional and behavioral consequence. For example, if we return to the scenario presented in chapter one of being raised in a home where mom and dad set unrealistically high expectations on performance in school, sports, chores, etc. No matter how hard the children worked, the parents were ultracritical of their child's performance. Out of adversity, this person develops perfectionistic beliefs; they lump their behavior into one of two categories—perfect or failure. Because nobody outside of God is perfect, to one degree or another, they come to view everything they do as a failure. The behavioral consequence of this belief is a compulsivity to achieve impossible goals. In such cases, one ties their own worth to accomplishments and productivity. Yet, because the goals are impossible, this mode of thought and behavior proves to be self-defeating. The result is an unmerited sense of worthlessness. In such a state, love, joy, and peace are stymied. So, too, is God's purpose for that individual's life.

Meet Tyler

Tyler was the youngest of four children. As a young boy, he learned to be seen but not heard. Whenever he attempted to express his thoughts or feelings, he was quickly silenced through the ridicule of his older siblings. Tyler's father was gone more than not, working to support his family. When he was home, he was tired and irritable. His mother was a harsh woman—critical of her children. As a result, Tyler believes it is best if he does not express his thoughts and feelings. In his marriage, he experiences distress whenever his wife expresses herself and then expects him to do the same. The emotional consequence is his feeling of confusion and frustration, while the behavioral consequence is his effort to avoid communicating with her.

As a result of his childhood distress, Tyler formulated certain beliefs about communicating with others. Now, in adulthood, he tries not to think about the struggles in his marriage. This, of course, is simple denial. But as tension builds, Tyler takes on additional tasks at work and is home less often. This behavior is really an act of repression that further exasperates his wife and increases the frequency with which she asserts her needs. Ultimately, he rationalizes his dysfunctional behavior by telling her things like, *"They need me at work," "I am just not a talker," "If I tell you what I think, it's only going to lead to an argument."* In his mind, these statements serve as justification for his stoic approach to communicating. In reality, his wife's needs are real and reasonable, but he seeks to alter this reality by convincing himself otherwise.

This line of thinking leads Tyler into sin due to his lack of consideration for his wife's needs. The apostle Peter provided guidance in such matters when he wrote: "Husbands, in the same way be considerate as you live with your wives, and treat them with respect as the weaker partner and as heirs with you of the gracious gift of life, so that nothing will hinder your prayers."[5] Tyler is engaged in a well-entrenched process of self-deception of which he is only minimally aware. The lack of love and security he felt in his family caused him great distress as a child. As a means to survive, he learned he could experience less emotional pain if he kept quiet. The results of this coping mechanism served as positive reinforcement for what is otherwise considered negative behavior. Conversely, whenever Tyler did speak up, the emotional punishment he received from his family members served as a negative aversion to functional behaviors like communicating thoughts, emotions, and needs. While his sin might not be an act of omission, where he knowingly defies God's will, it nonetheless is sin to which there will be negative consequences. The Lord seeks to steer Tyler away from such dynamics, because the negative consequences inhibit fulfillment of his purpose.

There are times when Tyler thinks about his wife's unmet needs. In these brief moments of heightened awareness, an opportunity is made available for him to choose differently. On occasion, he thinks about seeking help from a Christian counselor, but quickly falls back into his self-deceptive practices as a means to cope with the distress. He is likely to continue living his life this way until: (1) he sees the importance of changing his beliefs to align with God's will, and (2) commits to replace his dysfunctional modes of thought and behavior with healthier, more functional modes.

For the believer in Christ, the Holy Spirit is active in this process, convicting us of the ways we are living outside of God's will, not as a means to punish us, but because it is in our best interest that we live in accord with our Lord's will. Consider the words of Jesus:

> Which of you, if his son asks for bread, will give him a
> stone? Or if he asks for a fish, will give him a snake? If
> you, then, though you are evil, know how to give good

gifts to your children, how much more will your Father
in heaven give good gifts to those who ask him![6]

God wants to give us good gifts. He desires for us to experience the
abundant life of love, joy, and peace. But when we practice self-
deception through rationalization, these states-of-being become
stymied. So we must be willing to die as to our flesh. We need to ask
God to search our mind and reveal to us the ways we are conditioned
to think and behave that do not align with His plan for our life.

Meet Sheila

From the moment she first got high, it appeared as though
Sheila was hooked. The fact that she ever tried drugs was a shock to
most people, especially her family. Sheila was raised in a loving home
with her father, mother, and older sister. Dad ran a successful business
enterprise started by his great-grandfather. His motto was: God first,
family second, then comes work. So more than not, he made sure to be
home at night, and there was not one extracurricular event of his
daughters' that he missed. Mom was equally involved as well. She
loved her children, managed the household, and volunteered her time
to those in need. Sheila was raised in an upper-class neighborhood
with lots of friends. Life was good, or so it seemed. For as long as she
could remember, there was this persistent sense that God favored her
sister Gwen more than He did her. Sheila believed she lived in Gwen's

shadow. Her sister was one of those straight-A students who seemingly did not have to work hard for good grades. She excelled in athletics and was amazing on stage when it came to performing in school dramas. It is not that Sheila did not love her sister; she did. And, at most times, she felt very close to her. Gwen was one of those vivacious types whose energetic spirit was contagious. For instance, even though they were three years apart, teachers who had Gwen for a student would rave about her when Sheila later became a student of those same teachers. When she entered high school as a freshman, she could not help but see the banners on the gymnasium wall displaying the athletic achievements of fellow students. Gwen's name could be found next to many records she had set—records that were destined to stand for years to come. Her former coaches often reminded Sheila that she had some big shoes to fill.

It was not that Gwen was smug or prideful in all of this; in fact, she was quite the opposite. It was not a matter that her parents showed favoritism either. Sheila never felt anything other than being loved and supported by her family. She was not angry with Gwen either; she did not fault her for being who God made her to be. But she was angry with the Lord. Why would a loving God put her in this position? It seemed mean-spirited. In her mind, she believed she would always be relegated to her sister's shadow. Even though her parents had money to send both of their girls to fine universities, Gwen received generous scholarship offers to some of the most prestigious schools in the nation. That was an achievement Sheila believed she could not duplicate. She also believed her sister would one day take over as CEO of the family business. It was a position Gwen seemed destined for. In Sheila's mind, it was black and white; Gwen was destined for greatness because God favored her.

She unwittingly coped with her distress by denying the reality of her thoughts and feelings. Never once did she talk with her parents about her struggles. There was not one teacher she confided in. She felt powerless and trapped. She just simply denied her distress most of the time. But on occasion, reality would come crashing through in a big way, and there it was—the overwhelming sense that God had blessed Gwen beyond measure, but He had been less generous to her. Why? What was it about her sister that God favored so much? During these times, Sheila would employ repressive types of behavior as a means to cope. She had taken extra assignments at school and doubled-up on her practices for sports, whatever it took to avoid the painful thoughts that God favored Gwen over her.

But then it happened. Toward the end of her sophomore year in high school, while spending the night at a friend's house, Sheila was introduced to marijuana. The relief it brought seemed to hook her instantly. Prior to getting high, she was working to preoccupy her mind so as not to think about her sister's return home from college for the summer. Gwen's homecomings had proven to be distressing for Sheila; they were a stark reminder of what she believed to be God's favoritism. However, on that particular evening, it no longer seemed to matter once she was high. The whole experience felt so freeing. By the end of that summer, Sheila had developed a full-blown addiction. During her junior year, her grades fell sharply. Her parents, more than a little concerned over this change, were shocked to learn that she was not showing up to her sports practices after school. When they confronted her on these issues, Sheila flew into a rage. Her mom and dad were absolutely stunned! A few days later, the school counselor suggested to her mother that such dramatic changes in behavior could indicate drug use. Fearful of what she might find, she waited and prayed for a couple of more days. What she uncovered in Sheila's belongings crushed her heart. There, tucked away in the back of a bottom drawer, was her stash. Not only did she find pot, she discovered pills as well, for which she had no prescription.

That night, Sheila's parents confronted her. Amazingly, she did not deny her drug use; rather, she justified it, telling them, "Yah, that stuff is mine, so what! I have done everything you've asked of me. Now, it's my turn to do what I want." Where had their sweet, innocent girl gone? The more they questioned her, the more embittered and cynical she became. Her parents quickly realized they were in over their heads and sought Christian counseling. Sheila was uncooperative. On the days she was to attend counseling sessions, she purposely came home hours late. Her father attempted to pick her up after school a few times so that he could take her to the appointment, but when she saw him, she would turn and run. Clearly, the situation was out of hand. Sheila was flunking out of school. Just about every word that came out of her mouth seemed to be a lie. Her parents even noticed that items were missing from around the house. When they questioned Sheila, she brashly admitted to stealing, saying, "What do you expect? You stopped giving me my allowance."

In this account, we see how sin can become entrenched through rationalization. When we develop such strong addictions, our sole intent is to do whatever it takes to continue in our addictive behaviors. For Sheila, that involved reasoning from false premises. In effect, her self-disparaging approach of "to hell with it" served as justification for her continued drug use. It is a trick we play on ourselves. Intrinsically, we know that what we are doing is wrong, but we do not want to stop, so we justify our actions. We find excuses in an attempt to convince ourselves and others that our actions do not matter, even though we know they do. Sometimes we might rationalize our continuing in sin because we convince ourselves that we just cannot stop, so we give in to our compulsions. At other times, we practice self-deception with the notion that we are managing the behavior. But in reality, it is the other way around. The distress Sheila experienced as a result of her misperceptions resulted in distorted beliefs about her importance to God, which consequently led to her feeling worthless.

A Biblical Example of Rationalization

Let's look at how the religious leaders of Jesus' day rationalized their own behavior. To make the following example meaningful, we must first visit the book of Leviticus, where the Lord spoke to Moses and said:

> [B]eginning with the fifteenth day of the seventh month, after you have gathered the crops of the land, celebrate the festival to the LORD for seven days; the first day is a day of rest, and the eighth day also is a day of rest. On the first day you are to take choice fruit from the trees, and palm fronds, leafy branches and poplars, and rejoice before the LORD your God for seven days. Celebrate this as a festival to the LORD for seven days each year. This is to be a lasting ordinance for the generations to come; celebrate it in the seventh month. Live in booths for seven days: All native-born Israelites are to live in booths so your descendants will know that I had the Israelites live in booths when I brought them out of Egypt. I am the LORD your God.[7]

The celebration of this ordinance came to be known as the Feast of Booths. More than 1,400 years later, Jesus was facing opposition in the middle of the feast when He taught on several key points, specifically: (1) His authority comes from the Father, (2) His origin is from the

Father, and (3) when He departs, He will return to the Father. On the last day of the feast, Jesus further asserted He is the "living water." Those who heard these teachings were divided. Following the Feast of Booths, a woman was caught in adultery and thrown at Jesus' feet. The religious leaders taunted Him to condemn her and join them in stoning her to death. But Jesus would have none of that. He challenged them to search their hearts, which convicted them of their own sinfulness. After saving this woman's life, Jesus left the scene and later announced He was the "light of the world." He then healed a blind man, and eventually proclaimed He was the "good shepherd."[8]

Question: In the face of such powerful teaching and in light of the miracles Jesus performed throughout His ministry, what was it that kept the religious leaders of His day from accepting Him as the Messiah? After all, these were intelligent men; if any group was equipped to identify Christ, it seems as though the Pharisees would have been the most probable to do so. Perhaps, if we put ourselves in their place, we might find the answer. If you and I were Pharisees in Jesus' time, we would have spent countless hours studying the Torah, the first five books of what is today the Old Testament. These books comprise the entire body of the Law. In addition, we would be steeped in the writings of the prophets and praises of the psalmists. Our life would have been dedicated to living by the Law, following it with a sacrificial type of discipline. Over the course of time, we would have heard and read about the promise of a Messiah—that one day, God would raise a great leader to set captive Israel free.

As Pharisees, you and I would have lived in an oppressive society ruled by Romans. We most likely would have seen or heard about the kind of atrocities that occur under tyrannical occupation, like rape, murder, acts of intimidation, manipulations, and coercions—all at the hands of the Romans, as well as the Jewish leaders who conspired with our oppressors. This would be our reality. But as you and I studied the word of Yahweh—God—our hope would lie in such passages of the Scripture as this:

> You are the most excellent of men and your lips have been anointed with grace, since God has blessed you forever. Gird your sword upon your side, O mighty one; clothe yourself with splendor and majesty. In your majesty ride forth victoriously in behalf of truth, humility and righteousness; let your right hand display awesome deeds. Let your sharp arrows pierce the hearts of the king's enemies; let the nations fall beneath your feet.[9]

This passage, as well as several others pertaining to the Messiah, would have been stored in our memory. Every time we thought about Him, we would likely perceive of a strong, courageous man who would rise up as a great military leader against the tyranny of the Roman Empire. Certainly, such a man would rise up from among us

Pharisees, right? We'd believe the entire world would then stand in awe at the great work Yahweh had done. After the Romans were crushed, life as we knew it would end; the oppression, the tyranny—all of it—would be gone.

But we would have been off the mark. While we had it right that the Messiah would make a stand against tyranny, the notion that He would conquer the Roman Empire was not entirely accurate. The Messiah was sent from the Father to deal with the tyranny of the devil. Yes, captives have indeed been set free from the oppression of evil and the bondage of sin. Our debt has been paid, and the Father sends His own Spirit to live inside of those who choose to invite Him in. Filled with His Spirit, we have been given wisdom, knowledge, power, and strength from beyond this world. In Christ, the abundant life of love, joy, and peace is ours to partake of regardless of our circumstances. Yet, as Pharisees, this most likely would never have occurred to us.

From this perspective, we can better relate with the shock and outrage the religious leaders must have felt when Jesus appeared on the scene. He did not seem to be the great military leader they had envisioned; rather, He was a poor man from an insignificant town called Nazareth. In fact, when Philip was called into discipleship by Jesus, he went and found Nathanael. After he told him about Jesus being the Messiah, and that He was from Nazareth, Nathanael replied, "Nazareth! Can anything good come from there?"[10] This touches upon another interesting point, namely, the kind of disciples Jesus called to

His side. From our perspective as Pharisees, these men would have been the least likely for a great leader to call upon. None of them were men of power; not one held any kind of office or prestige that could have assisted a man in his rise to leadership. Who among Jesus' disciples knew anything about warfare? In fact, Jesus' own brother, James, thought for a time that He was out of His mind.[11] How could this group possibly represent the inner circle of the Messiah? Surely, Jesus had to be an impostor, right?

Yet there He was, teaching with authority, casting out demons, and healing the sick,[12] as well as professing He is the living water, the light of the world, and the good shepherd. Clearly, Jesus did not represent who the religious leaders of His day believed He would be. But having witnessed such awesome power to teach, heal, and set the people free, what was it that kept the leaders from believing Jesus is the Messiah? The answer is found in their entrenched modes of self-deceptive thought and behavior. Simply denying Jesus to be the Messiah would not have been enough for us as Pharisees; after all, we could hear His teachings and witness the miracles He was performing. Repression would have proven to be more effective for maintaining our hard line; however, that too would not suffice. As we religious leaders continued to witness the ministry of Christ, we would have been overcome with the truth. We simply could not have diverted our thoughts and emotions enough to effectively avoid the fact that miracles were occurring right before our eyes. On one hand, we would want to deny Jesus was the Messiah. But then He would do the most amazing things, like giving sight to a man blind since birth.[13] Reports were coming in from all over the countryside. Jesus was healing people, raising the dead, forgiving sins, and more. Repression would not have proven effective enough for us Pharisees to avoid the truth, so we would need to employ rationalization as a means to cope.

Having scriptural knowledge, as Pharisees, we could have very well stepped back and reassessed what we were witnessing. Had we done so, it is likely that some, if not a majority, of our leaders would have concluded Jesus was in fact the Messiah. But many of our leaders had already been conditioned into entrenched modes of self-deception. Jesus' own teaching of a Pharisee named Nicodemus exemplifies how this group of leaders had been blind to spiritual matters.[14] It is not that God had blinded them; rather, they were blinded on account of their own greed and self-righteousness. Consider the words of Jesus in the following passage:

> "No servant can serve two masters. Either he will hate the one and love the other, or he will be devoted to the one and despise the other. You cannot serve both God and Money." The Pharisees, who loved money, heard all this and were sneering at Jesus. He said to them, "You are the ones who justify yourselves in the eyes of men, but God knows your hearts. What is highly valued among men is detestable in God's sight."[15]

When we justify our sin, we are attempting to prove that our thoughts, feelings, and behaviors are just, right, and valid.[16] To consider ourselves as being just is to believe we are honorable and fair in our dealings and actions, that we are consistent with what is morally right.[17] Through justification, we attempt to demonstrate that our thoughts, feelings, and behaviors are well-grounded, that our premises are logical.[18] In effect, we are declaring ourselves to be free from blame, to be absolved.[19] But as we covered in Chapter Two, on this side of the Fall, we are a long way from the holy dispositions that our first parents, Adam and Eve, originally possessed. Post-Fall, we all have sinned and come up short on righteousness.[20]

This is not an easy reality to live with; not for the Pharisees of Jesus' day, and not for us living in the present. While pride can be defined as having a proper sense of our own value,[21] it would be wise for us to consider what the proper sense of our value is. Inevitably, we fail to answer this question correctly when we lean on our own understanding. But when we lean on the word of God, we discover the truth. The Scripture reveals that as believers:

- We are like a pearl of great value[22]
- There is value in our being disciples[23]
- We are worthy of our calling[24]
- There is meaning to our suffering[25]
- Our walk with the Lord produces fruit[26]

In all of this, we can see that the proper sense of our value is rooted in Christ Jesus, not anyone or anything of this world. We have value because God created us. Indeed, the cross serves as the ultimate symbol of how much our heavenly Father loves us. But we can take this value and become prideful. If we do not remain vigilant, we will start to believe that more of the credit goes to us and less to God. This would have been one of the greatest challenges you and I would have faced as Pharisees—pridefulness.[27]

There is something else to consider in all of this. Recall, I asserted in previous chapters that the closer we draw to our Creator, the more challenging this experience tends to be. This happens because our flesh nature seeks self-preservation. The thought of dying so that we can draw nearer to God can provoke fear and distress. Our fallen nature does not want to die; it wants what it wants when it wants it. As we, Pharisees, studied the word of God and observed its ordinances with precision, we would likely have struggled with our own possible death. Enter the defense mechanisms of denial, repression, and rationalization.

Self-Assessment

As with the previous two chapters, you have another opportunity to assess the degree to which you might practice self-deception. Below, you will find several statements about rationalization. Check the ones you believe apply to the ways you currently think and behave.

_____ When I get angry, I lash out at others, but believe I am justified in doing so because of their own actions.

_____ I know that the way I behave on a particular matter is wrong, but then I convince myself it is all right to do it anyway.

_____ There are times when I know I drink too much alcohol.

_____ Overall, the problems I face in my relationships are caused by other people's dysfunction.

_____ When I go shopping, I tend to spend more money than I can afford, but I always seem to talk myself into doing it.

_____ In reading this book, I find myself thinking how this information applies to people I know, but I have been less willing to apply it to my own life.

_____ What comes around goes around. People have taken from me, so it is all right that I take from others.

_____ I have issues with people that I know I need to address, but I seem to talk myself out of doing so.

_____ I use illicit drugs, but I have gotten it under control.

_____ Even though I grew up in a home where I was abused, it does not bother me now that I am an adult.

_____ I have justified why I thought it was all right to bully kids when I was younger.

_____ I recognize that I abuse the drugs prescribed to me, but I have good reasons for doing so.

_____ I allow people to mistreat me, but then I justify why it is okay for them to do so.

_____ I believe I am justified in cutting corners on my taxes.

_____ I know I should not try to rescue people from facing the consequences of their own behavior, but I feel so guilty and afraid that I simply must try to help.

_____ I realize I am hurting those I love through a particular behavior, but nobody really knows what it is like for me.

_____ I really do not see how my suffering abuse in the past impacts my life today. I put it all behind me.

_____ I have learned from my parents' alcoholism, so my drinking is under control.

_____ One way or another, I believe I have been justified in the crimes I have committed.

_____ I have justified my use of pornography.

Scoring

Count the number of items you checked and enter the amount here: _____.

If you checked less than 3: It is likely you have a mild to moderate tendency toward rationalization, and may be fearful to bring a particular issue out into the light.

If you checked 3 – 5: You most likely have a moderate tendency toward rationalization. There is at least one significant issue in your life you do not want to face. It is not uncommon for those who score in this range to battle compulsivity. If this is the case, your justification for continuing with the compulsive behavior has become a source of distress.

If you checked more than 5: Your tendency to rationalize is considered to be high. There are significant issues in your life that you are actively seeking to avoid. Your self-deceptive modes of coping are deeply entrenched and a source of significant distress.

Naturally, if you are struggling with a problem you cannot solve, seeking assistance from a minister, pastor, or professional Christian counselor is recommended. As noted in previous chapters, your clergy may be able to provide you with a referral to a professional Christian counselor. Another resource can be found through The American Association of Christian Counselors: www.aacc.net. Select the tab titled, FIND A CHRISTIAN COUNSELOR.

Summary

This chapter opened with the following passage: "There is a way that seems right to a man, but in the end it leads to death."[28] The Hebrew word used here for death is *maveth* (maw'-veth), which literally means just that—the dead, their place or state. However, *maveth* figuratively relates to pestilence or ruin.[29] There really are ways that seem right to us, but in the end they lead to pestilence, ruin, and, in some cases, death. While denial is an attempt to refuse reality, and repression is striving to avoid it, rationalization is a process through which we seek to alter reality. It is a self-satisfying, but irrational type of behavior aimed at maintaining our own will. When we rationalize, we *will* for things to be a certain way. In Tyler's case, he rationalized as a means to keep from getting hurt. Sheila turned to drugs to ease her distress. But when her parents brought the issue out into the light, she sought to justify her behavior through cynicism. The Pharisees rationalized to maintain their rigid mind-set and hardened hearts. The more we rationalize, the less reason we exercise. When we seek to justify a harmful behavior, our ability for sound thinking is inhibited, and we cease operating within the bounds of God's will. What sense did it make for the Pharisees to maintain their hard line of thinking in the face of the miracles and powerful teachings of Jesus? For the person struggling with a compulsion, what sense does it make for them to continue in their destructive behavior as opposed to seeking help?

To one degree or another, we all engage in the self-deceptive practice of rationalization. In most cases, we do so because we are fearful. We are afraid to face reality, scared things will not go the way we want them to, dread the thought of giving up control, and anxious we might get hurt. But at the heart of our self-deceptive practices, we come to see that the issue is spiritual. When we choose to do our will as opposed to the will of the Father, we can be assured rationalization is present. Doing God's will is not easy, but it is always best. While we might not know the finer points of the Lord's will in a given matter, when we engage in sinful behavior, we sense something is wrong deep within our spirit. At times, we might deny this sense. Other times, we might attempt to avoid it. But when denial and repression prove ineffective, rationalization provides a tweak to reality, which allows us to continue in our own willfulness.

Engaging in self-deceptive practices may initially result in a decrease of distress, but denial, repression, and rationalization can only offer temporary relief at best. At worst, these self-deceptive practices prevent us from experiencing the abundant life our heavenly Father has always intended for us; leading us into dysfunction and disease. Recall that God created us to live in a balanced state called homeostasis, but self-deceptive practices never create harmony; they only disrupt it. For this reason, there is little of the abundant life found in our self-deceptive thoughts and behaviors. The enemy seeks to burden us with his yoke of slavery by capitalizing on our practices of deception. Conversely, the Lord desires to lessen our burdens.[30] But God will not force Himself upon us; we must choose to submit to His ways. This means we will need to break through our self-deceptive practices and accept reality.

In the first part of this book, we looked at God's intent for humanity, the complexity of sin, and the ways we are conditioned by it. The second part has focused on the self-deceptive practices we engage in when we attempt to cope with sin through our own willfulness. In the third and final part of this book, we will look at ways to best resist the devil; the different capacities Christ serves as our Shepherd, Mediator, High Priest, and King; and the ministry of the Holy Spirit. We've seen the outcome of what happens when we lean on our own understanding. Now, be prepared to lean on our Creator's understanding and truly overcome the crippling effects of sin and guilt.

Chapter Seven

Resisting the Devil

Submit yourselves, then, to God. Resist the devil,
and he will flee from you.

James 4:7

In part one, we looked at how God's plan for humanity had gone awry when Adam and Eve willfully chose to think and behave in ways that the Father had never intended. The imputation of sin was thus set in motion. Humankind's first parents did not just sin one time; rather, it very much became a part of who they were. This nature—the sin nature—was then passed along to each of us. In part two, we took a detailed look at what this nature involves, and how sin conditions us to think, feel, and behave. Now, in this third and final part, we spend time delving into the spiritual realm of sin, and how best to overcome its crippling effects.

In this lifetime, we are constantly at war with a cunning adversary who seeks to enslave our will. If Satan can get us thinking in ways that come against the will of God, then he can get us to act out sin through our behaviors. The opening scriptural passage of this chapter advises us to resist the devil. In certain respects, the word *resist* might seem kind of weak. But the Greek word James used here is *anthistemi* (anth-is'-tay-mee), meaning, to stand against; to oppose.[1] To assess how best to resist the devil, we need first to understand the significance of biblical typology, which is the systematic classification of types that have characteristics or traits in common.[2] Throughout the Bible, all sorts of typologies can be found. For example, Adam was a type of Christ in that he was representative of the whole human race. Adam's representation led humanity into sin. Christ, as the propitiator, the one who paid for our sins, represents the way to salvation.[3] Another example of biblical typology can be seen in the Tabernacle, which is representative of Christ dwelling among His people and of His atonement for our sins.[4] Through the Tabernacle, God connected with His people in a very real way; so, too, did He dwell with humanity through the life of Jesus.[5]

The most prominent typology of the devil is found book of Isaiah:

> How you have fallen from heaven, O morning star, son of the dawn! You have been cast down to the earth, you who once laid low the nations. You said in your heart, "I will ascend to heaven; I will raise my throne above the stars of God; I will sit enthroned on the mount of assembly, on the utmost heights of the sacred mountain. I will ascend above the tops of the clouds; I will make myself like the Most High."[6]

The typology here is found in the commonality between the Babylonian empire, which in the Scripture is representative of tyrannical and self-idolizing power, and the characteristics of a prideful Lucifer.[7] With respect to the "morning star," the Hebrew term used here is *heylel* (hay-lale'),[8] which is derived from *halal* (haw-lal'), a primitive root that means "to be clear."[9] Prior to his fall from heaven, Lucifer reflected the glory of God as an archangel. His praises to the Lord were clear and beautiful, perhaps among the purest and most beautiful of sounds. However, over time, Lucifer began to take on a nature of pride, which is also what *halal* came to be associated with— the making of a show, to boast, and thus to be clamorously foolish.[10]

God's original intent for Lucifer was for him to serve within His kingdom in wonderful and mighty ways. But from Isaiah's passage, it is clear that this archangel had other plans. Ultimately, he sought to place himself above our heavenly Father—to be "above the tops of the clouds." Once this seed of pride took root, a sinister evil grew in Lucifer's heart. In the end, he sought to make himself "like the Most High." Once he was cast out of heaven, his pride turned to hatred. Lucifer had fallen from his high place as the morning star to that of Satan—adversary of God.

It is important to note that in His loving and gracious ways, God did not immediately restrict the devil from approaching His throne.[11] Even in light of the fact that Lucifer appeared as the accusing adversary of mankind, our heavenly Father demonstrated patience and mercy. Some biblical commentators have suggested that perhaps God allowed a time for Lucifer to repent of his ways.[12] But following Christ's crucifixion and ascension, he was *judicially* cast out of God's court.[13] The apostle Paul stated it this way:

> Who will bring any charge against those whom God has chosen? It is God who justifies. Who is he that condemns? Christ Jesus, who died—more than that who was raised to life—is at the right hand of God and is also interceding for us. Who shall separate us from the love of Christ? Shall trouble or hardship or persecution or famine or nakedness or danger or sword? As it is written: "For your sake we face death all day long; we are considered as sheep to be slaughtered." No, in all these things we are more than conquerors through him who loved us. For I am convinced that neither death nor life, neither angels nor demons, neither the present nor the future, nor any powers, neither height nor depth, nor anything else in all creation, will be able to separate us from the love of God that is in Christ Jesus our Lord.[14]

Satan may indeed continue to accuse us, but it is Christ who finds fault with his accusations and renders them baseless. Which brings us to a vitally important matter: why, specifically, would an all-loving, all-powerful God allow for the existence of evil in the first place?

The Challenge of Evil

The Bible clearly states that God is omnipotent, omniscient, omnipresent, as well as ever-loving.[15] This raises a quandary. Given the fact that evil clearly exists, how can it be justified that God—with all of His love, wisdom, and power—could allow such a thing? The Greek philosopher, Epicurus (341 B.C. – 270 B.C.), wrestled with this issue and asserted:

> Either God wants to abolish evil, and cannot; or he can, but does not want to; or he cannot and does not want to. If he wants to, but cannot, he is impotent. If he can, but does not want to, he is wicked. But, if God both can and wants to abolish evil, then how come evil is in the world?[16]

The Bible is clear on the fact that God will abolish evil. Indeed, our heavenly Father has made provision for an advocate through Christ Jesus. As we previously studied, immediately after the Fall, God addressed the serpent stating: "I will put enmity between you and the woman, and between your offspring and hers; he will crush your head, and you will strike his heel."[17] Following the introduction of sin into the world, God is found to be making provision to correct the issue. We know the "offspring" God was talking about is Christ. While Satan struck Christ's "heel," so to speak, in that He was crucified, Christ crushed Satan's head by conquering death, ultimately defeating sin and evil. God does allow the struggle between good and evil to play out, but the fact is the end is already decided—the devil is defeated.[18] All the while, the Father has chosen to suffer alongside with us. So, we come to see that the issue is not about God failing to abolish evil; rather, the issue is about how God is working this out in His own timing.

Nonetheless, we struggle with this fact, as did the prophet Habakkuk. Listen to the anguish in his heart as he petitioned the Lord:

> How long, O LORD, must I call for help, but you do not listen? Or cry out to you, "Violence!" but you do not save? Why do you make me look at injustice? Why do you tolerate wrong? Destruction and violence are before me; there is strife, and conflict abounds. Therefore the law is paralyzed, and justice never prevails. The wicked hem in the righteous, so that justice is perverted.[19]

God gave the following answer to the prophet's petitions: "[T]he revelation awaits an appointed time; it speaks of the end and will not prove false. Though it linger, wait for it; it will certainly come and will not delay."[20] Here we can further see that God has a plan and is working it out in His own timing. Consider the following passage, "my thoughts are not your thoughts, neither are your ways my ways," declares the LORD.[21] Our Father operates in His own timing. Job also came to understand the truth in all of this as a result of his afflictions, concluding:

> I know that you can do all things; no plan of yours can be thwarted. You asked, "Who is this that obscures my counsel without knowledge?" Surely I spoke of things I did not understand, things too wonderful for me to know.[22]

Suffering caused by evil does not negate an all-loving God. Indeed, there are countless examples of good resulting from suffering. The apostle Paul wrote: "we rejoice in our sufferings, because we know that suffering produces perseverance; perseverance, character; and character, hope."[23] Even in the case of Jesus, it is written: "He learned obedience from what he suffered."[24] To think that Christ *allowed* His scourging and crucifixion to happen so our sin debt would be paid in full—and that a way could be made for us to reconnect with heaven—blows the mind. Just look at what good came of Jesus' suffering! If good can come from Christ's suffering, good likewise can come from our own pain and anguish. Through life's trials, we are given the opportunity to experience the love of the Father on deeper levels. We come to the understanding that we were never truly alone in our anguish; the Lord, too, has suffered right along with us. It is not because He has to, but because He chooses to. All in all, we come to experience the perfection of God's strength in our weakness.

After ten million years spent in the loving presence of our heavenly Father, we will look back on the here and now and view what we have experienced in this lifetime much differently. This eternal perspective is precisely what Paul was touching upon when he wrote: "Now we see but a poor reflection as in a mirror; then we shall see face-to-face. Now I know in part; then I shall know fully."[25] God is indeed all-powerful; He is surely dealing with evil and will bring it to an end in His time. God is all-loving, going to the most extreme lengths to extend His love, grace, and mercy our way. The Father has made provision for us to experience His loving presence here and now, as well as into eternity. Yet we must not idly sit by allowing Satan to work his deceptive practices on us; we are called to fight.[26] To prove effective in this regard, we must study the ways of our adversary.

The Characteristics of Satan

The Devourer

The apostle Peter wrote: "Be self-controlled and alert. Your enemy the devil prowls around like a roaring lion looking for someone to devour."[27] To be self-controlled and alert, it is important to assess the ways sin has impacted us. This is no easy task. It really is not a question of if we have been conditioned by sin, but to what degree we engage in self-deceptive practices surrounding our sin. Through denial, repression, and rationalization, we keep the unfruitful works of darkness in the dark. Unless we bring these issues out into the light of God, the polluting elements of sin remain, inhibiting our relationship with our heavenly Father and robbing us of the abundant life of love, joy, and peace. We must understand that Satan actually seeks to devour us. Perhaps one of the most significant ways he accomplishes this feat is by consuming our hope. If he can succeed in this respect, he has rendered us ineffective in our God-given purpose. Without hope we are lost. Without hope, what use is there in going on? Stranded in such a state, we become mired down, and the enemy gains ground in our mind.

The Deceiver

The apostle John wrote: "The great dragon was hurled down—that ancient serpent called the devil, or Satan, who leads the whole world astray."[28] When we are deceived, we are led into believing something that is not true. We can clearly see this with Adam and Eve. The serpent got them focusing on the very thing God advised them to avoid. He managed to do this by asking a question that was actually a lie. "Did God really say, 'You must not eat from any tree in the garden'?"[29] Note the significance of this approach. The serpent took the command of God—to eat of *any* tree in the garden, *except* from the tree of the knowledge of good and evil—and twisted it around, asking Eve if God said they should not eat from *any* tree. Once he got them focused on the forbidden fruit, their own willfulness took over. Sure, it was appetizing, but they also understood something much more significant—that it was a means by which they could gain wisdom.[30] Adam and Eve were tempted with the notion that wisdom gained from eating the fruit could give them godlike power. Satan did not need to twist Adam and Eve's arms into eating the fruit; he was fully aware something more subtle and cunning could be used to lead them into believing his lie. In many respects, our adversary continues in this same characteristic way. He speaks lies into our lives, and if we are not careful, we can be deceived. This illustrates the fundamental importance of being aware of our thoughts, feelings, and needs. The greater our ability to be aware, the more effective our resistance of the devil will be. Conversely, the greater our self-deceptive practices, the less effective we are at standing firm against the devil.

The Father of Lies

Jesus said: "He [the devil] was a murderer from the beginning, not holding to the truth, for there is no truth in him. When he lies, he speaks his native language, for he is a liar and the father of lies."[31] Satan did not force Adam and Eve into sin, but he played a significant role in bringing them to the threshold. He was the catalyst for humanity's fall. There is no truth in Satan. He is an aberration,[32] a deviation fully perverted from what he was originally created to be. He is *nontruth*, continuing to seek a place above God, which is, and forever will be, a fallacy.

The Intentions of Satan

Undo God's Work

Now that we have studied the characteristics of our adversary, let us move forward and address his intentions. In the Parable of the Sower,[33] Jesus provided the following detail regarding Satan's intention: "Some people are like seed along the path, where the word is sown. As soon as they hear it, Satan comes and takes away the word that was sown in them."[34] Here we see one of our adversary's chief intentions—*to undo God's work*. Several biblical commentators call attention to the condition of the hearer's heart in this parable, specifically, how their hardness hinders God's word from finding a fertile place to take root. While this is an important point, we must not overlook the fact that our adversary will do all he can to steal God's word from us.

Why would it be so important for Satan to keep the word of God from taking root in our mind? Paul addressed this matter in his letter to the Romans when he wrote: "I am not ashamed of the gospel, because it is the power of God for the salvation of everyone who believes: first for the Jew, then for the Gentile."[35] Our adversary understands that the gospel of Christ leads to salvation. To believe in Christ, one must have faith in Him, and faith comes by way of hearing the word of God.[36] So it makes sense that the devil would seek to rob us of God's word anytime he has the opportunity. On an even deeper level, salvation paves the way for us to experience sanctification, the means by which we grow in holiness. In praying to His heavenly Father, Jesus said: "Sanctify them by the truth; your word is truth."[37] The Greek word used here for sanctify is *hagiazo* (hag-ee-ad'-zo), which means "to make holy."[38] But *hagiazo* also applies to veneration, which involves a deep feeling of respect and reverence. Satan loses as Christ gains a soul, for there is one more person in the world to experience growth in holiness through veneration of God and reflect His glory into this darkened world.

Another example of Satan's attempt to undo God's work can be found in the account of Jesus in the desert. After Christ was baptized, the Holy Spirit led Him out into the wilderness for forty days, where He was tempted by Satan.[39] For about a month and a half, he attacked Jesus in the most extreme ways. Here's a glimpse into what some of those attacks involved. After Jesus had not eaten for forty days, Satan said: "'If you are the Son of God, tell this stone to become bread.'"[40] On one hand, the enemy was tempting Christ to be prideful—*if you are the Son of God...* Jesus had nothing to prove to Satan. Prior to His being led out into the dessert by the Holy Spirit, Jesus' father had already stated, "This is my Son, whom I love; with him I am well pleased."[41] Nonetheless, this taunting by the devil would have been a temptation to Jesus, in that, He truly is the Son of God, but He was fully human as well. As a man, Jesus was tempted to prove He is who He is.

On the other hand, living without food for this length of time requires pushing the human body to the extreme limits of survival. Jesus was the God-man, fully God but also fully man. As a man, Jesus was nearing the final throes of starvation after more than a month of eating nothing. Those who have experienced such extreme starvation report that the pains of hunger are intense and nonstop. Jesus' muscles would have ached intensely from atrophy. He would have been exceedingly irritable, with a heightened sensitivity to the elements, especially sound. At some point, a significant degree of apathy would have settled in.[42]

However, because He was also fully God, He could have turned the very stones before Him into bread. This would have been an exceedingly tempting thing for Christ to do. All of us have experienced hunger pains at one time or other. But consider how intense those pains would be after not eating for weeks on end. Clearly, this was not some minor temptation—to turn a rock into bread. Jesus was on the verge of physical death as a result of starvation. Every human fiber of His being would have been tempted to perform this miracle. Yet, if Jesus was to binge on carbohydrates while in starvation mode, it would have likely resulted in physical death from what is known as refeeding syndrome. When the body is starved, it first feeds on its glycogen stores, which get depleted rapidly. Next, the body feeds on its fat stores, along with protein found in muscle. A sudden shift in starvation mode, i.e., from fat and protein metabolism to carbohydrate metabolism, results in a rapid increase in insulin levels and significant imbalances in blood serum electrolytes. Refeeding syndrome can result in cardiac irregularities, coma, and death.[43] It was no coincidence that Satan tempted Jesus with bread, a high source of carbohydrates. Clearly, the enemy knew what he was doing when he made the suggestion.

But why should Christ go through this hardship in the first place? As the God-man, what would such a feat serve? Certainly, it was the will of the Father that Jesus go through these trials. Recall it was the Spirit who led Him out into the desert. While Christ was filled with the Spirit at His baptism,[44] it was in the desert that the Spirit of God was galvanized with the Son of Man. To galvanize is to stimulate or shock; to arouse to awareness or action.[45] Consider the awareness Jesus developed as the Son of Man while in the desert. It was there that He came to fully understand His utter dependence on the Father. He was stretched to His physical limits as a man and came to see it would only be by the power of God's Spirit that He could fulfill His ministerial duties. Even at the point of starvation unto death, Jesus is found to be submitting to the will of the Father. There was the devil, seeking to undo God's work; and there, too, was the Son following after the ways of His Father. What comfort we can take in the assurance that Christ knows our sufferings!

Secure Our Worship

Satan did not just tempt Christ to pridefully produce food during His time of starvation to prove He was the Son of Man. He tempted Him with power as well. The devil took Jesus to a place where all the kingdoms of the world could be seen and said: "I will give you all their authority and splendor, for it has been given to me, and I can give it to anyone I want to."[46] What a temptation! There was Jesus, born into the lowest of circumstances, a poor boy raised in an impoverished town, being offered the kingdoms of the world. This would have been alluring to Christ's humanity. Just think of the good He could do with this kind of power. Consider the poor people He could reach and help. He would be in charge of it all. Yet Jesus sensed the falsity of Satan's offer, and the evil intent of the devil became clear to see—he wanted the Son of Man to worship him. Again, we see Satan's attempts to rise above the clouds and make himself like the Most High. The apostle Paul further clarifies this point:

> Don't let anyone deceive you in any way, for (that day will not come) until the rebellion occurs and the man of lawlessness is revealed, the man doomed to destruction. He will oppose and will exalt himself over everything that is called God or is worshiped, so that he sets himself up in God's temple, proclaiming himself to be God.[47]

While he may one day sit in the temple of God here on earth, it will not be as the Lord, but as an impostor. Nonetheless, Satan will use every means in his power to secure our worship. He will take it in any form we are willing to give it. As long as we hold onto our idols, the people or things we revere above God, the devil inadvertently secures our worship.

Entice Us to Turn Away from God

Consider the following passage:

One day the angels came to present themselves before the LORD, and Satan also came with them. The LORD said to Satan, "Where have you come from?" Satan answered the LORD, "From roaming through the earth and going back and forth in it." Then the LORD said to Satan, "Have you considered my servant Job? There is no one on earth like him; he is blameless and upright, a man who fears God and shuns evil." "Does Job fear God for nothing?" Satan replied. "Have you not put a hedge around him and his household and everything he has? You have blessed the work of his hands, so that his flocks and herds are spread throughout the land. But stretch out your hand and strike everything he has, and he will surely curse you to your face."[48]

From Satan's perspective, nobody could ever really worship God without looking for something in return. The notion that anyone would be willing to give of themselves for no other reason than love is not a reality he accepts. The devil is the epitome of selfishness; he cares only for himself. The thought that people worship the Lord out of love is something he detests. When it came to Job, Satan's accusation was that he only worshiped God because of the material blessings he received. The devil wanted him to curse God and prove that he worshiped something other than his Creator.

Instigates Evil

A clear example of Satan's instigation of evil can be found in the account leading up to Jesus' arrest. "The evening meal was being served, and the devil had already prompted Judas Iscariot, son of Simon, to betray Jesus....As soon as Judas took the bread, Satan entered into him."[49] It is important to understand that Satan's promptings of Judas began prior to that evening:

> Six days before the Passover, Jesus arrived at Bethany, where Lazarus lived, whom Jesus had raised from the dead. Here a dinner was given in Jesus' honor. Martha served, while Lazarus was among those reclining at the table with him. Then Mary took about a pint of pure nard, an expensive perfume; she poured it on Jesus' feet

and wiped his feet with her hair. And the house was filled with the fragrance of the perfume. But one of his disciples, Judas Iscariot, who was later to betray him, objected, "Why wasn't this perfume sold and the money given to the poor? It was worth a year's wages." He did not say this because he cared about the poor but because he was a thief; as keeper of the money bag, he used to help himself to what was put into it.[50]

Judas had been entrusted to manage the group's money, but he was pilfering from the treasury. Judas's angst in the matter had more to do with his considering how much he could have skimmed off the sale of the perfume. With the door open, Satan took the opportunity to instigate evil through Judas, preying upon his covetous desires and enticing him to seek a ransom for the arrest of Jesus. All along, during this time, Satan was gaining ground in Judas's mind, until the time came when he could enter it fully and take complete control. The devil's instigation of evil in this matter ensured that Christ would be turned over to His accusers. Unless we are willing to resist the devil, in many respects we, too, would end up in the same boat as Judas, conditioned by sin. In such a state, the mind is left open to attack. Before we know what has transpired, our adversary has built a stronghold.

The Methods of Satan

Masquerades

Thus far, we have studied the characteristics and intentions of Satan. Now we shift our focus toward the methods by which he operates. In his second letter to the church at Corinth, the apostle Paul makes the following statement: "Satan himself masquerades as an angel of light."[51] In the Scripture, light is synonymous with the word of God: "Your word is a lamp to my feet and a light for my path."[52] In this darkened world, the Father's word illuminates our way, making our journey less treacherous. It enables us to find the path of righteousness and equips us to stay the course: "Light is shed upon the righteous and joy on the upright in heart."[53] From this perspective, we can better understand the significance of Satan's masquerading as an angel of light. Angels are messengers.[54] Those who are from God always bring His word. By disguising himself as such a messenger, Satan works to deceive and lead us astray. This is why we are to take thoughts captive for Christ[55] and not give the devil a footing.[56] While we are God's workmanship,[57] Satan's aim is to pervert the Lord's original design and intent for our lives. By getting us to turn away from the purpose our heavenly Father has fashioned us with, the devil knows he has the best chance at fulfilling his own intentions.

Insinuates Doubt

When we doubt, we struggle with being decisive; we become skeptical and might disbelieve and not trust in a given matter. If Satan can get us second-guessing God's truth, he can then affect our belief and trust in the Lord. Without vigilance, the devil knocks us off course, diverting our time and energy onto some other path that God never intended for us to travel down. At first, all may seem well, but as we proceed down the paths of the enemy, we may find ourselves encountering increasingly treacherous terrain. Before long, we are no longer familiar with our surroundings; we become disoriented and confused on which way to go. The only way out of such places is through the illuminating light provided by God's word, which is why our adversary seeks to keep us in doubt. It is how he keeps us in the dark.

Schemer

A clear example of the devil's scheming can be found in a situation that occurred within the church at Corinth:

> It is actually reported that there is sexual immorality among you, and of a kind that does not occur even among pagans: A man has his father's wife. And you are proud! Shouldn't you rather have been filled with grief and have put out of your fellowship the man who did this? Even though I am not physically present, I am with

you in spirit. And I have already passed judgment on the one who did this, just as if I were present. When you are assembled in the name of our Lord Jesus and I am with you in spirit, and the power of our Lord Jesus is present, hand this man over to Satan, so that the sinful nature may be destroyed and his spirit saved on the day of the Lord. Your boasting is not good. Don't you know that a little yeast works through the whole batch of dough? Get rid of the old yeast that you may be a new batch without yeast—as you really are. For Christ, our Passover lamb, has been sacrificed. Therefore let us keep the Festival, not with the old yeast, the yeast of malice and wickedness, but with bread without yeast, the bread of sincerity and truth.[58]

Breaking this matter down for analysis, we see that the apostle was addressing the issue of a man in the church who was having sex with a woman who was likely his stepmother. Paul's notation that such immorality does not occur among pagans, most likely indicates that this type of arrangement would not have been legally permitted under Roman law. However, it is rather probable that the immoral Corinthian culture would have turned a blind eye in such instances. Nonetheless, the law sought to address the societal debauchery that ensues from these types of relationships. Even more disconcerting was the church's response to this man's actions—they were proud. Paul dealt with this matter like a surgeon deals with a tumor; working to cut it out so that its malignancy would not spread.

Note that the apostle did not give license to the Corinthian congregation to spew judgmental hatred upon this man; rather, he encouraged them to be grieved over the situation. He wanted the church at Corinth to view this issue through the eyes of Christ. His desire was for them to see that God never intended this man to live a life so far apart from his purpose. With such sin, this man would have been separated from the love of his heavenly Father. This is not to say that God withdrew His love from him; rather, like a clogged water pipe, his sin was inhibiting the flow of God's love into his life. It is never God's desire for us to be separated from His love. As I have well-established in previous chapters, our Creator longs for a close, intimate relationship with each one of us. Yet He leaves it up to us to choose Him freely or follow our own will and separate ourselves. There is no love to be found in matters of sexual immorality, where one person takes from one another. Sin opens the door for evil to pervade our mind and further the intentions of our adversary, hardening our heart to the point where love grows cold. For these reasons, Paul instructed the Corinthians to be saddened by the loss of love in this matter.

His direction served as an opportunity for them to resist the ways of the devil so that they could stand firm, but at the same time offer this man the opportunity to repent. Such an opportunity would not have existed had the congregation been anything other than grieved. Any one of them could have found themselves in the same boat as this young man. Instead of playing into the schemes of the enemy, Paul wisely instructed them to search their own hearts— precisely what was required for them to truly grieve. The apostle's challenge was for the Corinthians to understand that without the grace and mercy of the Lord, they, too, were no better off.

In his second letter to the Corinthians, Paul continues his address of this matter, stating:

> The punishment inflicted on him by the majority is sufficient for him. Now instead, you ought to forgive and comfort him, so that he will not be overwhelmed by excessive sorrow. I urge you, therefore, to reaffirm your love for him. The reason I wrote you was to see if you would stand the test and be obedient in everything. If you forgive anyone, I also forgive him. And what I have forgiven—if there was anything to forgive—I have forgiven in the sight of Christ for your sake, in order that Satan might not outwit us. For we are not unaware of his schemes.[59]

This is an interesting turn of events. In his first letter, Paul directed the Corinthians to confront this man on his sin, *but only after searching their own hearts.* Having done so, it would appear that the man had a change of mind. If he had not, the end result would have been his continued expulsion from the congregation. But this action was no longer necessary. The logical conclusion would be that the congregation's love for this man won him over. While there was an obvious consequence to his sin, the apostle saw fit to direct his brothers and sisters in Christ to forgive and comfort him.

Consider for a moment what the long-term implications could have been if Paul had not challenged the Corinthians to search their own hearts and truly grieve for this man. In many respects, this man's challenge was the same as each of them faced. Indeed, given our dichotomous nature, we all face the challenge of willfulness. Out of pride, the Corinthians might very well have placed themselves above this individual. Some of the people could have rationalized that because they had not sinned in the same way, they were immune from temptation. Others would have undoubtedly rationalized their own sins, comparing theirs to his and mistakenly conclude they were not as bad off. But pride precedes destruction.[60] Left unchecked, this matter would have spread throughout the congregation like a cancer. Had God not worked through Paul to effectively deal with this issue, there would be no telling the long-range implications. In the end, the systematic scheme of Satan was thwarted.

Casts Down

The word *afflict* is derived from the Latin *afflictum,* a past participle of *affligere,* which means "to cast down."[61] This is precisely what Satan seeks to do in our life. He works to cast us down any way he can. Let's look at an example:

> On a Sabbath, Jesus was teaching in one of the synagogues, and a woman was there who had been crippled by a spirit for eighteen years. She was bent over and could not straighten up at all. When Jesus saw her, he called her forward and said to her, "Woman, you are set free from your infirmity." Then he put his hands on her, and immediately she straightened up and praised God. Indignant because Jesus had healed on the Sabbath, the synagogue leader said to the people, "There are six days for work. So come and be healed on those days, not on the Sabbath." The Lord answered him, "You hypocrites! Doesn't each of you on the Sabbath untie your ox or donkey from the stall and lead it out to give it water? Then should not this woman, a daughter of Abraham, whom Satan has kept bound for eighteen long years, be set free on the Sabbath day from what bound her?" When he said this, all his opponents were humiliated, but the people were delighted with all the wonderful things he was doing.[62]

Theologically, we tend to look at the broader context of this matter, namely, that the synagogue ruler was indignant over Jesus' healing this woman on the Sabbath.[63] The Sabbath was intended by God to be a day of rest, where we take time to contemplate the ways He blesses us. In doing so, we bring honor and glory to our Creator as we give Him the due credit, which opens us up to the opportunity for greater intimacy. However, this concept became perverted within the Hebrew culture by religious leaders seeking to force people into conformity through legalism.

Understanding the significant damage a spirit of religion can cause is vitally important, but we must not lose sight of Christ's focus in this passage—the woman who had been afflicted by a "spirit" for so many years. The Greek word used here for "crippled" is *astheneia* (as-then'-i-ah), which pertains to a feebleness of mind or body.[64] It is possible this woman was afflicted mentally or physically, perhaps both. Regardless, by afflicting us, Satan seeks to achieve his evil intentions. Consider for a moment how the devil's actions in this woman's life might have stifled her in doing God's work, how her energy had been drained and her purpose diverted. Through such sufferings, we can become angry with God, erroneously concluding that He does not care. In these instances, Satan can achieve his aim of getting us to turn away from our Creator. Once this is accomplished, our adversary has a greater chance at securing our worship. Instead of turning to God as our source of strength, we end up turning to other means of worship to ease our pain and anguish, like alcohol, sex, shopping, and more. As Satan gains ground in our mind, he builds strongholds by which he can then instigate evil in and through our lives. The result: we become enslaved to the evil intents of our adversary.

Where the Battle Lies

It should be apparent at this point that we are engaged in a very real spiritual battle. By utilizing the methods noted in this chapter, Satan infiltrates our mind and uses worry, doubt, disunity, mental/spiritual disturbances, and weariness as building blocks for his strongholds. He knows that if he can get us worrying about the future, our focus is taken off God, which robs us of His strength in that given moment. This is why Jesus encouraged us not to be anxious for tomorrow.[65] Staying focused on the moment allows for optimum use of God's power.

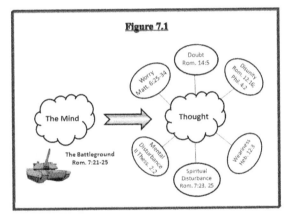

If we are not careful, each type of thought listed in Figure 7.1 will manifest in behavior shown in Figure 7.2. For this reason: "We demolish arguments and every pretension that sets itself up against the knowledge of God, and we take captive every thought to make it obedient to Christ."[66] To be effective in this regard, we must be able to discern clearly. When we are conditioned to deny, repress, and rationalize, we are then inhibited in our ability to: (1) assess what it is we are thinking and feeling, (2) determine why we are thinking and feeling that way, and (3) conclude what God's will is with respect to our thoughts, feelings, and behaviors.

Resisting the Devil

New Attitude

Now that we have studied the characteristics, intentions, and methods of Satan, we turn our focus toward ways of best resisting his attempts to gain ground in the battle for our mind. Consider the following passage:

> You were taught, with regard to your former way of life, to put off your old self, which is being corrupted by its deceitful desires; to be made new in the attitude of your minds; and to put on the new self, created to be like God in true righteousness and holiness.[67]

The inherent danger is that we can fall back into this old nature if we are not careful. Some may ask how this is possible. What about passages like: "[I]f anyone is in Christ, he is a new creation; the old has gone, the new has come!"[68] Is this not proof that we are free from sin once we become believers in Christ? The answer is *no.* Our belief in Christ does not mean we can no longer sin. Just because our debt of sin was paid through the blood of Jesus does not mean we cease to think and behave in ways that fall outside of God's will. As we examined earlier, this is precisely what Paul was addressing in his letter to the Romans.[69] To effectively live our life as a new creation in Christ, we must first develop an *awareness* of the ways we are conditioned to think and behave that do not align with the Father's will. Second, we must be willing to *accept* that we are conditioned in these ways. It is only through developing awareness and acceptance that we can then work to put our old self aside and put on the new.

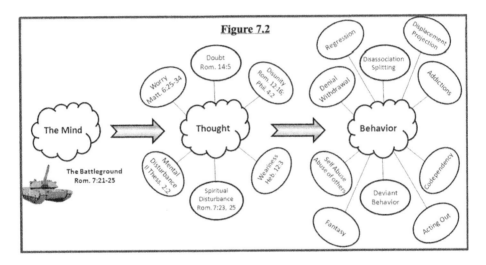

Figure 7.2 illustrates some of the common manifestations of behavior that result from the thoughts depicted in Figure 7.1. For example, it is not uncommon for survivors of sexual abuse to experience intense fears even years after the abuse has stopped. In her workbook, *Growing a Passionate Heart,* Wendy Mahill observes:

Because we have tied our deep longings for love and acceptance to our abuse, we also carry a deep sense of shame over the way God has made us to need and enjoy relationships. Illegitimate shame can develop into an all-consuming fear of being exposed. This all-consuming fear is problematic in that it keeps us from looking at the legitimate sin issues that flow from our human depravity, hindering our relationships and growth in the Lord. Our fear is that if some really know us, they will find us either defective, or unlovable.[70]

Mahill points out the significance of fear for survivors, a fear that is rooted in extreme forms of worry and doubt, as well as mental and spiritual disturbances. Clearly, it is not God's plan that the unfruitful works of darkness would be kept a secret;[71] however, worry and doubt plague the mind of the sexual abuse survivor. In such cases, it is not uncommon for survivors of abuse to experience dissociation, a severing of mental processes involving an individual's thoughts, memories, emotions, behaviors, and sense of identity. At Kingdom Community Ministries (www.kcmcounseling.com), we have worked with many women who have been sexually abused, whom recounted that, prior to treatment, they unwittingly put themselves back into danger as a result of their dissociated state. In effect, they were disconnected from their sense of impending harm. Mahill writes:

We learned to do this [i.e., dissociate] to get away physically and/or emotionally from the abuse. This is a beautiful tool and helped us to be safe and survive what was happening to us at the time. But, now that we are adults, it could be dangerous. We might dissociate when there is a stressor and not respond to something that is happening in a way that can keep those in our care or us safe. It is also a sin because we are escaping what God created us to be. Dissociation can hinder our ability to love and face the truth.[72]

So what does all of this have to do with resisting the devil? All too often, we develop habitually dysfunctional modes of thought and behavior as a result of our sin, as well as the sins of others perpetrated upon us. Yet, to be made new in the attitude of our mind, we must work to develop awareness of what our core issues in life are. The apostle Paul directed us to "put off falsehood and speak truthfully."[73] To do so, we must first get honest with ourselves. Unless we are willing to accept the truth about unresolved issues, we are not going to put off anything successfully. Our old ways of thinking and coping with life will persist on account of procedural memory. While freedom is ours in Christ, when we are affected in such ways by sin, we unwittingly submit to the enemy's yoke of slavery because we lack the awareness and acceptance to cope with the truth. The apostle James wrote: "Be self-controlled and alert."[74] But it is challenging to maintain such a state when we are conditioned to deny, repress, and rationalize.

Certainly, these factors are not just limited to our childhood. Even in adulthood, many people are affected by those around them who perpetrate sin. In like kind, people are affected by our sin as well. Regardless of when or how the sin occurs, it becomes an impossibility to resist the devil if we continue to practice self-deception. Our best option is to submit ourselves to God and pray that He will reveal the unresolved issues in our life that need to be dealt with. As He brings revelation, do not hesitate to seek professional help if needed. Your pastor/minister, as well as The American Association of Christian Counselors, can serve as good resources for locating counselors in your area. You can also go to www.aacc.net and select FIND A CHRISTIAN COUNSELOR.

Put On the Armor of God

Once we have developed enough awareness of the ways we are conditioned by sin, and worked to accept that we are indeed conditioned in these manners, we can then prepare to go to battle. The apostle Paul provided us with the following information on God's spiritual armor:

> Put on the full armor of God so that you can take your
> stand against the devil's schemes. For our struggle is
> not against flesh and blood, but against the rulers,
> against the authorities, against the powers of this dark

world and against the spiritual forces of evil in the heavenly realms. Therefore put on the full armor of God, so that when the day of evil comes, you may be able to stand your ground, and after you have done everything, to stand. Stand firm then, with the belt of truth buckled around your waist, with the breastplate of righteousness in place, and with your feet fitted with the readiness that comes from the gospel of peace. In addition to all this, take up the shield of faith, with which you can extinguish all the flaming arrows of the evil one. Take the helmet of salvation and the sword of the Spirit, which is the word of God.[75]

First and foremost, understand it is *God's* armor we are to put on. Any notion that we have the means to fight against such a formidable adversary as Satan on our own would amount to foolish pride. If Adam and Eve fell from their holy dispositions as a result of the schemes of the devil, how much more vulnerable are we? Any ground our adversary might have gained in our mind will not be given up without a fight. After we have geared up with the full armor of God, we are instructed to stand our ground. We are to be steadfast, not double-minded.[76]

The enemy will work to fill our mind with all kinds of thoughts. Unless we seek God's wisdom and make a stand against the devil, we will continue to cope in much the same manner as we always have. Past behavior really is an accurate predictor of future behavior;

that is, until we interrupt our faulty belief system. An example of this point is Laura, who has practiced alcoholism for more than four decades. Every key relationship in her life has been affected significantly by her drinking. Each day, Laura wakes up with an opportunity to seek help, but she chooses to do nothing other than continue to drink. While addiction is a complex issue involving spiritual and physiological factors, it still comes down to the individual accepting their life is unmanageable as a result of their addiction and choosing to seek help. The point here is that we must accept the truth and not allow the enemy to dissuade us from taking whatever action is necessary to move off our maladaptive ways of thought and behavior.

When we make our stand against Satan, we are to do so with the belt of truth around our waist. The symbolism of a belt is significant in this matter. In the days of the apostle Paul, ca. 2 B.C. – A.D. 68, people did not wear pants. Rather, in many of the Roman states, a tunic was worn—a one piece garment that typically went down to the knees on men, and further still on women. In some cases, a belt would be worn around the waist. This was the typical attire for Roman citizens and slaves. Citizens with the distinction of being "free" were also permitted to wear a large blanket known as a toga draped over one shoulder. During battle, Roman soldiers wore a tunic under their armor, with a belt to hike it up. This way, instead of the tunic hanging down around their knees, it would stop mid-thigh, allowing for greater mobility. Thus, the analogy could be made that the belt noted in Ephesians 6:14 equates to the mobility offered by the truth found in the word of God. While we are to stand firm on principle for the Lord, we also need agility when fighting a foe that is very much like a prowling lion. When issues go unresolved in our life, we are hindered like a Roman soldier would be if he were to allow his tunic to hang down to his knees. By putting on the belt of truth, we gain awareness and acceptance of our conditioned states and are then able to liberate our inhibited minds while battling the enemy.

In the armor of God, the "breastplate of righteousness" is intended to protect the heart, but not as one might imagine. Theologically, the heart symbolizes the center of spiritual activity, as well as all other facets of human life. When we lean on our own understanding, things really do seem right at times. Yet our heart is deceitful,[77] which is precisely why we need protection. On one hand, our adversary might attack us in thought using worry and doubt, which produces fear. In such a state, the enemy can render us inept in living out our God-given purpose. The Lord does not want to us to live as a slave to fear.[78] On the other hand, Satan might scheme to keep us so busy that we have little time to stop and assess what God's will is in a given matter. So we must protect our vulnerable heart with God's breastplate of righteousness. Here we can see the significance of being aware of what we think and feel, why we think and feel that way, as well as discerning what God wills for us to do with our thoughts and feelings.

Continuing with our assessment of God's armor, Jesus said: "Peace I leave with you; my peace I give you. I do not give to you as the world gives. Do not let your hearts be troubled and do not be afraid."[79] Any hint of peace this world has to offer is, at best, fleeting. Christ, on the other hand is our everlasting source of peace.[80] But the presence of peace does not always equate to the absence of adversity; rather, we find peace and comfort in the fact that we do not have to face adversity alone. Christ is with us, strengthening us.[81] Paul exhorts that our feet be fitted with readiness, which comes from the gospel of peace. We are to put on God's spiritual footwear, so that we can mentally and emotionally get a grip. Essentially, it is the gospel of peace that allows us to gain traction and maneuver away from our self-deceptive modes of thought and behavior that lead to, and keep us, in sin. God's word clearly says that He is not a God of confusion, but a God of peace.[82] The more we study His word, the greater the opportunity there is for us to actually experience peace: "the wisdom that is from above is first pure, then peaceful, gentle, reasonable, full of mercy and good fruits, without partiality, and without hypocrisy."[83]

Since its invention, the shield has played a key role in the makeup of a soldier's armor. As followers of Jesus Christ, we, too, are to work with a shield—the shield of faith, which Paul states can "extinguish all the flaming arrows of the evil one." Faith is having confident belief in the truth, value, or trustworthiness of a person, idea, or thing.[84] It is a belief that does not rest singly on logical proof or material evidence. Through faith amazing things happen.[85] By placing their faith in Jesus, a ruler's daughter who had died was brought back to life; a woman afflicted with a twelve-year hemorrhaging condition was healed; and the blind were given the ability to see.[86] Each of these individuals was healed of their afflictions because they believed Jesus could heal them. We, too, will receive healing from our afflictions by calling out to Christ. His ministry of intercession is as real and available to us today as it was when He walked the face of the earth more than two thousand years ago.

But faith is not without risk. I like how Dr. May summed it up:

[T]he purest acts of faith always feel like risks. Instead of leading to absolute quietude and serenity, true spiritual growth is characterized by increasingly deep risk taking. Growth in faith means willingness to trust God more and more, not only in those areas of our lives where we are most successful, but also, and most significantly, at those levels where we are most vulnerable, wounded, and weak. It is where our personal power seems most defeated that we are given the most profound opportunities to act in true faith.[87]

Exploring the ways we have been conditioned to think and behave requires faith. It may very well be that we are quite aware of what lurks below the surface of our life. Or it could be that we have been unaware that an issue remains unresolved. Either way, what will happen when we come face-to-face with these issues? Will they overwhelm us? Will we be hurt again? In these moments, I believe we receive the greatest degree of strength through faith in the Lord. Obviously, we have not understood what to do with these unresolved issues, or we would have already resolved them. Yet, in these moments, when we boldly step out in faith and confront our fears, we can stand firm and rest assured God's armor is sufficient for us to fight this battle and be victorious. Through these experiences, we have the opportunity to master our use of the shield. This is where learning God's word comes in. Jesus resisted the temptations of Satan through the use of His Father's word.[88] If it worked for Him, it will work for us.

In covering ourselves with God's armor, we are to put on the helmet of salvation as well. *Salvation* is preservation from destruction, difficulty, or evil.[89] Theologically, it is understood to be the deliverance from the power or penalty of sin. With the helmet of salvation, we can best protect our minds with the truth found in Christ. Jesus said: "I am the way and the truth and the life. No one comes to the Father except through me."[90] When we accept the truth that we are totally dependent upon our Creator for everything, we can more effectively accept the need for Christ to work in our life to set us free.[91] It is not that we are set free from having to work though unresolved issues. But through Christ, we are empowered to work out our salvation.[92] It is not a matter of whether Satan will attack us with words that provoke worry, doubt, and fear, but to what degree we will stand firm in the face of his attacks. During these times, we can best hold fast against the devil by making sure we are covered with all of God's armor, including the helmet of salvation. When we do, we can stand confident that we have His covering.

Additionally, we are instructed to use the sword of the Spirit—which is the word of God. The Holy Spirit is the author of God's word.[93] While Satan works to bring darkness to our life, God's Spirit illuminates the darkness by cutting through to reveal the truth:

> The Spirit searches all things, even the deep things of God. For who among men knows the thoughts of a man except the man's spirit within him? In the same way no one knows the thoughts of God except the Spirit of God. We have not received the spirit of the world but the Spirit who is from God, that we may understand what God has freely given us.[94]

We do not have to live in bondage to our past, bound by unresolved pain and anguish. No longer do we need to be timid about coping with our conditioned modes of thought and behavior. Along these lines, Paul wrote to his protégé Timothy, stating: "God did not give us a spirit of timidity, but a spirit of power, of love and of self-discipline."[95] With the full armor of God, we can stand firm against the tricks and schemes of the devil.

Summary

God had a different purpose for Lucifer than the one he chose to follow. As his pride grew, so too did his motivation to place himself above the Most High, which resulted in his eviction from heaven. Pride turned to bitterness, and bitterness to hatred. Over time, Lucifer's hatred transformed him into Satan, the father of lies and the antithesis of Christ Jesus. While God created Lucifer, He also gave him the freedom to choose whose will he would follow. Without a doubt, his choice perverted what our heavenly Father originally intended for His creation. However, the fact that this perversion now exists does not mean God is incapable of dealing with evil. Through systematic theology, we come to see that He has already dealt with the issue in His own way and timing. We can rest assured that God is in control and has worked matters out where evil is concerned. All we need do is look to the cross to confirm that our Father has indeed taken care of the issue. God is working out His plan, and we must persevere.

Characteristically, Satan is the father of lies, a deceiver, and our adversary in life. If he cannot do away with us altogether, then he will settle for making us minions for his evil intent. Through our encounters with sin, either our own or the sin of others, we are conditioned in ways that unwittingly open the door of our mind for Satan to enter and pervert God's purpose for our life. In effect, he deceives us by telling us lies. If we do not stay alert, we begin to believe what he tells us. Believing our adversary's lies has devastating effects. At times, Satan sets us up for a fall with lies that puff up our pride. Other times, he erodes our sense of worth with lies that tell us we are not good enough. These are but two of a myriad of schemes he employs to divert us from our God-given purpose. Regardless of the approach, his intentions are always the same: (1) to undo God's work, (2) to make us turn away from our heavenly Father, and (3) to instigate evil—all as a means to make us ineffective for the kingdom of God. Our adversary is clever, disguising himself as an angel of light. He is constantly at work to insinuate doubt. He has even been known to misuse the Scripture as a means of accomplishing his evil will.

Satan battles for our mind. Once infiltrated, he then works to steal our peace, kill our hope, and ultimately destroy our ability to carry out the purpose God placed on our life. Because of this, we must work diligently to resist our adversary. To be effective in our efforts, we need to change the way we once thought. We must submit our thoughts to the Lord and be willing to allow God to search our mind, so that He can reveal conditioned modes of thought and behavior that do not line up with His will. As we gain greater awareness, we can then work toward accepting the truth and lean on the Lord for strength as He works to transform us. Through this process, we become conditioned to take thoughts captive for the Lord. We make choices to behave in ways that coincide with the will of our Creator. We stop submitting to a yoke of slavery. Putting on the full armor of God, we stand firm on His word and walk in freedom. While the devil continues to prowl around like a roaring lion, we need not fear Satan, for there is Christ in our life, and the Spirit of God is living inside of us. Yes, he is a formidable foe, never to be underestimated or completely ignored, but through Christ we are victorious.

Now that we have thoroughly assessed Satan's characteristics, intentions, and methods of operation, as well as the most effective means of resisting him, we can move forward and study the antithesis of our adversary—Christ Jesus. In the next chapter, we will look at Christ in the roles of Shepherd, Mediator, High Priest, and King.

Opportunity for Reflection

1. What was God's original intent for Lucifer? What was it that caused Lucifer to turn against his Creator?

2. How could an all-knowing, all-powerful, all-loving, and ever-present God allow evil to exist?

3. Satan has been called the devourer, deceiver, and father of lies. How have you personally encountered these characteristics of the devil?

4. Review the section on Satan's intentions. In what ways has the devil attempted to fulfill these intentions in your own life?

    _____

    _____

5. Satan battles for our mind. Review Figures 7.1 and 7.2. Describe the ways the devil has attacked your thoughts. What were the resulting behaviors of those attacks?

    _____

    _____

6. What new attitudes might you need to develop with respect to resisting the devil?

    _____

    _____

7. How proficient are you at putting on the *full* armor of God? What can you do to further increase your proficiency?

    _____

    _____

Chapter Eight

Christ the Shepherd, Mediator, High Priest, and King

The Word became flesh and made his dwelling among us.

We have seen his glory, the glory of the One and Only,

who came from the Father, full of grace and truth.

John 1:14

In this chapter, we will look at our glorious Savior in four splendid typologies of Shepherd, Mediator, High Priest, and King. Each represents a separate facet of our heavenly Father's love for us; the One who ultimately created you and I in love so that we, too, would choose love. But true love cannot exist without free will. This is understood to be true, because the very essence of love requires a decision to be made—a decision to give of oneself. Not out of selfish ambition, but out of a true desire for what is good and right. Such a decision cannot be robotic in nature. For it to be of love, we must first have the freedom to choose. In this, we will have a glimpse of our Creator's original intent for humanity, along with the moral character we were designed to represent, for which we would be given the free will to choose God's love and thus become extensions of His love. When this flow of love is inhibited to too great a degree, disease is the result. In truth, love with excessive conditions is not really love at all, but an attempt by one person to control another. So the psychopath lashes out as a result of the injustices committed in the name of love. The obsessive seeks to control their life and others as a means to corral love, to bind it in hopes of being able to hold onto it. Those who tend toward emotionalism cry out, saying, "Love me!" They will be whatever they believe they need to be to please others in exchange for love. Because these types of individuals incorrectly harbor their self-worth in other people as opposed to placing it in Christ, their sense of worth is in a constant state of flux. So they use up love's energy as a means to bolster a distorted sense of self.

While each of us can most likely see our own *tendencies* toward the characteristics found in the psychopath, obsessive, and emotional personality types, we come to observe in Jesus the ultimate model of a life lived in love. The observance of such a matter is glorious! The uninhibited love of the Father, flowing freely though the life of His Son, is so full of grace that all one can do is stand in awe.

Christ the Shepherd

A shepherd is one who herds, guards, and tends sheep.[1] Long ago, the prophet Isaiah foretold the following about Christ: "He tends his flock like a shepherd: He gathers the lambs in his arms and carries them close to his heart."[2] As our Shepherd, Jesus cares for us with a tender heart and a great concern for our needs. He leads us to green pastures and gives us rest.[3] Within the green pastures of God's word, we can pause for a while, grazing on its rich spiritual sustenance. Recall that we were not created to live on bread alone.[4] We are more than mere physical beings; we have a soul, and our soul requires nourishment, the kind of nourishment that comes only from the word of God. What the world has to offer leaves us unfulfilled and wanting more. But God's word is wholesome and satisfying; it contains all that we need. Within the green pastures of His word, we can relax; there is no need to hurry on. We can recharge the energy zapped by the trials and pressures we face in this world. It is Christ Jesus, our Shepherd, who leads us to the word of God, for He is the revealer of God.[5] As we work to address our dysfunctional states of thought and behavior, we come to better understand the significance of this facet of God's love reflected in Christ as our Shepherd. The process of reconditioning our mind is arduous at times. Entrenched modes of thought and behavior require serious effort to change. To be effective, we are going to need the rich, fertile pastures of God's word to reenergize.

Another way the Shepherd tends to us as His flock is when He provides living water for our soul. While traveling through Samaria, Jesus stopped at a place known as Jacob's well. It was there that He asked a woman to draw up some water so He could have a drink. Instead of fulfilling Jesus' request, the woman focused on the prejudices that had long existed between Jews and Samaritans. Jesus' response to her was: "If you knew the gift of God and who it is that asks you for a drink, you would have asked him and he would have given you living water." Of the water in the well, Jesus said: "Everyone who drinks of this water will be thirsty again, but whoever drinks the water I give him will never thirst. Indeed, the water I give him will become in him a spring of water welling up to eternal life."[6]

Our physical thirst can be quenched by water, but we will eventually thirst again. However, our spiritual thirst can be completely satisfied through the indwelling of God's Spirit. Once we drink of this living water, the Source is made ever-present within us. Our Shepherd knows exactly what we need, not just our physical needs, but our spiritual, mental, and emotional needs as well. It is for this reason that He leads us to quiet waters.[7]

With regard to Christ as our Shepherd, Jesus Himself proclaimed: "I am the good shepherd. The good shepherd lays down his life for the sheep."[8] The Greek word used here for good is *kalos* (kal-os'), pertaining to that which is right, beautiful, fine, or excellent.[9] In this context, being right means to conform to morality, the quality of being in accord with standards of good conduct.[10] So when Jesus says He is the good Shepherd, He is indicating that His quality of life is in harmony with God's standards of conduct. Christ is not just good because He laid down His life for us. He is good because He never wavers from the Father's will. Our Creator is love. Therefore, His will is rooted in love. The more we live by His standards of conduct, the less we inhibit the flow of His love. From this perspective, we can see the beauty of Christ as our Shepherd. We can observe how the love of the Father flows so purely through the Son and out into this world. As we follow Christ, we come to experience His quality. No one else could ever lead us with such superiority. There is none who is higher in rank or importance than Christ. He is worthy of all merit. While tempted, Jesus never yielded; He never deviated from the Father's will. Jesus is excellent! This is what He meant when He said: "I am the good shepherd."

Yet, Christ does not make this proclamation from a position of arrogance. Note the very next thing He says: "The good shepherd lays down his life for the sheep." Here we find the utmost of humility. The good Shepherd, the One who is right, beautiful, fine, and excellent, gives His all for us! In the life of Christ, we find the will of God manifested and carried out to the fullest extent. No sin was found in Christ.[11] Though He submitted to the complete punishment for humanity's sin, at no time has He ever ceased being our good Shepherd.

In addition to ensuring His flock is well fed and saturated with love, Christ offers protection. In the wilderness, there are predators that make easy prey of a flock of sheep. But the actions of the shepherd thwart the predator's intent. In the days of Jesus, shepherds carried a rod—a club carved from a thick tree branch—which was used to fend off attackers. In their attempt to protect the flock, many shepherds laid down their life. Thus, Jesus' statement about being the good Shepherd and laying down His life had significance to those He was speaking to. Because Christ is our Shepherd, we are not in want. He knows our needs and avails Himself to us as our Provider and Protector.[12] He is the one we want to follow. Jesus can be trusted!

Jesus has also been called the Chief Shepherd: "And when the Chief Shepherd appears, you will receive the crown of glory that will never fade away."[13] The Greek word for *appear* is *phaneroo* (fan-er-o'-o), which means "to render apparent," or "manifestly declare."[14] When something is manifested, it is shown or demonstrated plainly.[15] When Jesus becomes manifest in our life, we come to understand that He truly is our Shepherd, and we learn His voice. Jesus said:

> The watchman opens the gate for him [the shepherd], and the sheep listen to his voice. He calls his own sheep by name and leads them out. When he has brought out all his own, he goes on ahead of them, and his sheep follow him because they know his voice.[16]

This is a significant passage. In agrarian societies, shepherds pull their flocks together where there is greater safety in numbers. This is a common practice during the evening hours, where shepherds rotate turns as watchmen. In the morning, each shepherd calls to his individual flock, and because his sheep are familiar with his voice, they come to him, and only him, each flock to its shepherd. Once the shepherd has gathered his flock, he then leads them out to pasture and water. This is one of the reasons why it is important for the follower of Christ to stay in God's word; in this way, we come to know our Shepherd's voice. And what a Shepherd indeed! Listen to the words of the prophet Micah with respect to Christ:

> He will stand and shepherd his flock in the strength of the LORD, in the majesty of the name of the LORD his God. And they will live securely, for then his greatness will reach to the ends of the earth. And he will be their peace.[17]

Note that He stands and shepherds His flock in the strength and majesty of our heavenly Father. There is nothing in this world that can overcome God. In Christ we live secure. This is not to say we will not face trials and hardships, but we are assured that Jesus is always there for us, interceding with the Father so that we might be strengthened.[18] He is our source of love and peace. Because He is never failing, we can rely solidly on Him. When we open our mind to the love of God, we experience revelation and can more effectively discern the things that inhibit our reception and transmission of love. We can count on the Chief Shepherd to guide and direct us in this regard: "He guides me in paths of righteousness for his name's sake."[19]

Christ as Mediator

To mediate is to resolve or settle differences by working with all of the conflicting parties in a given matter.[20] We have learned that the Bible contains many typologies. When it comes to mediation, Moses can be seen as a typology of Christ. Consider the following passage with respect to the Israelites being given the Ten Commandments:

> Moses summoned all Israel and said: Hear, O Israel, the decrees and laws I declare in your hearing today. Learn them and be sure to follow them. The LORD our God made a covenant with us at Horeb. It was not with our fathers that the LORD made this covenant, but with us, with all of us who are alive here today. The LORD spoke to you face to face out of the fire on the mountain. (At that time I stood between the LORD and you to declare to you the word of the LORD, because you were afraid of the fire and did not go up the mountain.)[21]

Moses was a type of Christ in that he mediated between God and His people. As is seen in the above cited passage, God had spoken with His people, but they feared Him, so He worked through Moses to deliver the foundation of a new covenant—the Ten Commandments. Three key points are found in this covenant: (1) we cannot live a sinless life, (2) our sin is an actual transgression, a violation against God's will, and (3) we are absolutely dependent upon Him to save us from the punishment of sin—which is death.[22] Through the Law, we come to see our need for a mediator, and not just anyone who is willing to step in between God and mankind. We need a mediator who is without sin. While Moses and his brother Aaron were appointed to be priests, they were nonetheless men who struggled with their own sin. But Jesus is the perfect Mediator to fulfill the Law, because He was found to be without sin.[23] God Himself served as the ultimate sacrifice through the life and ministry of Jesus Christ, so that the sins of humanity could finally be dealt with: "we have been made holy through the sacrifice of the body of Jesus Christ once for all."[24] Through Christ, a new covenant was formed between God and humanity, a superior covenant to all others.[25]

A powerful example of Christ's mediation can be found in the words He spoke to Peter: "Simon, Simon, Satan has asked to sift you as wheat. But I have prayed for you, Simon, that your faith may not fail. And when you have turned back, strengthen your brothers."[26] Note that Jesus did not say He would prevent such an act; rather, He prayed that Peter's faith would not fail. The reference here to sifting wheat is significant. To do so, the stalk, along with its head, must first be cut off. Peter experienced a cut off from Christ in the garden of Gethsemane. This must have been a frightening and confusing event for him. He understood Christ to be the Messiah,[27] so why would Jesus allow these men to take Him captive? Why would the Son of God, with all of His power, allow such a thing? We can all relate to Peter in this matter. We, too, often ask ourselves similar questions. But we do not always realize that Christ is doing something. In Peter's case, Jesus not only prayed that his faith would not fail, but also that he would serve as a source of strength to those who followed him.

In relation to wheat, chaff is made of dry bracts known as husks that enclose the mature grain. Before wheat is processed into eatable forms, the chaff must be separated from the grain through a process known as threshing. Here the stems and husks are vigorously beaten. No doubt, Peter felt the threshing of his soul as he denied Christ not once, but three times. One can only imagine the fear and utter confusion Peter felt as he was being threshed by Satan.

But the attack did not stop there. Remember, the devil had asked to *sift* Peter, the implication meaning to be ground down and screened into a fine power. In Jesus' time, this involved grinding grain between stones. Once the grinding occurred, the ground wheat would then be set out to dry and later passed through a sieve, an instrument with a mesh or perforated bottom that further separated the coarse parts from the fine parts.

Satan's intent was to sift Peter into a finely ground powder, and God allowed it! In His infinite wisdom and power, God used this trial to refine Peter into what He desired him to be. The same holds true for each one of us. God uses anything and everything to refine us. Nothing gets wasted. Right there in the middle of it all is Christ Jesus, our Mediator, interceding on our behalf, praying for us that our faith will not fail, so that one day, we, too, might turn and strengthen our brothers and sisters.

The apostle Paul wrote: "there is one God and one mediator between God and men, the man Christ Jesus, who gave himself as a ransom for all men—the testimony given in its proper time."[28] The Greek word used here for ransom is *antilutron* (an-til'-oo-tron), which means " a redemption price."[29] To redeem is to recover ownership of something by paying a specified sum.[30] The sum owed for humanity's sins was a perfect sacrifice:

> Just as man is destined to die once, and after that to face judgment, so Christ was sacrificed once to take away the sins of many people; and he will appear a second time, not to bear sin, but to bring salvation to those who are waiting for him.[31]

Christ, as the representative Man, holds tremendous importance with respect to His mediation on our behalf.[32] By taking on the nature of man, Jesus is best able to empathize with our plight. Who better to understand the specifics of our struggles than the One who has walked a mile in our shoes, who knows the burdens we carry in life.[33]

> When you were dead in your sins and in the
> uncircumcision of your sin nature, God made you alive
> with Christ. He forgave us all our sins, having canceled
> the written code, with its regulations, that was against
> us and that stood opposed to us; he took it away, nailing
> it to the cross. And having disarmed the powers and
> authorities, he made a public spectacle of them,
> triumphing over them by the cross.[34]

Here Paul used the Greek word *paraptoma* (par-ap'-to-mah) for sin, which pertains to a lapse or deviation.[35] In other words, when we deviate from God's original design and intent for our life, we are sinning, which is not in our best interest. It is a harsh reality to accept at times, but we must come to terms with the fact that we become ineffective for the kingdom of God on our own choosing.

This is precisely what Paul was noting in his statement about our uncircumcised sin nature. To circumcise is to cut around. Yet, without the strength of the Lord, we lack the ability to cut out our own sinful behaviors. In effect, we are bent toward performing our own will. But Christ rectifies our sin nature. In the above cited passage, Paul employed the Greek word *suzoopoieo* (sood-zo-op-oy-eh'-o), which means "to reanimate conjointly."[36] It is important to understand that prior to receiving Christ as our Savior, we were on our way to an eternal physical and spiritual separation from our Creator. But through the saving work of Jesus, we are conjointly made alive with Christ; we are joined together with Him as heirs to the kingdom of God.

Recall that to mediate is to resolve or settle differences by working with all of the conflicting parties in a given matter. Through His work on the cross, Christ resolved the differences between God and mankind. Not only did Jesus resolve the issues of the "written code," the Law, He also dealt with the issue of usurped authority. In the Garden of Eden, Adam and Eve relinquished their God-given authority, and Satan seized upon the opportunity to take charge.[37] But on the cross, Christ paid our sin debt in full and disarmed the powers of Satan. From this perspective, the significance of *suzoopoieo* can be better understood. In Christ, we are joined together with Him in power. Now, we have the authority to take our thoughts captive, and no longer submit to our conditioned modes of immoral thought and behavior. We can work to develop an awareness of the ways we are conditioned to sin. As we develop this awareness, we can then move toward acceptance that we are conditioned in such ways, and that changes are necessary. Once we have accepted our current state, we can best tap into God's strength, power, and authority to change our conditioned state of being. We no longer need to engage in maladaptive modes of coping through self-deception. We can open ourselves up to the love of the Father. Now that Christ has mediated for us, we can stand together with Him in His authority over our adversary, and no longer submit to his yoke of slavery. If there are unresolved issues in our past that are painful and frightening, we can stand firm in the knowledge that God has already made provision through Christ for us to face the pain and to heal and grow.

Christ the High Priest

In the fourteenth chapter of Genesis, we find Abram encountering Melchizedek, the king of Salem and priest of God Most High:

> Then Melchizedek king of Salem brought out bread and wine. He was priest of God Most High, and he blessed Abram, saying, "Blessed be Abram by God Most High, Creator of heaven and earth. And blessed be God Most High, who delivered your enemies into your hand." Then Abram gave him a tenth of everything.[38]

In this passage, we find a typological precedent being set for Christ, namely, that He is both King *and* High Priest.[39] To better understand the significance of this typology, we'll need to look at the seventh chapter of Hebrews. Here we find that Christ, as our High Priest, is superior to all who preceded Him: "If perfection could have been attained through the Levitical priesthood (for on the basis of it the law was given to the people), why was there still need for another priest to come—one in the order of Melchizedek, not in the order of Aaron?"[40] The answer to this question is that perfection could not be attained through the Levitical priesthood, because it was made up of men who suffered from a sin condition themselves. While their duties in serving God and His people were not insignificant, they could not propitiate for their own sins, let alone the sins of God's people.

The system of sacrifice God had put in place was a means by which the Hebrews could come to understand their complete and total need for Him. They offered animal sacrifices as an expression of their understanding that they were born of a sinful nature and needed God's redemption. They needed God to deal with what they themselves could not. The system of sacrifice brought home the reality that sin is costly. An individual's time and resources were required to raise a suitable sacrifice to offer for one's own sin. Bringing the living sacrifice to the tabernacle, participating in the actual act of sacrifice, and witnessing the immense bloodshed of the sacrifices would have been a sobering experience, a significant reminder of the price to be paid for sin.

The opportunity to experience humility as a result of sacrifice is a key factor in our walk with Christ. It affords a sense of humility with respect to our place within the Father's creation. Such a sense allows for the opportunity to drop our pride and submit to the ways of God. Through submission, we come to more clearly understand the significance of God's grace and mercy. We are then able to experience greater degrees of our Father's love, joy, and peace. When we experience His love on deeper levels, pathologies—the manifestations of disease—are diminished. As we rest more upon God and submit to

His will, we sin less and become reflections of His love to a world in desperate need of such light.

However, the old system of sacrifice was a stopgap measure, a temporary system put in place by God as a substitute until the appointed time of Christ:

> And what we have said is even more clear if another priest like Melchizedek appears, one who has become a priest not on the basis of a regulation as to his ancestry but on the basis of the power of an indestructible life. For it is declared: "You are a priest forever, in the order of Melchizedek." The former regulation is set aside because it was weak and useless (for the law made nothing perfect), and a better hope is introduced, by which we draw near to God.[41]

Under the old system of sacrifice, people were still separated from their Creator by sin. While the Law gave commandments, it could not give life.[42] Until humanity's sin debt was paid in full, the penalty of death remained. Certainly, God demonstrated His forbearance with respect to sin;[43] but it was not until Jesus presented Himself as the perfect sacrifice that the debt of sin was finally paid. The blood of Christ was exactly what was required. His atoning work on the cross covered all sins for all times—past, present, and future.[44] Yet Jesus' work as High Priest is not finished. He continues to intercede for us, "because Jesus lives forever, he has a permanent priesthood. Therefore he is able to save completely those who come to God through him, because he always lives to intercede for them."[45]

Through the sacrificial offering of our High Priest, we have been reconciled with our Creator and can now freely approach His throne.[46] Christ empathizes with our plight in life: "Because he himself suffered when he was tempted, he is able to help those who are being tempted."[47] The Greek word used here for tempted is *peirazo* (pi-rad'-zo), which means "to test," i.e., endeavor, scrutinize, entice, or discipline.[48] To endeavor is to make a conscientious or concerted effort toward an end.[49] Jesus endeavors in His priestly duties, interceding with the Father on our behalf, and teaching us the truth about God and His plan for humanity. Clearly, Jesus was scrutinized. His every move was critically examined by the religious leaders of His day. Christ was enticed by Satan, and He was brutally disciplined for false accusations leveled against Him. But the criticisms did not stop there. Jesus continues to this very day to be criticized; yet He remains unthwarted in His priestly duties. In this lifetime, we cannot escape our flesh, the side of our nature that is full of our own will. For this reason, we are in continual need of Jesus to make intercession with the Father. We need the atoning work of His priestly duties to cover our continuing violations of the Father's will.

In all of this, our High Priest seeks to bless us. Consider the words of the apostle Peter: "When God raised up his servant, he sent him first to you to bless you by turning each of you from your wicked ways."[50] While Peter was addressing a Jewish audience, it can be seen that God not only sought to bless the Israelites, but all of humanity as well.[51] The word used here for bless is *eulogeo* (yoo-log-eh'-o), which means "to speak well of."[52] Indeed, our High Priest does speak well of us to the Father, and His words are a literal blessing upon us. Coffman put it this way: "The great blessing Jesus came to deliver was not a re-establishment of the old Solomonic empire, but a spiritual blessing marked by the forgiveness of sins, the reception of God's Spirit, and a turning of the people away from their wickedness."[53]

Through the intercession of our High Priest, we are judicially represented in the highest court of all—before the throne of God Almighty. Standing at the throne, each of us is examined by the Father, every deed in our life exposed. In effect, we are asked the question: "What did you do with My Son Jesus?" In other words: "Did you believe enough to invite Him into your life?" Understand that our Creator does not ask this question in hopes of punishing us; rather, He does so more along the lines of: "Please, tell Me that you believe in My Son. Tell Me that your mind and heart are open to Him, because if this is so, then I can call upon Him this very moment to make things right in your case. I so desire for that to happen—I want the record to be set straight so that we can move forward with an eternal relationship!" What a wonderful concept—our High Priest standing before the throne of the God Most High, interceding on our behalf. In turn, God declares us to be forgiven of our sins and justified in the strictest sense of the Law, all because our High Priest was able to offer the perfect sacrifice—Himself. Thus, we see the workings of our Creator in ways beyond our comprehension. Yet, one day, we will actually stand before the throne of our heavenly Father, and we will know love like we never have before. We will comprehend completely the price that was paid for our sin. In that moment, we will fully experience the blessings of our Father's grace and mercy. Viewing things from the eternal perspective, all of our struggles in life and all of the trials we endured will make sense, and we will finally be home!

Christ the King

Now that we have studied the typology of Melchizedek as priest of God Most High, let us turn our focus to Melchizedek as king. Recall that he was king of Salem,[54] which in the Hebrew language means "peaceful."[55] Clearly, this king's peaceful demeanor was witnessed in his provision of bread and wine to Abram. Melchizedek seemed to understand exactly what Abram needed in that moment, the sustenance of bread after an exhausting battle and wine to settle his nerves. Yet consider the typology here with respect to bread representing Christ's body and wine His blood. Could it be that Abram was given a revelation that was fantastically wonderful to behold—perhaps a glimpse into true salvation? Abram's encounter with Melchizedek moved and inspired him to display his reverence by offering a tithe, wherein the first and finest portions of his spoils from battle were offered to God. When we draw close to our King and sense His love; we feel moved to reciprocate our love by giving Him the first and finest of what we have.

There are numerous examples of Christ being revered as King. One such instance was the visit of the magi from the East, who, upon arriving in Jerusalem inquired: "Where is the one who has been born king of the Jews? We saw his star in the east and have come to worship him."[56] Not only were these men early astronomers, they were also part of their king's council, serving as his advisors.[57] It was this same sort of office that Daniel is believed to have held while in Babylonian captivity.[58] The phenomena the magi were observing in the sky leading up to the Christ's birth, in conjunction with their familiarity of Hebrew messianic prophecy, led them to conclude that a great King was soon to be born in Israel. Their trek would not have been an easy one. Travel from Persia, or perhaps Arabia, required many days of journey over inhospitable terrain. Roving marauders were also a very real threat to this group of dignitaries.

It is interesting to note the use of the Greek word *proskuneo* (pros-koo-neh'-o) in the above cited verse, which means "to fawn over," "to adore," or "to revere."[59] This tells us the magi were filled with awe at the sight of Christ. They understood what it meant to be in the presence of royalty. Regardless of the humble setting they found

Jesus birthed into, the sublime nature of the child before them brought them to their knees.

Much can be learned about a king by studying his kingdom. In this regard, the Scripture reveals that the kingdom of Christ is not of this world. In the eighteenth chapter of John, we find Pilate questioning Jesus on some key points:

> Pilate then went back inside the palace, summoned Jesus and asked him, "Are you the king of the Jews?" "Is that your own idea," Jesus asked, "or did others talk to you about me?" "Am I a Jew?" Pilate replied. "It was your people and your chief priests who handed you over to me. What is it you have done?" Jesus said, "My kingdom is not of this world. If it were, my servants would fight to prevent my arrest by the Jews. But now my kingdom is from another place." "You are a king, then!" said Pilate. Jesus answered, "You are right in saying I am a king. In fact, for this reason I was born, and for this I came into the world, to testify to the truth. Everyone on the side of truth listens to me."[60]

In this passage, the Greek word used for kingdom is *basileia* (bas-il-i'-ah), which means "royalty"; abstractly, it relates to rule, but more specifically it pertains to a realm.[61] When Jesus said that His kingdom is not of this world, He meant it in every sense. Jesus' human lineage may have been from a royal line,[62] but His authority to rule is not of this world; it is from a source infinitely more powerful than any human government could establish. While Satan is permitted to rule here for the time being, Christ will one day return and take up His rightful place on earth, and the devil will be dethroned.[63]

The Scripture also reveals that Christ's kingdom will be universal: "He will rule from sea to sea and from the River to the ends of the earth."[64] The prophet Zechariah proclaimed: "The LORD will be king over the whole earth. On that day there will be one LORD, and his name the only name."[65] The day is coming when all the inhabitants of the world will clearly understand who Christ is, and we will gladly worship Him.[66] But He will not be worshiped in the same way that oppressed people fane worship of a dictator; we will worship Christ freely because of our love for Him. Our hearts will be filled with joy, and we will praise our King!

The apostle John wrote:

> The seventh angel sounded his trumpet, and there were loud voices in heaven, which said: "The kingdom of the world has become the kingdom of our Lord and of his Christ, and he will reign for ever and ever."[67]

Think of the security we'll experience when our loving King returns and establishes His rule here on earth for all eternity. No longer will we need to fear foreign invaders and evil despots corrupted by power. We will serve a loving King—the King of Salem. Humanity will finally be restored to its rightful place with our Creator. Secure in our identity as children of the Most High God, our willfulness will transform into willingness and align with our heavenly Father's morality. We will experience purity of mind and will live again as representatives of our Creator's moral character. Indeed, when our King returns, His perfect love will cast out all fear; we will be free from anxiety as we experience true everlasting peace.

The kingdom of Christ will be a righteous one: "Your throne, O God, will last for ever and ever; a scepter of justice will be the scepter of your kingdom."[68] The Hebrew term used here for scepter is *shebet* (shay'-bet), which means "to branch off."[69] However, *shebet* is also indicative of a scion, a descendent or heir. While *shebet* is literally understood to be a stick used for a myriad of things, such as fighting, punishing, walking, and writing, it could be asserted that the scepter of justice pertains more to the branch from which true justice will be derived, namely Christ Jesus. Isaiah wrote: "See, a king will reign in righteousness and rulers will rule with justice."[70] The prophet was writing about Christ. The Hebrew word used here for righteousness is interesting. It is *tsedeq* (tseh'-dek), which means "right," i.e., natural, moral, or legal. Abstractly, *tsedeq* means "equity"; figuratively, it relates to prosperity.[71] The reign of Christ will feel natural to us. We will come to see that this is the way God always intended it to be. As our King, Christ demonstrates the Father's moral character, which is forever good and virtuous. King Jesus rules with a just, impartial, and fair disposition. Through His rule, we will experience a life of prosperity—a life filled with an abundance of love, joy, and peace. Listen to the words of our Father, spoken through the prophet Jeremiah: "The days are coming," declares the LORD, "when I will raise up to David a righteous branch, a king who will reign wisely and do what is just and right in the land."[72]

We need not wait for the Second Advent; Jesus can rule as King in our life today. We can break with our fears and anxiety that stem from unresolved issues and present troubles, and follow His lead. Because Christ is just in His kingly duties, we can entrust ourselves to His leadership. If He calls us to break through our denials and accept truth, then we can trust He does so for good reason. We can trust in our King; no longer must we maintain our repressive ways and avoid reality. Our attempts to rationalize dysfunctional behavior break down at the throne of Christ. In the end, we will come to see that He has come to set us free.

Summary

The inclination to avoid painful memories is common for many of us. Who wants to go back and relive the hurt? But as was covered in Chapter Three, our mind wants to resolve what is unresolved. If we grew up in a home where dysfunctional or abusive behaviors stifled love, then our mind will seek to resolve the matter. If there are painful experiences we have had outside of childhood, our mind will cope with the psychic distress one way or another. To experience resolution of these painful matters, we must turn and face them. But we need not do so alone. With a tender heart and great concern, Christ, our Shepherd, comes to us. He leads us to the fertile pastures of God's word where we find the sustenance needed to sustain us on our spiritual journey. In such a place, we discover the truth that we are loved by our Creator and have tremendous worth in His eyes.[73] Through Jesus, our spiritual thirst for love is completely satisfied. He is our good Shepherd, our chief Shepherd, continually protecting us. As we strive to resolve the painful matters of our past, Christ walks with us step-by-step, pulling us out of the ruts we fall into and saving us from the evil predator of this world.

Jesus mediates for us. He seeks to bolster our faith when surely, on our own, we would falter and crumble. On our behalf, Christ speaks directly to the Father, to the Source of all power, so that we might be strengthened and persevere. Being tempted in every way as a man, Jesus empathizes with our trials in life. He knows firsthand what it is like to walk in our shoes. Because of this understanding, He is able to intercede with exactly what we need to make it through to victory. While we might pray a painful issue in life would pass us by, Jesus petitions the Father so that we might be strengthened to stay with the issue, working it through to resolution. Other times, we might find ourselves involved with unwarranted behaviors. There as well, we find Christ mediating with the Father, so we will be equipped to give up attempts to control others. Jesus mediates for us in ways that are always in our best interest. He leads us in paths of righteousness, to places of right standing with our Creator. While the journey is not always easy, Jesus' goal is to bring us to a place where we can live a life of power, love, and sound mind.

As we look back at the unresolved issues in our life, Jesus is there to guide us and is continually interceding on our behalf. No longer need we submit to a yoke of slavery, led around by our conditioned states of thought and behavior. Christ mediated on our behalf during His time here on earth, and He continues to do so now at the right hand of the Father. Through Him, we have conjoint authority and can best resist the schemes of the devil. We can learn to operate within the power of our Lord and take every thought captive for Him. But first, we must work to resolve what remains unresolved in our life. We must be willing to allow God to search our mind and heart, asking Him to reveal the ways we have been conditioned by sin. As we work to clear away these obstacles to God's love, we can rest assured Christ Jesus will be mediating on our behalf.

Apart from our heavenly Father, there is really nothing we can do about our issues with sin. We need Jesus' work as High Priest in our life. His priestly work does not end when we receive Him as Lord and Savior. His work at the altar is continual on our behalf because of our dichotomous struggles. There's a side of us that really wants to follow the will of God, but there is another side that wants to do what we want, when we want. Living a life detached from God's will is not the same as living a life that is free. Such a life only equates to focusing our willful desires on the things of this world. Solomon told us that this type of behavior amounts to nothing more than vain exploits.[74]

In effect, we were created with a God-shaped hole in our heart that only He can fill. If we are not careful, we'll end up experiencing all sorts of trials, pains, and anguish as we attempt to fill this void with anything other than His love. Praise Christ Jesus as He continues in His priestly duties! His sacrificial work affords us the opportunity to humble ourselves. When we think of all He has done for us, we are moved from a mind-set of pride and arrogance to one of humility and adoration. We must be willing to break down our thought processes and assess our behaviors in light of God's word. This is no easy task because we are not able to be fully objective with ourselves. We need Jesus, our High Priest, to assist us in the area of humility. We need Him to demonstrate the cost of operating outside of the Father's will. Then we are more apt to surrender. We can work through the unresolved issues in our life with Christ as our High Priest. With the love of God flowing less inhibited into our life, we can best relate with our Creator and allow Him to fill that God-shaped hole in our heart.

Christ as King leads us in total righteousness. We can relax and trust in Him to rule over us with a moral character that is just and fair. When we open our heart to God, His love, grace, and mercy flow into our life. We can actually feel secure in the present moment because we choose Christ as our King. As we submit to His leadership, we can stand confident that He will not lead us astray. With Christ's kingly leadership, we can experience the abundant life. This is true because Jesus leads us away from our maladaptive states. If we are willing to allow Christ to guide us, then victory over our dysfunctional modes of thought and behavior will be achieved. How reassuring it is to know that we do not have to attempt to lean on our own understanding; we can lean on Christ as He leads us to green pastures and streams of pure flowing water.

As we close this chapter, it is my sincere prayer that you come one step closer in preparing your mind to face the sin you have been seeking freedom from. In the following chapter, we turn our focus to the ministry of the Holy Spirit.

Opportunity for Reflection

1. Read Isaiah 40:11 and John 10:11. What do these verses mean to you?

_____

_____

2. Read John 10:3, 4. How well do you know the voice of your Shepherd? How might you come to know His voice even better?

_____

_____

3. Review the three key points about the Ten Commandments found on pages 236-237. How might these points impact your relationship with Jesus?

   _____

   _____

4. Are the self-deceptive practices involving denial, repression, and rationalization stifling the work of Christ as High Priest in your life?

   _____

   _____

5. What are some of the characteristics found in Christ as King?

   _____

   _____

6. In what ways do you revere Christ as King in your own life?

   _____

   _____

7. Have you prayed to receive Jesus Christ as your Lord and Savior? If not, study the following passages:

   · Jesus said, "Whoever acknowledges me before men, I will also acknowledge him before my Father in heaven."[75]

   · "[I]f you confess with your mouth, "Jesus is Lord," and believe in your heart that God raised him from the dead, you will be saved. For it is with your heart that you believe and are justified, and it is with your mouth that you confess and are saved."[76]

· "If anyone acknowledges that Jesus is the Son of God, God lives in him and he in God."[77]

Do you believe Jesus Christ really was God in the flesh, that He died on a cross for your sins, was buried but arose again on the third day, and now sits at the right hand of the Father in heaven? If you have never prayed to receive Christ as your Lord, I invite you to do so now. Based on the above cited passages, formulate your own personal prayer to God about your profession of Christ as Savior in your life. Invite Him to be your Lord. If you do not belong to a church, I recommend that you find a Christ-centered, Bible-teaching church in your area. A good resource for advice and direction after making a decision for Christ is to call 1.800.Need.Him (1.800.633.3446), or visit the following websites: www.needhim.org, and www.chataboutjesus.com.

Chapter Nine

The Ministry of the Holy Spirit

If you love me, you will obey what I command. And I
will ask the Father, and he will give you another
Counselor to be with you forever—the Spirit of truth.
The world cannot accept him, because it neither sees
him nor knows him. But you know him, for he
lives with you and will be in you.

John 14:15–17

I n the previous chapter, we learned of the myriad ways that
Christ intercedes on our behalf as our Shepherd, Mediator, High
Priest, and King. In the passage above, we find further evidence
of Jesus' intercession for us when He asked the Father to send another
Counselor—His Holy Spirit. In our effort to prepare our minds for
action and cope with the pain and anguish in our life, we come to this
critical juncture in which we submit to God's will by allowing His
Spirit to work in and through us. Let's begin by taking a look at what it
means to have the Spirit of God live inside of us.

Indwell

In the eighth chapter of Romans, we find Paul's exposition of a life lived through the Holy Spirit. The apostle opens hard and fast with the following assertion: "Therefore, there is now no condemnation for those who are in Christ Jesus, because through Christ Jesus the law of the Spirit of life set me free from the law of sin and death."[1] Paul begins his statement with the adverb *therefore,* which signifies a consequence. This was in light of his earlier statement where he indicated: "I myself in my mind am a slave to God's law, but in the sinful nature a slave to the law of sin."[2] In other words, (1) we are dichotomous—we have two opposing natures, but (2) as a result of being conjointly raised up with Christ Jesus, there is now no condemnation. Our Lord not only provides for our salvation, but His work on the cross ushered the office of the Holy Spirit into our lives. All we need to do is open our hearts and receive Him. In this, we find evidence of our unification with God through the joining together with His Holy Spirit, wherein we are set free from the law of sin and death. This does not mean that as believers in Christ we can no longer sin, but it does signify that our sin debt has been paid in full and we are now unified with God. Jameison, Faussett, and Brown put it this way:

> As Christ, who "knew no sin," was, to all legal effects,
> "made sin for us," so are we, who believe in Him, to all
> legal effects, "made the righteousness of God in Him;"[3]

and thus, one with Him in the divine reckoning....But this is no mere legal *arrangement:* it is a union in *life;* believers, through the indwelling of Christ's Spirit in them, having one life with Him, as truly as the head and the members of the same body have one life. [4]

Paul moves forward with his line of reasoning declaring:

Those who live according to the sinful nature have their minds set on what that nature desires; but those who live in accordance with the Spirit have their minds set on what the Spirit desires. The mind of sinful man is death, but the mind controlled by the Spirit is life and peace; the sinful mind is hostile to God. It does not submit to God's law, nor can it do so. Those controlled by the sinful nature cannot please God.[5]

To live in accord with God is to conform to Him; it is us living in agreement with our Creator. All of this sounds good and well, only we fall short of agreement when we practice self-deceptive modes of thought and behavior that do not align with God's will. Because we tend not to challenge the validity of our premises, we need the indwelling of the Holy Spirit. Left to our own vices, we are hard pressed to arrive at the truth of matters.[6] We deny certain facts, avoid reality, and construct justifications as to why it is all right for us to remain in sin. But when the Holy Spirit comes and lives in us, He gives life and peace by pointing us toward the supreme reality, the ultimate meaning and value of our existence.

To live in accord with God's Spirit is to experience peace. Yet, all too often, we mistakenly assume that experiencing peace means there should be no struggle. We are going to fight in our pursuit of God's will, but this does not preclude us from experiencing peace at the same time. For example, it might be challenging to confront someone who has hurt. We might fear their reaction, or perhaps we might fear our own. But when we overcome our fear and confront in love, bitterness and resentment are rooted out, and the devil is not given a foothold. Is it challenging for us to confront in love? Many times the answer is yes. But this does not mean we cannot also experience peace of mind in doing so.

In all of this, we come to see that the indwelling of the Holy Spirit brings balance to our mind. Paul stated: "[T]he sinful mind is hostile to God. It does not submit to God's law, nor can it do so. Those controlled by the sinful nature cannot please God."[7] The Greek word used here for hostile is *echthra* (ekh'-thrah), which means "enmity," i.e., deep-seated hatred.[8] Little peace can be found in such a state of mind. We tend to dislike not being able to practice our own will. There may even be times when we feel hostile toward God in this regard. This is why Paul asserted that the sinful mind cannot submit to God's Law. Let's face it, living in the flesh, i.e., our own will can be pleasurable, albeit a fleeting pleasure.

If we are not careful, though, our quest to maintain a sense of pleasure in the things of this world can lead us into a state of compulsion. In such a state, we deny, repress, and rationalize in significant ways, which in turn inhibits our experience with love, joy, and peace. Ultimately, we are left feeling empty, and a vicious cycle develops. We attach our desires to people, places, or things and wind up addicted. Trapped in our addiction, we loath ourselves and God, blaming Him for the mess *we* created! Sounds absurd does not it? This is one of the many troubling states of mind that sin can lead us into, which is why we *need* the Holy Spirit to indwell us. We need the Spirit to help us submit to God's will, so that we can experience the abundant life and have it overflow into the lives of others.

Anoint

Once the Spirit of God indwells us, He then sets to work on anointing our mind. This is really an act of consecration in which our mind is set apart *for* God. Such a matter also relates to veneration, which is precisely why we tend to experience a newfound reverence and heartfelt change toward the Father when the Holy Spirit comes to live within us. Regarding this point, the apostle John wrote:

> [Y]ou have an anointing from the Holy Spirit, and all of
> you know the truth...the anointing you received from
> him remains in you, and you do not need anyone to

teach you. But as his anointing teaches about all things and as that anointing is real, not counterfeit—just as it has taught you, remain in him.[9]

In this passage, John was addressing the issue of antichrists, opponents of Christ; hence, his point with respect to not needing anyone to teach us. In other words, the apostle was encouraging the followers of Christ not to lean on the understanding of those opposed to Him, but to follow the promptings of the Holy Spirit. The Greek word John used here for *remain* is *meno* (men'-o), which means "to stay," such as in a given place, state, relation, or expectancy.[10] We are not to allow the forces of this world to push us out of our state of mind in Christ, which, again, is why we have been instructed to take every thought captive for Him.[11] As we shift from our self-deceptive practices to those involving awareness and acceptance of God's will, we increase in sensitivity to the promptings of the Holy Spirit. The more we can sense the will of the Spirit, the less likely we are to be pushed around by the happenings of this world. With such sensitivity, we can stand firm and not allow the enemy to enslave us again.

The above cited passage also tells us that God's Spirit anoints our mind. The Greek word used here for anointing is *chrisma* (khris'-mah), which means "a special endowment."[12] When one is endowed, they are equipped or supplied with a talent or quality.[13] The anointing of the Holy Spirit endows with knowledge and gifts, which enable us in key ways.[14] Solomon was considered to be one of the wisest individuals throughout all time, but even he made a special petition for discernment. One night, in a dream, the Lord appeared to him saying: "Ask for whatever you want me to give you."[15] Here was Solomon's response:

> You have shown great kindness to your servant, my father David, because he was faithful to you and righteous and upright in heart. You have continued this great kindness to him and have given him a son to sit on his throne this very day. Now, O LORD my God, you have made your servant king in place of my father David. But I am only a little child and do not know how to carry out my duties. Your servant is here among the people you have chosen, a great people, too numerous to count or number. So give your servant a discerning heart to govern your people and to distinguish between right and wrong. For who is able to govern this great people of yours?"[16]

Solomon understood he was not going to govern God's people effectively without the ability to discern His will. The Hebrew term used here for discerning is *shama`* (shaw-mah'), which means "to hear intelligently."[17] When the Holy Spirit anoints us with discernment, our ability to acquire knowledge of God's will is increased. The Spirit then prompts us to *apply* this knowledge, which is precisely what intelligence is: the ability to acquire and apply knowledge. Consider the words of the apostle Paul in his first letter to the followers of Christ in Corinth:

> The Spirit searches all things, even the deep things of God. For who among men knows the thoughts of a man except the man's spirit within him? In the same way no one knows the thoughts of God except the Spirit of God. We have not received the spirit of the world but the Spirit who is from God, that we may understand what God has freely given us. This is what we speak, not in words taught us by human wisdom but in words taught by the Spirit, expressing spiritual truths in spiritual words. The man without the Spirit does not accept the things that come from the Spirit of God, for they are foolishness to him, and he cannot understand them, because they are spiritually discerned. The spiritual man makes judgments about all things, but he himself is not subject to any man's judgment: "For who has known the mind of the Lord that he may instruct him?" But we have the mind of Christ.[18]

The Holy Spirit is an investigator, searching the deep things of God, as well as our own heart and mind. While we desire to know the deep things of our Creator, we tend to steer away from matters that have been proven challenging to us. On one hand, we like the notion of our Father wanting us to be free from the bondage of sin. On the other hand, we tend not to think in depth about such matters because it is distressing. And what are we humans apt to do with matters that cause distress? Resist. And how are we apt to resist? Denial. Repression. When these acts have been proven ineffective, we attempt to adapt to the distress by rationalizing. We want to be set free from the pain and anguish, from fear, as well as from the guilt of past events. It is not that we do not try; we pray, we petition, but somehow the pain remains. We profess we have been made new in Christ and assert there is now no condemnation, but as was discussed in Chapter Five, because of the nature of episodic memory, we cannot effectively forget painful events. The key then is to commit to working *through* the painful emotions attached to the distressing memories.

When we deny, repress, or rationalize, we are seeking a worldly answer to the issues of our life. But the Holy Spirit is prompting us to deal with whatever remains unresolved. When we make the conscious decision to resolve sin, regardless of whether it is our own sin or that which others have perpetrated upon us, the Holy Spirit anoints us with the knowledge to achieve resolution. Where deeply rooted issues are concerned, God's Spirit can prompt us to the right counselor who is equipped to assist in such matters.

Comfort

Three times in the Gospel of John, Jesus spoke of the Holy Spirit as our *Parakletos* (par-ak'-lay-tos), which in the Greek means, "intercessor," "counselor," "advocate," or "comforter."[19] An *intercessor* is one who makes entreaty, an earnest request or petition for others who are in need.[20] What a comforting thought! God's very Spirit lives on the inside of us and is providing support in the form of intercession. But our *Parakletos* does more than intercede; He is understood to be our Counselor, advising us on all matters. The counsel of God is a great thing. The prophet Jeremiah wrote: "O great and powerful God, whose name is the LORD Almighty, great are your purposes and mighty are your deeds."[21] The saying, "great are your purposes" is derived from the Hebrew expression of *gadowl 'etsah* (gaw-dole' • ay-tsaw'), which means "great advice."[22] God's advice is infinitely greater than any human being could give. We also learn from the prophet Isaiah that God's counsel is faithful and wonderful.[23] For the Christian, the counsel of God is rendered through His communing Spirit. The *Parakletos* is our Advocate, fighting for our rights as children of God. In all of this, the Spirit of God is the greatest source of comfort we will find in this world. As we prepare our minds to face the unresolved issues in life, we can rest assured the Holy Spirit will be there every step of the way, interceding, counseling, advocating, and comforting us.

Jesus said: "When the Counselor comes, whom I will send to you from the Father, the Spirit of truth who goes out from the Father, he will testify about me."[24] Prior to speaking these words, Christ informed His disciples that they would face adversity for having faith in Him.[25] No doubt, such news was disheartening, but Jesus did not leave His followers hopeless—we have the Counselor, the Spirit of truth. It is the work of the Holy Spirit to testify about Christ Jesus. None of us are promised an easy road in this lifetime; however, we are promised the aid of God's Spirit to help us through anything that comes our way. As we work to resolve the issues that cause us pain and condition us to think and behave in ways that God never intended, the devil is sure to make his stand and accuse us. When we stop submitting to the enemy's yoke of slavery, we can count on him to attack us. Thus, we need the work of the Holy Spirit to overcome; we need His intercession, counsel, and comfort. In such times, we need the Spirit of God to testify to us that our salvation lies in Christ and nobody else.[26] We need the Holy Spirit to remind us that we are coheirs with Christ—conjoint participants in His authority.[27]

With respect to the *Parakletos,* Jesus also had this to say:

Now I am going to him who sent me, yet none of you asks me, 'Where are you going?' Because I have said these things, you are filled with grief. But I tell you the truth: It is for your good that I am going away. Unless I go away, the Counselor will not come to you; but if I go, I will send him to you. When he comes, he will convict the world of guilt in regard to sin and righteousness and judgment: in regard to sin, because men do not believe in me; in regard to righteousness, because I am going to the Father, where you can see me no longer; and in regard to judgment, because the prince of this world now stands condemned.[28]

Surely, this was a confusing time for Christ's disciples. While they had come to the understanding that He was the Messiah, they still had little understanding that His ministry was about dealing with the issues of sin and restoration. But Jesus graciously worked to prepare His disciples for what was to come and continued to instill hope in them. They first heard that it is for their own good that Jesus was going away; in doing so, the Counselor would come. I like Matthew Henry's commentary on this point:

[T]he presence of Christ's Spirit in his church is so much better, and more desirable, than his bodily presence, that it was really expedient for us that he should go away, to send the Comforter. His corporal presence could be but in one place at one time, but his Spirit is everywhere, in all places, at all times, wherever two or three are gathered in his name. Christ's bodily presence draws men's eyes, his Spirit draws their hearts....[29]

Jesus taught that upon the arrival of the Holy Spirit, the world would be convicted of guilt with respect to sin. To clearly see this point, we need to develop a right understanding of what it means to be convicted of sin. The Greek word for convict is *elegcho* (el-eng'-kho), which means "to confute."[30] When someone is confuted, he or she has been proven to be wrong or in error.[31] Coffman put it this way: "The Spirit convicts of sin, revealing man's fallen estate and bondage to Satan, and showing his total helplessness to achieve through his own efforts any healing of his condition."[32] The choice is ours. Will we heed the promptings of the Spirit, or will we stubbornly insist on having our way? Can we accept our fallen, broken state? Will we come to terms with the fact that we are helplessly lost in our sin without the assistance and direction of the Holy Spirit? Or will we lean on our own understanding?

With respect to the Spirit's convicting in righteousness, we find here the use of the Greek word *dikaiosune* (dik-ah-yos-oo'-nay), which is a rather interesting application. *Dikaiosune* means "equity" (of character or act).[33] When we talk about equity with respect to character, we are really touching upon the state, quality, or ideal of being just, impartial, and fair.[34] The Holy Spirit convicts the world with respect to Jesus' equity. Here we find another example of our ways not being anything like the ways of the Father. The world tends to view the notion of being convicted as negative. But in God's kingdom, being convicted by His Spirit is good. His conviction keeps us from eternal doom and gives us a leader in Jesus who has ideal character. Is not this what we really desire, someone we can trust to lead us to a place of right standing? We all want peace of mind, which is precisely what the Holy Spirit brings us when we are convicted in the righteousness of Christ Jesus. Coffman further wrote: "The Spirit also convicts of righteousness by revealing the mystery of how a man may acquire a righteousness not his own, that being the righteousness of Christ, available to all who receive and obey the gospel, thus being inducted 'into Christ,' and identified with Christ as Christ."[35] As we turn and face the deeply rooted issues of our life, working to identify and overcome the ways sin has conditioned us, we find solace in the conviction of the Holy Spirit.

Let us examine further the matter of conviction with respect to judgment. Jesus said that the Holy Spirit would do so "because the prince of this world now stands condemned."[36] The Greek word for judgment is *krisis* (kree'-sis), which means "decision," subjectively or objectively—for or against; by extension, it means "a tribunal"; by implication, *krisis* means "justice" (especially, divine law).[37] Christ's work on Calvary was very much judicial, having everything to do with the administration of justice. Satan figuratively struck Christ on the heel by working to harden the hearts of those who falsely accused Him, then stood by while He was scourged and crucified. At that time, it appeared to be a fatal blow. But three days later, Christ had proven the prophecy to be true when He rose from the grave in glorified form.[38] Indeed, Jesus had struck a crushing blow to Satan. Christ's work on the cross vindicates us from the accusations of our adversary. We are now justified in the right standing of Jesus Christ. This third point drives home the comforting fact that God's manner of conviction is nothing like that of this world. As we prepare our minds for action, let us fully embrace the comfort afforded us through the gracious work of the Holy Spirit.

Regenerate

The word *regenerate* is derived from the Latin root *regenerāre,* which means "to reproduce," "to create again."[39] In Chapter Two, we investigated how humanity was originally intended to be most representative of God's moral character, and that morality pertains to a right way of thinking. In Chapter Three, we studied how the mind is a component of the soul. Regeneration then brings about correction of thought processes and behaviors, resulting in a state of mind that aligns more with God's right way of thinking.[40] This, too, is part of the Holy Spirit's work—to bring about correction of thoughts and behaviors that fall outside of the Father's will. And it was what Jesus spoke to Nicodemus about:

> Now there was a man of the Pharisees named Nicodemus, a member of the Jewish ruling council. He came to Jesus at night and said, "Rabbi, we know you are a teacher who has come from God. For no one could

perform the miraculous signs you are doing if God were not with him." In reply Jesus declared, "I tell you the truth, no one can see the kingdom of God unless he is born again." "How can a man be born when he is old?" Nicodemus asked. "Surely he cannot enter a second time into his mother's womb to be born!" Jesus answered, "I tell you the truth, no one can enter the kingdom of God unless he is born of water and the Spirit."[41]

The Greek word used here for born is *gennao* (ghen-nah'-o), which figuratively means, "to regenerate" or "to be delivered of."[42] The Greek word used here for see is *eido* (i'-do), which is a primary verb and is generally used only in certain past tense applications. By implication, *eido* means "to know" or "to be aware of."[43] Through lexical analysis, we come to understand that Jesus was stating no one is going to know, or effectively be aware of the kingdom of God, without the indwelling of the Holy Spirit. Which is what Christ goes on to clarify for Nicodemus: "[N]o one can enter the kingdom of God unless he is born of water and Spirit." Note how Jesus first stated that no one can *see* the kingdom of God unless he is born again, but on the second assertion He said no one can *enter* without the Holy Spirit. Without the Spirit of God indwelling us and anointing our mind, we cannot effectively know God or be aware of His kingdom. Because the kingdom of God is not of this world, we can neither see it nor enter into it without the mind of God intersecting with our mind via His Spirit.

Coming into contact with our Creator's Spirit affords the opportunity for great change to our state of mind. Through the process of regeneration, the opportunity exists to develop a preference for doing the Father's will. I say *opportunity* because the freedom to choose always exists. Inherent in all of this is the issue of our conditioned modes of thought and behavior. When I first accepted Jesus as my Lord and Savior back in March of 1990, I was still entrenched in maladaptive modes of thought and behavior. During the first years of my walk with Christ, I recall struggling intensely with feelings of fear and guilt. I feared that God was waiting for me to mess up so He could strike me down. When the pastor preached about God's unfailing love, I was inhibited to receive this truth. I honestly believed the love of the Father was available to others but not to me; I was too far gone and had done too much wrong. Needless to say, my walk with the Lord was rather rocky. It remained this way for a decade, until I was able to surrender my fear and guilt to Him. I so longed for a close relationship with my heavenly Father that I made the decision to stand still long enough for Him to deal with me. This was not easy to do, but it was at this point in my walk with the Lord that I truly began to experience His love, grace, and mercy. This experience changed the condition of my mind.

I relate this because I believe it is important to exemplify the significance of our conditioned modes of thinking. There are times when the Holy Spirit prompts us to deal with a specific issue we are in bondage to, yet many are conditioned toward self-deception. In this state, we automatically default to modes of thought and behavior, as well as emotional responses, that do not line up with God's perfect and loving intent for our life. The Spirit prompts and we deny Him. The Spirit moves and we repress. The Spirit convicts and we rationalize. The battle goes on and on until we reach the end of ourselves. Like the father of the prodigal son, it is painful for our heavenly Father to see us go our own way. His desire is for us to turn our heart toward Him and enter into a deep, meaningful relationship. For such an act to be of love, it must be entirely our choice to surrender to Him. But this is not to say that He does not prompt us with His Spirit, impressing upon our thoughts and emotions as a means to uproot the things that inhibit our relationship with Him. The true nature of regeneration is more of a *process* as opposed to an event.

Empower

Micah was a prophet who lived during a dark time in Israel's history between 735 and 710 B.C. The northern portion of Israel had adopted perverse acts, idol worship, infanticide, practice of cultic type of prostitution, and more.[44] The influence of the north was spreading southward into Judah, and the Lord saw it fit to work through prophets to address the sins of His people. Micah came from Moresheth-gath,[45] a small agricultural community about twenty-five miles southwest of Jerusalem. To those who lived in the more populated cities, Micah must have appeared to be a backward country bumpkin. While he was not as astute on political matters as were the prophets Isaiah and Daniel, Micah's heart for God's people was just as big. But how was it that a man from the country could take on the suave, sophisticated, and fraudulent leaders of his day? What or who filled Micah with such power to face the prevailing authorities? Micah himself made the profession: "I am filled with power, with the Spirit of the LORD, and with justice and might, to declare to Jacob his transgression, to Israel his sin."[46] Micah stated that he had been filled with *koach* (ko'-akh), the Hebrew term for vigor.[47] The Spirit of the Lord had filled Micah with a mental energy that gave him the strength to follow through with what he was called upon to do.

A majority of the people in Micah's day would not have wanted to hear what the Lord had to say through this prophet. Persecution and death were very real possibilities he had to face. But through the Holy Spirit, Micah received new capacities for reasoning. The Spirit of God had invigorated him with a deeper logic and rationale, the evidence of which can be seen in his writings. While the Israelites were God's chosen people,[48] throughout the Bible, we can see a pattern by which God showed them His love, which they welcomed initially. As they followed their Creator, He blessed them with great leaders, inspired prophets, the priesthood, the Law, Messianic promises, the Temple, His covenants, and more. [Note: let's remove the term—oracles—its redundant with "inspired prophets"].[49] But over time, they would lean on their own understanding and turn away from the ways of the Lord. Before they knew it, the Israelites would fall back into idolatry, hypocrisy, disobedience, externalism, unbelief, and many other dysfunctions.[50]

As we study these matters, the tendency is to wonder why God's chosen people could not stay the course. What was it that repeatedly led the Israelites away from the Lord? I believe the answer is found within each one of us. To one degree or another, we are all like the Israelites; our Father blesses us, but we fall back into our entrenched modes of thought and behavior. Our Lord desires for us to revere Him in worship;[51] such an act brings us closer.[52] But instead, we worship idols. The Creator of the cosmos says, "[C]onsecrate yourselves and be holy, because I am holy."[53] Instead, we follow after our own ways and end up in hypocrisy. The Lord asks that we obey Him, but we practice disobedience. God desires for us to focus on the internal, but that is too much work, so we focus on the external and lose ourselves in the process. Our heavenly Father prompts us to believe in Him, but we choose otherwise.

In all of this, we can see the immense need for the invigorating work of the Holy Spirit. We cannot do the things of God on our own; though we try and try, we fall short. But the Spirit of God brings logic and rationale where it is much needed. His power provides us with the mental energy that helps us see the way sin has conditioned us. Through the promptings of the Holy Spirit, we come to see how illogical it has been for us to run from the issues of our past. As the

Spirit of God anoints our mind, we are empowered with a rationale that brings about soundness. Is this not what we so desperately desire? To be of sound mind, having a firm, unshakable basis by which we can live free from the chaos brought about by sin? The peace we long for is made available through the love of our Father, who sends His Holy Spirit, imbuing us with His logic and infusing us with His powers, which ultimately bring about His lasting peace.

Gives Joy

In the twelfth and thirteenth chapters of the book of Romans, the apostle Paul addressed a number of matters we are to concern ourselves with as Christians, such as responsibilities toward God, society, and government.[54] After making these assertions, Paul transitions into the principles of Christian liberty, stating:

> Accept him whose faith is weak, without passing judgment on disputable matters. One man's faith allows him to eat everything, but another man, whose faith is weak, eats only vegetables. The man who eats everything must not look down on him who does not, and the man who does not eat everything must not condemn the man who does, for God has accepted him.[55]

Paul was addressing how some Christians in Rome were breaking fellowship with other Christians over differences of opinion. In Rome, the Messianic Jews were holding fast to their traditions with respect to food and particular days of celebration.[56] Regarding the issue of food, Jews were not to eat meat that had previously been offered to idols. In Jewish tradition, simply partaking of such food would be considered a violation of the Law.[57] Because there was no guarantee that idol worship had not been conducted with meat purchased in the Roman marketplace, some Jews had adopted the practice of vegetarianism.

Messianic Jews who engaged in this practice were then condemning their non-Jewish Christian brothers and sisters for eating meat. On the flip side, the non-Jewish Christians were looking down at their Jewish brothers and sisters as being what they considered weak-minded. Paul sought to address this matter by redirecting their focus to the major point at hand—namely, that God accepts equally all of those who are in Christ:

> He who regards one day as special, does so to the Lord. He who eats meat, eats to the Lord, for he gives thanks to God; and he who abstains, does so to the Lord and gives thanks to God. For none of us lives to himself alone and none of us dies to himself alone. If we live, we live to the Lord; and if we die, we die to the Lord. So, whether we live or die, we belong to the Lord....Therefore let us stop passing judgment on one

> another. Instead, make up your mind not to put any
> stumbling block or obstacle in your brother's way. As
> one who is in the Lord Jesus, I am fully convinced that
> no food is unclean in itself. But if anyone regards
> something as unclean, then for him it is unclean. If your
> brother is distressed because of what you eat, you are
> no longer acting in love. Do not by your eating destroy
> your brother for whom Christ died. Do not allow what
> you consider good to be spoken of as evil.[58]

The issue Paul was addressing here is a good example of how differentness is often viewed as threatening. When we are secure in our place with Christ, we can then love others regardless of their differences, just as Jesus does. Clearly, people on both sides of this issue were distressing one another through judgment and pride. Paul went so far as to state they were "no longer acting in love."

Consider the entrenched modes of thinking on each side of this issue. Generation after generation of Jews had worked to follow the Law, the leading principle of which was rooted in what is known as *theocratic character*. Such character pertains to the thoughts and behaviors of a society relating directly and immediately to the will of God.[59] It is not just about a rule of conduct, but the revelation of God's nature and divine order. From a Jewish perspective, it embraces God as being the Head of the Israeli nation. Perhaps the most significant facet of theocratic character is the goodness the Law seeks to impress upon the people.[60] Devotion and reverence to God is of the highest order. For the Jew, it is out of piety that righteousness and love come, not only toward God but also toward others.

Yet they were so entrenched in their theocratic mode of thinking that they could not grasp the concept that Christ had already fulfilled the Law once and for all.[61] In this regard, piety of the Law was no longer the single most important facet in the demonstration of righteousness and love. Faith in Christ trumps piety. In similar fashion, many of us have thought like the Jews. We believed we could achieve a certain degree of holiness through pious acts. We thought if we got involved enough with ministerial efforts we would become more holy and less affected by our past. But this will never be the case because our mind is wired for homeostasis; denying the unresolved pain of our past does not bring about balance. While practicing spiritual formation techniques—such as those involved in the disciplines of abstinence and engagement—proves beneficial in our drawing closer to God,[62] they will not erase our unresolved issues. As a matter of fact, the closer we draw to our heavenly Father, the more His Spirit impresses upon us the need to deal with matters that inhibit our relationship with Him and others.

If we delve further, we can see our tendency to be like the Gentile Christians as well, looking down our nose at those who struggle with issues that we ourselves do not. These Christians were not caught up with the issue of piety, because it was not as ingrained in them as it was for their Jewish brothers and sisters. But look how easily their perspective turned to harmful pride. As much as the Messianic Jew's judgmental stance inhibited love, so too did the prideful stance of the Gentile Christians.

Having exhorted both sides of the issue, Paul then stated: "For the kingdom of God is not a matter of eating and drinking, but of righteousness, peace and joy in the Holy Spirit, because anyone who serves Christ in this way is pleasing to God and approved by men."[63] Here, again, we find the Greek word *dikaiosune.* Recall that we touched upon this earlier with regards to the Holy Spirit rendering comfort in our lives. Paul was asserting that the kingdom of God is really not a matter of ceremonial actions centered on eating and drinking; it is about being upright in moral character—thinking and behaving more like Christ Jesus, and less like ourselves. Yet the kingdom of God is also representative of peace. The Greek word used here is *eirene* (i-ray'-nay), which, by implication, applies to prosperity, being one with God, or resting in the Lord.[64] Paul then hits upon a third facet of God's kingdom—joy in the Holy Spirit. It is the *chara* (khar-ah') or cheerfulness of the Holy Spirit. Consider for a moment what it means to experience cheer. When we feel cheerful, there is a lifting of our spirit. There really is a wonderful delight in experiencing the encouragement of the Holy Spirit. Coffman summed it up well when he wrote: "The great concern is not the exercise of liberty in such matters as food and drink, but the holy joy of the sacred communion of the fellowship in Christ."[65] Note Paul's tie-in: "anyone who serves Christ is pleasing to

God." The great joy in all of this is our connection with the Lord through the presence of His Spirit living within us.

As we work to develop an awareness of the unresolved issues in our life and the ways we have been conditioned by sin, we can then work toward accepting the need for resolution. As we do so, we become less inhibited in following the ways of our Father. His character lives through us in increasing measure, perpetuating greater degrees of love, joy, and peace. As we work to die in the old ways of coping with life, we then sense a growing prosperity and can better rest in the Lord. As we experience resolution from our past issues, a fullness of cheer overtakes us. Our spirit feels less burdened, like a heavy load has been removed. When we achieve such a state, we experience joy unlike anything of this world. In these moments, gone is the need to posture for position, to create strife or dissension. We are at one with our heavenly Father; His love flows with considerably less restriction, and we are filled with joy.

Summary

This study has not been all-inclusive of the Holy Spirit's ministry. While points such as baptism, sanctification, bearing witness, or fruits of the Spirit were not covered, they are no less important factors. Indeed, entire books have been written on the specifics of the Holy Spirit, but time and space simply do not permit such detail here. Nonetheless, the six points covered in this chapter sufficiently demonstrate the depth to which our Father will go to achieve relationship with us.

It is in our best interest that we learn to live in accord with His Spirit. There must be a willingness on our part to conduct an honest inventory of our lives. With the discernment afforded us through God's Spirit, we can move toward acknowledging the sin that inhibits our relationship with the Lord and others. This can be accomplished through the anointing work of the Spirit by which our thoughts are set aside *for* God. The Spirit of God is our Counselor and Advocate, the ultimate Source of comfort, especially as we struggle through the valleys of life.

The presence and anointing work of the Spirit ushers in the process of regeneration, through which we enter into the kingdom of God. The Holy Spirit enables transformation of our conscious state by which we comprehend in greater degrees those areas of our life that the Lord desires for us to change. This is not because He is a dictatorial God. But He does desire for us to be healthy and functional, so that we can best relate with Him and allow His gracious love to flow into and through our lives. The Spirit of God invigorates our mind, empowering us to do the will of the Father. We can count on the Spirit to provide the resources needed to resolve our issues. Just as He did with Micah, the Lord can work in our life to bring about change. Inherent in such change is joy. As we are set free from the bondage of our mental and emotional pain, we experience an upwelling of cheer.

In this state, we are significantly less inhibited to receive and extend the Father's love.

With this chapter, we bring the third and final part of this book to a close. In Chapter Seven, the characteristics, intentions, and methods of Satan were studied. We learned that the best way to resist the devil is by taking on the mind of Christ and putting on the full armor of God. Chapter Eight covered the different facets of Christ's character as Shepherd, Mediator, High Priest, and King. Our in-depth look at the ministry of the Holy Spirit rounds out part three. In the final chapter, I offer my concluding thoughts.

Opportunity for Reflection

1. Read Romans 8:1, 2. What does this passage personally mean to you?

   _____

   _____

2. The Holy Spirit has been likened to an investigator, searching the deep things of God and of our own mind. How does this apply in your own walk with God?

   _____

   _____

3. Jesus taught that upon the arrival of the Holy Spirit, the world would be convicted of guilt with respect to sin. In what ways might denial, repression, and rationalization factor into His point?

_____

_____

4. How have you experienced the Holy Spirit as Comforter in your walk with the Lord?

_____

_____

5. In what ways has the Holy Spirit worked in your life to regenerate your mind?

_____

_____

6. The prophet Micah serves as a good example of how the Holy Spirit can empower people. Have you experienced an empowering through God's Spirit? Are there self-deceptive practices in your life that inhibit your use of this power?

_____

_____

7. What joy have you experienced in life as a result of the workings of the Holy Spirit?

_____

_____

Chapter Ten

Repentance

It is for freedom that Christ has set us free. Stand firm,
then, and do not let yourselves be burdened
again by a yoke of slavery.

Galatians 5:1

Is the follower of Jesus Christ set free from their debt of sin by the Lord's redeeming work on the cross? The answer is: absolutely. But is this the question we should be asking? What if I were to ask, "To what degree does the believer in Christ *possess* freedom?" Jesus said: "I tell you the truth, everyone who sins is a slave to sin. Now a slave has no permanent place in the family, but a son belongs to it forever. So if the Son sets you free, you will be free indeed."[1] We are not called to simply survive this life till we get to heaven; we are to live in the freedom and power afforded us through our relationship with Christ Jesus right here, right now. We are joint heirs with our Lord; it is important that we adopt this mind-set so that we can be strengthened to do that which God directs us to do.[2] In all of this, it is vitally important that we work to gain awareness of the ways sin conditions us to think and behave. Sin separates us from our

Father. It clogs the conduit through which His love flows into our life. Gaining awareness of the ways we have been conditioned by sin affords us the opportunity to surrender to God's will. As we do so, the Spirit of the Lord sets to work on reconditioning our mind.

In the mind of God, you were conceived before the beginning of time. He has always known of you; He has always loved you. You were born with your exact set of personality characteristics because He designed you with purpose. You fit perfectly into His plan. There has never been anyone like you before, and there never will be again. Your life has meaning, not just in the afterlife but in the here and now as well. You have always mattered to God. Because He is omniscient, He has forever known of you, and because God is love, He has always loved you. Your heavenly Father desires personal relationships. God so longs to share His love with you that He went all the way to the cross to make it possible.

It is for this purpose that God created us to be relational beings. Wired into us are specific needs like love and security, which drive us toward relationship. It is really not a matter of whether we want love; we need it to be fulfilled in our life. Because God is love, it could be understood that love is the greatest force in the universe. But when our need for love is not satisfactorily met, the results can turn pathological. We end up manifesting behaviors that are habitual, maladaptive, and compulsive.[3] As I have covered, three common personality styles that tend to develop out of a lack of love are psychopathic, obsessive, and emotional. When too many conditions are placed on love, a psychopathic mind-set can develop in which the individual learns to prohibit self-affirmation, resulting in the growth of hatred for themselves and society. Remember, that in the case of the obsessive personality style, the individual internalizes the belief that love can be gained only on the basis of performance and accomplishment. This individual attempts to willfully control both their internal and external life. When the flow of love is inhibited, the individual with an overly emotional personality style will turn their willfulness against themselves, suppressing their own needs and desires as a means to meet with the approval of others.

As we practice maladaptive coping mechanisms, they become etched into our procedural memory, making them habitual. Because these mechanisms are maladaptive, they become a source for further distress as we repeat the same sinful behaviors. General Adaptation Syndrome reveals that we cope with distress through the stages of alarm, resistance/adaptation, and exhaustion. Alarm triggers our fight-or-flight mechanism, but if the distress remains, we then engage in resistance/adaptation. It is during these periods of distress that our coping mechanisms become fine-tuned. We must ask ourselves: (1) Are we aware of unmet needs, and do we work to satisfy those needs in healthy manners? (2) Are we coping in such a way as to maintain God's morality, evidenced by the presence of the fruits of the Spirit?[4] If we can answer yes to these questions, then it could be concluded we are coping in healthy, functional ways. However, if we determine that our actions lean more toward habitually dysfunctional types of behavior, we must conclude we are not operating within God's will. When we persist in these modes of thought and behavior, we eventually experience exhaustion. This is where breakdown occurs and disease may set in. Such a state serves as evidence of sin's sickening nature.

What we learn in life affects the relationship between soul, mind, and body. Those who deny and repress their emotions will find this action affecting the way they think and behave. Stuffing emotions impacts our body in a myriad of different ways, such as tension headaches, stomach discomfort, elevated blood pressure, and more. Covering up our feelings stifles love, joy, and peace, which has a profound effect on our spiritual and mental proclivities. While the implications of what we learn can have negative consequences, the reverse is true as well. Learning to be more in touch with what we are feeling, why we are feeling that way, and what God wills for us to do with our emotions results in clearer thought processes, less tension in the body, and a more open and honest relationship with the Lord and others. Given all of this, it is important for us to develop a keen awareness of the ways we have learned to think, feel, and behave.

Nonassociative, associative, and deductive forms of learning serve as key factors in the process of sanctification. Habituation acts like an automatic default when it comes to thoughts, emotions, and behaviors. If you learned to cope with your fears by bullying others, it is likely that this line of thought and behavior will continue in your relationships. If you learned to withdraw from conflict, chances are you are still doing so; that is, unless enough awareness was developed to interrupt the pattern. As our processes of thought and behavior are enforced through operant conditioning, they become more procedural, even to the point where we are not consciously aware of them. Through classical conditioning, associations are formed between our senses, memories, and emotions. In turn, these associations cause us to react in ways that are procedural. If we discover these reactions are not in line with God's will, then we must lean on the help of the Holy Spirit to replace the old process of coping with the process the Father desires.

The way we cope with our thoughts and emotions impacts us neurologically as well. An example of this is found in the depressive and anxious states that often develop as a result of continually repressing our thoughts and feelings. Repression is an attempt to resist distress, but maintaining this state for too long proves exhaustive. The neurological ramifications are altered states in our electrochemical signaling, whereby disorderly moods occur. These altered states move us farther away from God's purpose for our life. Clearly, the Lord never intended to see us live a repressed life; it is for good reason He created us with the ability to think and feel. On one hand, through cognition, we can perceive of our Creator and His creation; we can reason and make judgments more in accord with the Father's will. On the other hand, our emotions serve as a gauge for our needs. Through emotions, we can more effectively ascertain the degree to which our needs are or are not being met. For instance, the feeling of loneliness acts like a signal that our need for relationship is not being fulfilled as God intended. If we have learned to cope through healthy, functional modes, we can then recognize our feelings, reason why they exist, and make judgments that best line up with the will of the Father for getting our needs met. The more aware we are of our thoughts and feelings, the greater opportunity we have of living out God's purpose for our life.

From this perspective, we can see the significance of sin's impact. How can we demolish arguments and pretensions set up against the knowledge of God if we are conditioned to cope through denial, repression, and rationalization? Perception, reason, and judgment are hampered when we are entrenched in self-deception. Through denial, we refuse to acknowledge reality, especially if the realization involves pain. Our perception must then be altered so as not to accept the truth. How can we effectively reason and conclude what our Father's will is if we are unwilling to allow ourselves to think and feel thoroughly? Justification for our behaviors that fall outside of God's will only serve to steep us further in sin.

Through personal and professional experience, I have come to understand that Satan might flee in the moment of our resistance, but he lingers in the shadows of our mind. This is why Peter encouraged us to be self-controlled and alert.[5] The more we practice denial, repression, and rationalization, the less alert we are; awareness is stymied, and so too is our self-control. Unless we bring these matters out into the light of God, the polluting elements of sin remain, inhibiting our relationship with our heavenly Father and robbing us of the abundant life. The devil knows this fully well, which is why he seeks to deceive us. He knows that if he can get our focus off God, he has a shot at injecting enough deception into a given situation to lead us astray. Recall that Satan's intention is to undo the work of our Creator. In doing so, he hopes to thwart our effectiveness for the kingdom of God here on earth. If he can entice us away from the will of the Father, he can better instigate evil through the life we live. So he masquerades as an angel of light. He insinuates doubt. The devil schemes in such ways as to cast us down from our rightful place of authority as children of God.

The battle is real; it cannot be avoided. Sticking our head in the sand as a Christian is folly. We must be prepared to follow our Shepherd. He gathers and carries us close to His heart. Jesus knows our needs, and He makes provision for them. We must be willing to submit to His leadership, lest we become separated from the fold. When we are lost and alone, our enemy can have his way with us. Further still, because we are dichotomous, we need a mediator, someone who can resolve the inner conflict that arises from our two opposing natures of flesh and spirit. The Ten Commandments clearly demonstrate we cannot live a sinless life; for whom among us (save Christ) has ever been able to live life without breaking at least one of the Commandments? We must come to terms with the reality that our sin is a violation against God's will, and that it always carries painful and destructive consequences. We are absolutely dependent on God to save us; we simply do not possess the power to save ourselves. We need Christ Jesus to mediate on our behalf. There is no other who is qualified for such work. He is our High Priest, interceding with the perfect offering to pay our debt of sin in full. Through the intercession of our Priest, we are judicially represented in the highest court of all—before the throne of God Almighty. The authority of Christ comes from beyond this world, from the Father Himself. Under His rule, we need not fear, for Jesus leads us with righteous character. As we operate under the authority of our King, we live the life He always intended for us to have—the abundant life filled with love, joy, and peace.

When we open our mind and heart to Christ, the very Spirit of God comes to live inside of us. Unified with the Holy Spirit, we can more readily live in accord with our Creator. His Spirit prompts us toward awareness of His will. As the Holy Spirit searches our heart, He reveals what we need to see about ourselves. He shows us what our own willfulness is reaping, and guides us toward reason and judgment that aligns with the will of the Father. In the middle of all of this is our own willfulness, our desire to do what we want, when we want. If we are to follow the ways of the Lord, there must be a willingness to do His will. The Holy Spirit can prompt us all day long, but if we are unwilling to follow these promptings, then we stay stuck in our sin. When we stifle the flow of God's love into our life, joy diminishes and peace becomes harder to attain.

Questions:

(1) Did Chapter Four reveal any practice of denial in your life?

(2) Through working the self-assessment in Chapter Five, have you learned something significant about the ways in which you might repress?

(3) In Chapter Six, did you come to see how you may be rationalizing sinful behaviors?

If you answered yes to any of these questions, now is the time to allow the counsel of the Holy Spirit to break through. What is He revealing to you in this very moment? Are you in need of help? If so, allow the Spirit of God to guide and direct you. Remember, it is for freedom that Christ has set us free. If you determine that your issues with sin are too ingrained to overcome on your own, follow the guidance of the Holy Spirit and get professional assistance. Otherwise, you are likely to continue with your submission to a yoke of slavery. This is your time of liberation! God wants to set free from your bondage. It is His desire that you experience regeneration and significant growth in holiness. Trust that He will empower you to do what is necessary. Talk with your clergy or visit www.aacc.net and select the link, FIND A CHRISTIAN COUNSELOR.

Repentance

Every act of sin involves a way of thought and behavior that is out of line with the Father's will. Because this applies to all people, except Jesus, our Creator has tolerated billions upon billions of sinful acts from humanity—mine and yours included. Talk about patience! The apostle Peter wrote: "The Lord is not slow in keeping his promise, as some understand slowness. He is patient with you, not wanting anyone to perish, but everyone to come to repentance."[6] Why is God so patient with us? The obvious answer is that He loves us. The act of repentance involves a sincere feeling of regret and sorrow for our sins.[7] This is otherwise known as being contrite. In such a state, we are most apt to turn away from our willfulness and head toward a willingness to live life God's way.

The case of Peter offers an excellent example of the transforming power contained within a contrite heart. This disciple denied the Lord three times the night of His arrest. He, too, could have chosen the same route as Judas and ended his life, but instead he allowed his breakdown to usher in a breakthrough. Following His resurrection, Christ appeared to His disciples on more than one occasion. The third time happened after Peter and some of the disciples had been out fishing all night. When morning arrived, they still had caught nothing. But then Jesus appeared on the shore and instructed them to cast the net on the right side of the boat.[8] The result was an enormous haul of fish. But once Peter learned it was Jesus, he jumped overboard and swam the length of a football field to meet Him.[9] One can only imagine Peter's angst. There on the shore was the Son of God, the One he professed he would die for yet ended up denying three times. Perhaps in Peter's mind, he thought: *This is it! This is where He really gives it to me for betraying Him.* One gets the sense that he could no longer stand the distress of it all. In that moment, his occupation mattered little. The excitement of the big haul of fish was of no importance to him. The moment he anticipated since he first discovered Christ had arisen was now at hand. Irrespective of the consequences, he had to know what would become of him? Was there any hope?

Instead of encountering an irate Lord eager to render judgment, he found a compassionate Savior who invited His disciples to sit and eat with Him.[10] It was only after they had their fill that Jesus addressed Peter, but not in the way he most likely expected. At that moment, the Prince of Peace asked him three questions. Here is the account:

> When they had finished eating, Jesus said to Simon Peter, "Simon son of John, do you truly love me more than these?" "Yes, Lord," he said, "you know that I love you." Jesus said, "Feed my lambs." Again Jesus said, "Simon son of John, do you truly love me?" He answered, "Yes, Lord, you know that I love you." Jesus said, "Take care of my sheep." The third time he said to

him, "Simon son of John, do you love me?" Peter was hurt because Jesus asked him the third time, "Do you love me?" He said, "Lord, you know all things; you know that I love you." Jesus said, "Feed my sheep."[11]

Note how Christ addressed him as Simon rather than Peter, the name He had bestowed upon him.[12] Again, we observe how the Lord meets us right where we are. More than likely, Peter was not feeling solid like a rock in that moment, let alone part of the foundation on which Christ was to build his church. The weight of his guilt must have been enormous. Gone was his former sense of pride. The man who once stood before Christ and proclaimed he would die for Him was now broken and thoroughly humbled.[13] This was not a condescending address on the part of the Lord. Use of the name Simon, as opposed to Peter, would have allowed for a moment of reflection, back to a time when this disciple first received the revelation that Jesus was the Son of the living God.[14] It was this understanding that led to his name change and a wonderful vision of what was to come. That time was now at hand.

There, in the midst of all of this, Jesus is found to be extending His grace and mercy toward Peter, asking him about matters of love. Three times he had denied his Lord, but now he was given three additional opportunities to profess his love for Christ. How Peter must have marveled at the patience of his Savior! What kindness. What gentleness. After all Peter had done, and as broken as he was, the Lord still saw fit to utilize him in the same manner He said He would. This was possible because Peter had been brought to a place in life where his dependency was strictly upon the Lord. In this place, he truly experienced the love, joy, and peace of being in Christ.

If Jesus was willing to meet Peter in his broken place after denying Him three times, then He will meet you in your brokenness as well. Indeed, I believe the Lord would have met Judas right where he was, but Judas decided his situation was hopeless. In the ultimate act of willfulness, he lashed out in anger at the world by killing himself. What Judas failed to see was that he, too, was a pearl of great value in the eyes of the Father. Christ did not want him to throw his life away; He wanted Judas to repent of his sins and take action so that he could get right with the Father.

May you never reach such a false conclusion in your own life; rather, you should always see yourself as the pearl Christ sold everything for. God has loved you both inside and outside of time. His greatest desire is to have a deep, intimate relationship with you. It is for this reason He has set you free. Perhaps Christ is standing on the shore of your life. Will you jump ship and swim to Him as Peter did? No matter the consequences, are you prepared to face your Savior and repent of your ways? Love, joy, and peace await you.

Notes

Chapter One

[1] Psalm 139:13–16
[2] Psalm 37:23
[3] Romans 8:28
[4] Genesis 1:26
[5] Wesley, J. John Wesley's Notes on the Bible.
http://wesley.nnu.edu/john_wesley/notes/genesis.htm#Chapter+I Commentary
on Genesis 1:28. (accessed: December, 2008). [Clarification added]
[6] A good resource for further study into unifying experiences with God is Dr.
Gerald May's book: Will and Spirit: A Contemplative Psychology. Harper
SanFrancisco (1982).
[7] Proverbs 29:18
[8] The Law is fulfilled by love; see Romans 13:8, 10. Love edifies; see 1
Corinthians 8:1. Love contains patience and kindness, but not envy, boastfulness
or pride; see 1 Corinthians 13:4. There is not rudeness, self-seeking, or record
kept in love, but there is self-control; see 1 Corinthians 13:5. Through love, we
rejoice in the truth, but do not delight in evil; see 1 Corinthian 13:6. Where there
is love, there is protection, trust, hope, and perseverance; see 1 Corinthians 13:7.
The more we know the love of Christ, the more we are filled with the fullness of
God; see Ephesians 3:19.
[9] Genesis 2:23
[10] See Malachi 2:13–15
[11] May, G. Will and Spirit: A Contemplative Psychology. New York, NY.
HarperSanFrancisco. 1982, p. 75.
[12] routine. Webster's New World Dictionary, Second Concise Edition. Nashville,
TN. The World Publishing Company. 1975.
[13] Ibid., see: familiar.
[14] Ibid., see: predictability.

Chapter Two

[1] Matthew 22:37–39
[2] John 8:42
[3] John 14:15
[4] 1 Peter 4:8
[5] Genesis 1:26, 27

6   radah. Strong's Hebrew Bible Dictionary. Electronic source: The SWORD Project, v. 1.5.9. CrossWire Software & Bible Society. Tempe, AZ. Word reference number: 7287.

7   tselem. Strong's Hebrew Bible Dictionary. Electronic source: The SWORD Project, v. 1.5.9. CrossWire Software & Bible Society. Tempe, AZ. Word reference number: 6754.

8   Genesis 2:16, 17

9   Ecclesiastes 7:29

10   yashar. Strong's Hebrew Bible Dictionary. Electronic source: The SWORD Project, v. 1.5.9. CrossWire Software & Bible Society. Tempe, AZ. Word reference number: 3474.

11   Romans 8:22, 23

12   Ecclesiastes 3:11

13   Romans 1:20

14   1 Corinthians 13:12

15   Genesis 1:1

16   See 1 Corinthians 13:12

17   Genesis 3:1–7

18   See Genesis 1:31

19   See Genesis 1:22, 28

20   See Song of Solomon 1:12–15; 3:1–5

21   See Genesis 3:8

22   See Genesis 14:18–20

23   See Exodus 3:2–4

24   See John 14: 9

25   Genesis 3:9

26   Genesis 3:10

27   yare'. Strong's Hebrew Bible Dictionary. Electronic source: The SWORD Project, v. 1.5.9. CrossWire Software & Bible Society. Tempe, AZ. Word reference number: 3372.

28   Genesis 3:11

29   Genesis 3:12

30   Genesis 3:13

31   impute. Webster's New World Dictionary, Second Concise Edition. Nashville, TN. The World Publishing Company. 1975.

32   Romans 5:12

33   Genesis 3:16

34   tshuwqah. Strong's Hebrew Bible Dictionary. Electronic source: The SWORD Project, v. 1.5.9. CrossWire Software & Bible Society. Tempe, AZ. Word reference number: 8669.

35   Genesis 3:17-19

36   Easton, M.G. Easton's Bible Dictionary. Electronic source: http://biblemaximum.com/About/?VERSION=1.4.0 Under the word: sin, citing Hodge.

Chapter Three

1   1 Peter 3:1, 2, 7
2   1 Peter 2:21
3   See Galatians 5:22, 23 for a list of fruits of the Spirit.
4   Galatians 5:19–21
5   See Ephesians 5:21–33; 1 Peter 3:1–7
6   Our spirit is the conduit through which God's energies flow, as demonstrated through; the spirit being the source of passions (see Ezekiel 3:14) as well as the source for volitions (i.e., our will) (see Proverbs 16:32).
7   The soul is the vital and animating principle of who we are in that it is able to keep itself (see Deuteronomy 4:9), seek the Lord (see Deuteronomy 4:29), love the Lord (see Deuteronomy 6:5), serve the Lord (see Deuteronomy 10:12), store God's word (see Deuteronomy 11:18), keep God's law (see Deuteronomy 26:16), obey God (see Deuteronomy 30:2, 6, 10), as well as get wisdom (see Proverbs 19:8).
8   mind. Dictionary.com. The American Heritage Dictionary of the English Language, Fourth Edition. Houghton Mifflin Company. http://dictionary.reference.com/browse/mind (accessed: January 10, 2009).
9   behavior. Dictionary.com. The American Heritage Dictionary of the English Language, Fourth Edition. Houghton Mifflin Company, 2004. http://dictionary.reference.com/browse/behavior (accessed: January 27, 2010).
10   associative learning. Dictionary.com. The American Heritage Dictionary of the English Language, Fourth Edition. Houghton Mifflin Company, 2004. http://dictionary.reference.com/browse/associative_learning (accessed: July 27, 2009).
11   operant conditioning. Dictionary.com. The American Heritage Dictionary of the English Language, Fourth Edition. Houghton Mifflin Company. http://dictionary.reference.com/browse/Operant%20conditioning (accessed: January 4, 2009).
12   habituation. Dictionary.com. The American Heritage Dictionary of the English Language, Fourth Edition. Houghton Mifflin Company. http://dictionary.reference.com/browse/habituation (accessed: January 4, 2009).
13   See Ephesians 5:11
14   sensitization. Dictionary.com. The American Heritage Dictionary of the English Language, Fourth Edition. Houghton Mifflin Company. http://dictionary.reference.com/browse/Sensitization (accessed: January 4, 2009).

[15] proposition. Dictionary.com. The American Heritage Dictionary of the English Language, Fourth Edition. Houghton Mifflin Company, 2004. http://dictionary.reference.com/browse/proposition (accessed: October 30, 2009).

[16] brain. The Columbia Encyclopedia, Sixth Edition. 2008. Encyclopedia.com. http://www.encyclopedia.com/doc/1E1-brain.html (accessed: December 30, 2008).

[17] action potential. Wikipedia, The Free Encyclopedia. Wikipedia.com. http://en.wikipedia.org/wiki/Action_potential (accessed: December 30, 2008).

[18] neuron. Wikipedia, The Free Encyclopedia. Wikipedia.com. http://en.wikipedia.org/wiki/Neuron (accessed: September 11, 2009). Note: This image is adapted from the work of the U.S. Federal Government, and is considered public domain under the terms of Title 17, Chapter 1, Section 105 of the U.S. Code.

[19] norepinephrine. Dictionary.com. The American Heritage Dictionary of the English Language, Fourth Edition. Houghton Mifflin Company, 2004. http://dictionary.reference.com/browse/norepinephrine (accessed: December 30, 2008).

[20] 2 Corinthians 10:3–5

[21] personality. Dictionary.com. The American Heritage Dictionary of the English Language, Fourth Edition. Houghton Mifflin Company, 2004. http://dictionary.reference.com/browse/personality (accessed: December 30, 2008).

[22] proclivity and inclination. Dictionary.com. The American Heritage Dictionary of the English Language, Fourth Edition. Houghton Mifflin Company. http://dictionary.reference.com/browse/proclivity and http://dictionary.reference.com/browse/inclination (accessed: January 6, 2009).

[23] Galatians 5:1

[24] Mark 12:29–31

[25] 2 Corinthians 10:5

Chapter Four

[1] John 16:33

[2] See Joshua 7:20, 21 for covetousness; 1 Samuel 2:22–25 for immorality; 1 Samuel 15:17–23 for rebellion; 1 Kings 12:26–33 for idolatry; and 1 Samuel 25:25–37 for folly.

[3] anakainosis. Strong's Greek Bible Dictionary. Electronic source: The SWORD Project, v. 1.5.9. CrossWire Software & Bible Society. Tempe, AZ. Word reference number: 342.

[4] renovate. Dictionary.com. The American Heritage Dictionary of the English Language, Fourth Edition. Houghton Mifflin Company, 2004.

http://dictionary.classic.reference.com/browse/renovate (accessed: June 03, 2009).

5   Henry, M. Matthew Henry's Concise Commentary on the Whole Bible. Electronic source: http://biblemaximum.com/About/?VERSION=1.4.0 Commentary on Romans 12:2. [clarification added].

6   denial. Dictionary.com. The American Heritage Dictionary of the English Language, Fourth Edition. Houghton Mifflin Company, 2004. http://dictionary1.classic.reference.com/browse/denial (accessed: May 12, 2009).

7   denial. Wikipedia, The Free Encyclopedia. Wikipedia.com. http://en.wikipedia.org/wiki/Denial (accessed: May 12, 2009).

8   Collins, Gary, R. Christian Counseling: A Comprehensive Guide, Revised Edition. W Publishing Group. Nashville, TN. 1988, pp. 353–353.

9   See Matthew 10:1–8

10 Jesus had cured the sick; see John 4:46–54; Matthew 8:1–11, 14–17, 9:20–22, etc. Jesus healed the lame; see Matthew 9:1–8, 12:10–13, etc. Jesus raised the dead; see Mark 5:23; John 11:38–44. Jesus fed multitudes from practically no food at all; see Luke 9:10–17, Mark 8:1–9. Jesus walked on water; see Matthew 14:25–33.

11 Jesus' talk about leaving; see John 12:20–36. Christ's role as servant; see John 13:1–17. See John 13:18–30 for Judas' betrayal, and 31–38 for Peter's denial.

12 John 14:5

13 Jesus' arrest, see John 18:12; His scourging, see John 19:1; His crucifixion, see John 19:16. On Christ being innocent, see Matthew 27:4; 2 Corinthians 5:21; 1 Peter 2:21, 22; 1 John 3:5.

14 John 20:19

15 See Isaiah 53, specifically verse five

16 See John 20:21–23

17 John 20:25

18 John 20:26

19 John 20:28

20 Ibid.

21 See 2 Samuel 11:1

22 2 Samuel 11:3–5

23 See 1 Chronicles 3:1–4

24 See 1 Chronicles 3:4–9

25 See 1 Kings 1:1–31

26 See Leviticus 20:10

27 See 2 Samuel, chapter eleven

28 See 1 Samuel 13:14 and Acts 13:22

29 See 2 Samuel 12

30 See I Samuel 13:14

31   Ephesians 5:9

32   Ephesians 5:11

33   See Genesis 4:1

34   quyin. Strong's Hebrew Bible Dictionary. Electronic source: The SWORD
      Project, v. 1.5.9. CrossWire Software & Bible Society. Tempe, AZ. Word
      reference number: 7014, but also 7013 and 7069.

35   See Whole Bible Commentary Critical and Explanatory by Jameison, Faussett,
      Brown (1871) comments on Genesis 4:1; as well as Matthew Henry's Complete
      Commentary on the Whole Bible (1706), Point I on Genesis 4:1.

36   Genesis 3:15

37   hebel. Strong's Hebrew Bible Dictionary. Electronic source: The SWORD
      Project, v. 1.5.9. CrossWire Software & Bible Society. Tempe, AZ. Word
      reference number: 1892.

38   See Genesis 4:3

39   Henry, M. Matthew Henry's Complete Commentary on the Whole Bible. 1706.
      Electronic source: The SWORD Project, v. 1.5.9. CrossWire Software & Bible
      Society. Tempe, AZ. Commentary on Genesis 4:3, point II, 3.

40   Genesis 4:6, 7

41   See Galatians 5:22, 23

42   Carter, L. and Minirth, F. The Anger Workbook. Thomas Nelson, Inc.
      Nashville, Tenn. 1993. p. 8.

43   See Matthew 22:39

44   chatta'ah. Strong's Hebrew Bible Dictionary. Electronic source: The SWORD
      Project, v. 1.5.9. CrossWire Software & Bible Society. Tempe, AZ. Word
      reference number: 2403.

45   expiate. Dictionary.com. The American Heritage® Dictionary of the English
      Language, Fourth Edition. Houghton Mifflin Company, 2004.
      http://dictionary.reference.com/browse/expiate (accessed: February 14, 2010).

46   Genesis 4:8

47   See Genesis 4:10, 11

48   See Genesis 4:13–16

49   dissonance. Dictionary.com. The American Heritage Dictionary of the English
      Language, Fourth Edition. Houghton Mifflin Company, 2004.
      http://dictionary.classic.reference.com/browse/Dissonance (accessed: June 02,
      2009).

50   cognitive dissonance. Dictionary.com. The American Heritage Dictionary of the
      English Language, Fourth Edition. Houghton Mifflin Company, 2004.
      http://dictionary.classic.reference.com/browse/Cognitive Dissonance (accessed:
      June 02, 2009).

51   God's will for this husband would be that he not abuse his wife, but that he
      would: love her, Ephesians 5:25, 28; honor her, 1 Peter 3:7; be faithful, Malachi
      2:15; be satisfied Proverbs 5:18, 19; provide for her, 1 Timothy 5:8; not allow

himself to fall into temptation, 1 Corinthians 7:5; that he would confer with his wife, Genesis 31:4–16; and that he would lead her with Christ-like character, 1 Corinthians 11:3.

52 See Ephesians 5:11
53 Galatians 6:4
54 2 Timothy 1:7
55 See 1 Samuel 13:5–8 for an example of how fear demoralized the army of Israel.
56 Galatians 5:1
57 Galatians 6:2
58 Ephesians 5:11
59 1 John 1:9
60 contrite. Dictionary.com. The American Heritage Dictionary of the English Language, Fourth Edition. Houghton Mifflin Company, 2004. http://dictionary.classic.reference.com/browse/contrite (accessed: June 07, 2009).
61 See Romans 12:2
62 Galatians 5:19–21
63 pharmakeia. Strong's Greek Bible Dictionary. Electronic source: The SWORD Project, v. 1.5.9. CrossWire Software & Bible Society. Tempe, AZ. Word reference number: 5331.

Chapter Five

1 repression. Dictionary.com. The American Heritage Dictionary of the English Language, Fourth Edition. Houghton Mifflin Company, 2004. http://dictionary.reference.com/browse/repression (accessed: June 14, 2009).
2 Erdelyi, M. H. The Unified Theory of Repression. Behavior and Brain Sciences (2006) 29:5. Cambridge University Press. Cambridge, MA., p. 499.
3 John 10:10
4 Ibid, 506.
5 memory. Dictionary.com. The American Heritage Dictionary of the English Language, Fourth Edition. Houghton Mifflin Company, 2004. http://dictionary.reference.com/browse/memory (accessed: June 15, 2009).
6 encoding. Dictionary.com. The American Heritage Stedman's Medical Dictionary. Houghton Mifflin Company. http://dictionary.reference.com/browse/encoding (accessed: June 15, 2009).
7 retrieval. Dictionary.com. The American Heritage Stedman's Medical Dictionary. Houghton Mifflin Company. http://dictionary.reference.com/browse/retrieval (accessed: June 15, 2009).
8 semantic memory. Dictionary.com. WordNet 3.0. Princeton University. http://dictionary.reference.com/browse/semantic memory (accessed: June 15, 2009).

9   episodic memory. Wikipedia, The Free Encyclopedia. Wikipedia.com.
    http://en.wikipedia.org/wiki/Episodic_memory (accessed: June 15, 2009).

10 implicit memory. Wikipedia, The Free Encyclopedia. Wikipedia.com.
    http://en.wikipedia.org/wiki/Implicit_memory (accessed: June 15, 2009).

11 Ashcroft, M.H. Human Memory and Cognition. Harper Collins Publishers.
    Glenview, IL. 1989.

12 Erdelyi, M. H. The Unified Theory of Repression. Behavioral and Brain
    Sciences (2006) 29:5. Cambridge University Press. Cambridge, MA. p. 509.

13 Ibid.

14 Proverbs 14:15

15 prudent. Dictionary.com. The American Heritage Dictionary of the English
    Language, Fourth Edition. Houghton Mifflin Company, 2004.
    http://dictionary.reference.com/browse/prudent (accessed: June 20, 2009).

16 Ephesians 4:25–27

17 Dokimazo pas katecho kalos. Greek translation of 1 Thessalonians 5:21.
    Strong's Greek Bible Dictionary. Electronic source: The SWORD Project, v.
    1.5.9. CrossWire Software & Bible Society. Tempe, AZ. Word reference
    numbers: 1381, 3956, 2722, and 2570.

18 test. Dictionary.com. The American Heritage Dictionary of the English
    Language, Fourth Edition. Houghton Mifflin Company, 2004.
    http://dictionary.reference.com/browse/test (accessed: February 23, 2010).

19 Psalm 26:2

20 Hebrews 12:1–3

21 See Matthew 26:36–46

22 See John 15:13

23 For a full account of what transpired between Jesus and His disciples in the
    garden, see Matthew 26:36–46.

24 May, G. G. Will & Spirit: A Contemplative Psychology. Harper SanFrancisco.
    New York, NY. 1982, p. 29.

25 Ibid, p. 30.

26 awareness. Wikipedia, The Free Encyclopedia. Wikipedia.com.
    http://en.wikipedia.org/wiki/Awareness (accessed: June 17, 2009).

27 empathy. Dictionary.com. The American Heritage Dictionary of the English
    Language, Fourth Edition. Houghton Mifflin Company, 2004.
    http://dictionary.reference.com/browse/empathy (accessed: June 17, 2009).

28 sympathy. Dictionary.com. The American Heritage Dictionary of the English
    Language, Fourth Edition. Houghton Mifflin Company, 2004.
    http://dictionary.reference.com/browse/sympathy (accessed: June 17, 2009).

29 reason. Dictionary.com. The American Heritage Dictionary of the English
    Language, Fourth Edition. Houghton Mifflin Company, 2004.
    http://dictionary.reference.com/browse/reason (accessed: June 09, 2009).

30 See Ecclesiastes 3:11 and Luke 11:9

31 Matthew 7:24, 25
32 judgement. Dictionary.com. The American Heritage Dictionary of the English Language, Fourth Edition. Houghton Mifflin Company, 2004. http://dictionary.reference.com/browse/judgement (accessed: June 12, 2009).
33 emotion. Dictionary.com. The American Heritage Dictionary of the English Language, Fourth Edition. Houghton Mifflin Company, 2004. http://dictionary.reference.com/browse/emotion (accessed: June 14, 2009).
34 Limbic system. Medline Plus: Medical Encyclopedia. nlm.nih.gov. http://www.nlm.nih.gov/medlineplus/ency/imagepages/19244.htm (accessed: June 14, 2009).
35 See Job 26
36 See Job 38:4–11
37 Hebrews 1:3
38 See Galatians 5:19–21
39 See Galatians 5:22, 23
40 epilanthánomai. Strong's Greek Bible Dictionary. Electronic source: The SWORD Project, v. 1.5.9. CrossWire Software & Bible Society. Tempe, AZ. Word reference number: 1950
41 2 Timothy 1:7
42 See 2 Corinthians 10:5
43 Philippians 4:11–13

Chapter Six

1 reasonable. Dictionary.com. The American Heritage Dictionary of the English Language, Fourth Edition. Houghton Mifflin Company, 2004. http://dictionary.reference.com/browse/reasonable (accessed: June 22, 2009).
2 rationalize. Dictionary.com. The American Heritage Stedman's Medical Dictionary. Houghton Mifflin Company. http://dictionary.reference.com/browse/rationalize (accessed: June 22, 2009).
3 Albert Ellis. AllPsych Online: The Virtual Psychology Classroom. Allpsych.com. http://allpsych.com/biographies/ellis.html (accessed: June 27, 2009).
4 Dryden W. and Neenan M. Essential Rational Emotive Behavior Therapy. Wiley Publishing. Hoboken, NJ. 2000.
5 1 Peter 3:7
6 Matthew 7:9–11
7 Leviticus 23:39–43
8 Regarding: Jesus' authority, origin, and return; see John 7:16, 17, 28, 29, 33–34. Christ as the living water; see John 7:37–39. Israel felt divided over Jesus' behavior; see John 7:40–44. Attempted stoning of the female fornicator; see John 8:1–11. Jesus' announcement that He is light of the world; see John 8:12.

For the Lord's healing the blind man and proclamation that He is the good shepherd; see John 9:1–7; 10:11.

9 Psalms 45:2–5

10 John 1:46

11 See Mark 3:20, 21

12 Teaching with authority; see Matthew 4:23, 7:29; Luke 13:22. Casting out demons and healing the sick; see Matthew 8:16, 14:14, 15:30.

13 See John 9

14 See John 3:1–10

15 Luke 16:14, 15

16 justify. Dictionary.com. The American Heritage Dictionary of the English Language, Fourth Edition. Houghton Mifflin Company, 2004. http://dictionary.reference.com/browse/justify (accessed: June 23, 2009).

17 just. Dictionary.com. The American Heritage Dictionary of the English Language, Fourth Edition. Houghton Mifflin Company, 2004. http://dictionary.reference.com/browse/just (accessed: June 23, 2009).

18 valid. Dictionary.com. The American Heritage Dictionary of the English Language, Fourth Edition. Houghton Mifflin Company, 2004. http://dictionary.reference.com/browse/valid (accessed: June 23, 2009).

19 justify. Dictionary.com. The American Heritage Dictionary of the English Language, Fourth Edition. Houghton Mifflin Company, 2004. http://dictionary.reference.com/browse/justify (accessed: June 23, 2009).

20 Romans 3:23

21 pride. Dictionary.com. The American Heritage Dictionary of the English Language, Fourth Edition. Houghton Mifflin Company, 2004. http://dictionary.reference.com/browse/pride (accessed: June 23, 2009).

22 See Matthew 13:45, 46

23 See Matthew 10:37–42

24 See Ephesians 4:1

25 See Acts 5:41

26 See Colossians 1:10

27 Matthew 6:1–5

28 Proverbs 14:12

29 maveth. Strong's Hebrew Bible Dictionary. Electronic Source: The SWORD Project, v. 1.5.9. CrossWire Software & Bible Society. Tempe, AZ. Reference number: 4194.

30 See Matthew 11:29, 30

Chapter Seven

[1] anthistemi. Strong's Greek Bible Dictionary. Electronic Source: The SWORD Project, v. 1.5.9. CrossWire Software & Bible Society. Tempe, AZ. Reference number: 436.

[2] typology. Dictionary.com. The American Heritage Dictionary of the English Language, Fourth Edition. Houghton Mifflin Company. http://dictionary.reference.com/browse/typology (accessed: January 13, 2009).

[3] See Romans 5:12–21

[4] See John 1:14

[5] See Matthew 1:23

[6] Isaiah 14:12–14

[7] Lucifer. Smith's Bible Dictionary. Electronic source: http://biblemaximum.com/About/?VERSION=1.4.0

[8] heylel. Strong's Hebrew Bible Dictionary. Electronic Source: The SWORD Project, v. 1.5.9. CrossWire Software & Bible Society. Tempe, AZ. Word reference number: 1966.

[9] halal. Strong's Hebrew Bible Dictionary. Electronic Source: The SWORD Project, v. 1.5.9. CrossWire Software & Bible Society. Tempe, AZ. Word reference number: 1984.

[10] Ibid.

[11] See Job 1:6, 2:1; Zechariah 3:1, 2

[12] Jameison, R., Faussett, A.R., Brown, D. Commentary Critical and Explanatory on the Whole Bible. Electronic source: http://biblemaximum.com/About/?VERSION=1.4.0 (accessed: January 15, 2009). Commentary on Revelation 12:7.

[13] Ibid.

[14] Romans 8:32–39

[15] See Jeremiah 32:17, 27 for omnipotent; 1 John 3:20 for omniscient; Psalm 139:7–12 for omnipresent; and John 3:16; Romans 5:5, 8:39; Titus 3:4; 1 John 3:16, 4:9 for ever-loving.

[16] Problem of evil. Wikipedia, The Free Encyclopedia. Wikipedia.com. http://en.wikipedia.org/wiki/Problem_of_evil (accessed: January 15, 2009); as cited in 2000 Years of Disbelief, by James A. Haught. Prometheus Books. 1996.

[17] Genesis 3:15

[18] See Revelation 12:9, 12; 20:2, 10

[19] Habakkuk 1:2–4

[20] Habakkuk 2:3

[21] Isaiah 55:8

[22] Job 42:2–3

[23] Romans 5:3, 4

[24] Hebrews 5:8

25 1 Corinthians 13:12
26 See Ephesians 6:10–17
27 1 Peter 5:8
28 Revelation 12:9
29 Genesis 3:1
30 See Genesis 3:6
31 John. 8:44 [clarification added]
32 Jameison, R., Faussett, A.R., Brown, D. Commentary Critical and Explanatory on the Whole Bible. Electronic source: http://biblemaximum.com/About/?VERSION=1.4.0 Commentary on John 8:44.
33 See Mark 4:3–9
34 Mark 4:15
35 Romans 1:16
36 See Romans 10:17
37 John 17:17
38 hagiazo. Strong's Greek Bible Dictionary. Electronic source: The SWORD Project, v. 1.5.9. CrossWire Software & Bible Society. Tempe, AZ. Word reference number 0037.
39 See Luke 4:1, 2
40 Luke 4:1–3
41 Matthew 3:17
42 Brozek, J. "Psychology of Human Starvation and Nutritional Rehabilitation." The Scientific Monthly, 70. 1950. pp. 270–274.
43 refeeding syndrome. Wikipedia, The Free Dictionary. Wikipedia.com. http://en.wikipedia.org/wiki/Refeeding_syndrome (accessed: August 28, 2009).
44 See Luke 3:21, 22
45 galvanize. Dictionary.com. The American Heritage Dictionary of the English Language, Fourth Edition. Houghton Mifflin Company, 2004. http://dictionary.reference.com/browse/galvanize (accessed: August 28, 2009).
46 Luke 4:6, 7
47 2 Thessalonians 2:3, 4
48 Job 1:6–11
49 John 13:2, 27
50 John 12:1–6
51 2 Corinthians 11:14
52 Psalm 119:105
53 Psalm 97:11
54 See Job 1:14; Luke 7:24; 9:52
55 See 2 Corinthians 10:5
56 See Ephesians 4:27
57 See Ephesians 2:10
58 1 Corinthians 5:1–8

59   2 Corinthians 2:6–11

60   See Proverbs 16:18

61   afflict. Dictionary.com. The American Heritage Dictionary of the English Language, Fourth Edition. Houghton Mifflin Company, 2004. http://dictionary.reference.com/browse/afflict (accessed: February 08, 2009).

62   Luke 13:10–17

63   See Luke 13:14–16

64   astheneia. Strong's Greek Bible Dictionary. Electronic source: The SWORD Project, v. 1.5.9. CrossWire Software & Bible Society. Tempe, AZ. Word reference number: 0769.

65   See Matthew 6:25–34

66   2 Corinthians 10:5

67   Ephesians 4:22–24

68   2 Corinthians 5:17

69   See Romans 7

70   Mahill, W. Growing A Passionate Heart: Help, Hope, and Healing for Women Wounded by Childhood Sexual Abuse. Xulon Press. Longwood, FL. 2007. p. 102.

71   See Ephesians 5:11

72   Ibid., p. 86. [clarification added]

73   Ephesians 4:24

74   James 5:8, 9

75   Ephesians 6:11–17

76   See James 1:8, 4:8

77   See Jeremiah 17:9

78   See 2 Timothy 1:7

79   John 14:27

80   See Ephesians 2:14–22

81   See Philippians 4:12, 13

82   See 1 Corinthians 14:33

83   See James 3:17

84   faith. Dictionary.com. The American Heritage Dictionary of the English Language, Fourth Edition. Houghton Mifflin Company, 2004. http://dictionary.reference.com/browse/faith (accessed: February 11, 2009).

85   See Hebrews, chapter eleven

86   See Matthew 9:18, 19, 23–26 for ruler's daughter; Matthew 9:20–22 for afflicted woman; Matthew 9:27–31 and Mark 10:46–52 for blind men receiving their sight.

87   Gerald May. Addiction & Grace: Love and Spirituality in the Healing of Addictions. HarperOne. New York, NY. 1988. p. 128.

88   See Matthew 4:1–11

89   salvation. Dictionary.com. The American Heritage Dictionary of the English Language, Fourth Edition. Houghton Mifflin Company, 2004. http://dictionary.reference.com/browse/salvation (accessed: February 11, 2009).

90   John 14:6

91   See John 8:31, 32

92   See Philippians 2:12

93   See Acts 28:25 and 2 Timothy 3:16

94   1 Corinthians 2:10–12

95   2 Timothy 1:7

Chapter Eight

1   shepherd. Dictionary.com. The American Heritage Dictionary of the English Language, Fourth Edition. Houghton Mifflin Company, 2004. http://dictionary.reference.com/browse/shepherd (accessed: February 15, 2009).

2   Isaiah 40:11

3   See Psalm 23:2

4   See Deuteronomy 8:2 and Matthew 4:4

5   See John 1:18

6   See John 4:5–14

7   See Psalm 23:2

8   John 10:11

9   kalos. Strong's Greek Bible Dictionary. Electronic Source: The SWORD Project, v. 1.5.9. CrossWire Software & Bible Society. Tempe, AZ. Word reference number: 2570.

10   morality. Dictionary.com. The American Heritage Dictionary of the English Language, Fourth Edition. Houghton Mifflin Company, 2004. http://dictionary.reference.com/browse/morality (accessed: March 18, 2009).

11   See 2 Corinthians 5:21; 1 Peter 2:21–25; 1 John 3:5

12   See Psalm 23:1 for wants; see Matthew 6:25–34 for needs; and John 10:28 for provider/protector.

13   See 1 Peter 5:4

14   Phaneroo. Strong's Greek Bible Dictionary. Electronic Source: The SWORD Project, v. 1.5.9. CrossWire Software & Bible Society. Tempe, AZ. Word reference number: 5319.

15   manifest. Dictionary.com. The American Heritage Dictionary of the English Language, Fourth Edition. Houghton Mifflin Company, 2004. http://dictionary.reference.com/browse/manifest (accessed: February 15, 2009).

16   John 10:3, 4 (emphasis added)

17   Micah 5:1–5

18   See Philippians 4:12, 13

19   Psalm 23:3

20 mediate. Dictionary.com. The American Heritage® Dictionary of the English Language, Fourth Edition. Houghton Mifflin Company, 2004. http://dictionary.reference.com/browse/mediate (accessed: February 15, 2009).

21 Deuteronomy 5:1–5

22 See Romans 6:23

23 See Hebrews 4:15

24 Hebrews 10:10

25 See Hebrews 8:6

26 Luke 22:31, 32

27 See Matthew 16:13–17

28 1 Timothy 2:5, 6

29 antilutron. Strong's Greek Bible Dictionary. Electronic Source: The SWORD Project, v. 1.5.9. CrossWire Software & Bible Society. Tempe, AZ. Word reference number: 0487.

30 redeem. Dictionary.com. The American Heritage Dictionary of the English Language, Fourth Edition. Houghton Mifflin Company, 2004. http://dictionary.reference.com/browse/redeem (accessed: February 16, 2009).

31 Hebrews 9:27, 28

32 Jameison, R., Faussett, A.R., Brown, D. Commentary Critical and Explanatory on the Whole Bible. Electronic source: http://biblemaximum.com/About/?VERSION=1.4.0 Commentary on 1 Timothy 2:5.

33 See Isaiah 53

34 Colossians 2:13–15

35 paraptoma. Strong's Greek Bible Dictionary. Electronic Source: The SWORD Project, v. 1.5.9. CrossWire Software & Bible Society. Tempe, AZ. Word reference number: 3900.

36 suzoopoieo. Strong's Greek Bible Dictionary. Electronic Source: The SWORD Project, v. 1.5.9. CrossWire Software & Bible Society. Tempe, AZ. Word reference number: 4806.

37 See Genesis 1:28

38 Genesis 14:18–20

39 The Holy Bible. The New International Version Student Bible, Revised. Study notes for Genesis 14:18. Zondervan. Grand Rapids, MI 2002. p. 19.

40 Hebrews 7:11

41 Hebrews 7:15–19

42 Jameison, R., Faussett, A.R., Brown, D. Commentary Critical and Explanatory on the Whole Bible. Electronic source: http://biblemaximum.com/About/?VERSION=1.4.0 Commentary on Hebrews 7:16.

43 See Romans 5:21–26

44 See Hebrews 9:13, 14

45   Hebrews 7:24, 25

46   See Hebrews 2:17

47   Hebrews 2:18

48   peirazo. Strong's Greek Bible Dictionary. Electronic Source: The SWORD Project, v. 1.5.9. CrossWire Software & Bible Society. Tempe, AZ. Word reference number: 3985.

49   endeavor. Dictionary.com. The American Heritage Dictionary of the English Language, Fourth Edition. Houghton Mifflin Company, 2004. http://dictionary.reference.com/browse/endeavor (accessed: February 21, 2009).

50   Acts 3:26

51   See Romans 3:29, 30

52   eulogeo. Strong's Greek Bible Dictionary. Electronic Source: The SWORD Project, v. 1.5.9. CrossWire Software & Bible Society. Tempe, AZ. Word reference number: 2127.

53   Coffman, J. Commentary of the New Testament. Electronic source: http://biblemaximum.com/About/?VERSION=1.4.0 Commentary on Acts 3:26.

54   See Genesis 14:18

55   salem. Strong's Hebrew Bible Dictionary. Electronic Source: The SWORD Project, v. 1.5.9. CrossWire Software & Bible Society. Tempe, AZ. Word reference number: 8004.

56   Matthew 2:2

57   Magi. Smith's Bible Dictionary. Electronic Source: http://biblemaximum.com/About/?VERSION=1.4.0

58   See Daniel 5:11

59   proskuneo. Strong's Hebrew Bible Dictionary. Electronic Source: The SWORD Project, v. 1.5.9. CrossWire Software & Bible Society. Tempe, AZ. Word reference number: 4352.

60   John 18:33–37

61   basileia. Strong's Greek Bible Dictionary. Electronic Source: The SWORD Project, v. 1.5.9. CrossWire Software & Bible Society. Tempe, AZ. Word reference number: 0932.

62   See Isaiah 9:7 and Luke 1:32, 33

63   See Ephesians 2:2 regarding Satan's level of rule. See Revelation 12:9 for the devil's dethroning.

64   Psalm 72:8

65   Zechariah 14:9

66   See Isaiah 45:23 and Philippians 2:10

67   Revelation 11:15

68   Psalm 45:6

69   shebet. Strong's Hebrew Bible Dictionary. Electronic Source: The SWORD Project, v. 1.5.9. CrossWire Software & Bible Society. Tempe, AZ. Word reference number: 7626.

70 Isaiah 32:1
71 tsedeq. Strong's Hebrew Bible Dictionary. Electronic Source: The SWORD Project, v. 1.5.9. CrossWire Software & Bible Society. Tempe, AZ. Word reference number: 6664.
72 Jeremiah 23:5
73 See Matthew 13:45, 46
74 See the book of Ecclesiastes
75 Matthew 10:32
76 Romans 10:9, 10
77 1 John 4:15

Chapter Nine

1   Romans 8:1, 2
2   Romans 7:25
3   2 Corinthians 5:21
4   Jameison, R., Faussett, A.R., Brown, D. Commentary Critical and Explanatory on the Whole Bible. Electronic source: http://biblemaximum.com/About/?VERSION=1.4.0 Commentary on Romans 8:1.
5   Romans 8:5–8
6   See Proverbs 14:12
7   Romans 8:7, 8
8   echthra. Strong's Greek Bible Dictionary. Electronic Source: The SWORD Project, v. 1.5.9. CrossWire Software & Bible Society. Tempe, AZ. Word reference number: 2189.
9   1 John 2:20, 27
10 meno. Strong's Greek Bible Dictionary. Electronic Source: The SWORD Project, v. 1.5.9. CrossWire Software & Bible Society. Tempe, AZ. Word reference number: 0500.
11 See 2 Corinthians 10:5
12 chrisma. Strong's Greek Bible Dictionary. Electronic Source: The SWORD Project, v. 1.5.9. CrossWire Software & Bible Society. Tempe, AZ. Word reference number: 5545.
13 endow. Dictionary.com. The American Heritage Dictionary of the English Language, Fourth Edition. Houghton Mifflin Company, 2004. http://dictionary.reference.com/browse/endow (accessed: March 26, 2009).
14 See 1 Corinthians 12:7–12
15 1 Kings 3:5
16 1 Kings 3:6–9
17 shama. Strong's Hebrew Bible Dictionary. Electronic Source: The SWORD Project, v. 1.5.9. CrossWire Software & Bible Society. Tempe, AZ. Word reference number: 8085.

[18] 1 Corinthians 2:10–16

[19] parakletos. Strong's Greek Bible Dictionary. Electronic Source: The SWORD Project, v. 1.5.9. CrossWire Software & Bible Society. Tempe, AZ. Word reference number: 3875.

[20] intercessor. Dictionary.com. The American Heritage Dictionary of the English Language, Fourth Edition. Houghton Mifflin Company, 2004. http://dictionary.reference.com/browse/intercessor (accessed: March 31, 2009).

[21] Jeremiah 32:18, 19

[22] gadowl and etsah. Strong's Hebrew Bible Dictionary. Electronic Source: The SWORD Project, v. 1.5.9. CrossWire Software & Bible Society. Tempe, AZ. Word reference numbers: 1419 and 6098.

[23] See Isaiah 25:1; 28:29

[24] John 15:26

[25] See John 15:18–25

[26] See John 14:6

[27] See Galatians 4:7

[28] John 16:5–11

[29] Matthew Henry's Complete Commentary on the Whole Bible. Electronic source: The SWORD Project, v. 1.5.9. CrossWire Bible Society. Tempe, AZ. Commentary on: John 16:8, point I [2] (2).

[30] elegcho. Strong's Greek Bible Dictionary. Electronic Source: The SWORD Project, v. 1.5.9. CrossWire Software & Bible Society. Tempe, AZ. Word reference number: 1651.

[31] confute. Dictionary.com. The American Heritage Dictionary of the English Language, Fourth Edition. Houghton Mifflin Company, 2004. http://dictionary.reference.com/browse/confute (accessed: April 01, 2009).

[32] Coffman, J. Commentary of the New Testament. Electronic source: http://biblemaximum.com/About/?VERSION=1.4.0 Commentary on John 16:8.

[33] dikaiosune. Strong's Greek Bible Dictionary. Electronic Source: The SWORD Project, v. 1.5.9. CrossWire Software & Bible Society. Tempe, AZ. Word reference number: 1343.

[34] equity. Dictionary.com. The American Heritage Dictionary of the English Language, Fourth Edition. Houghton Mifflin Company, 2004. http://dictionary.reference.com/browse/equity (accessed: April 01, 2009).

[35] Coffman, J. Commentary of the New Testament. Electronic source: http://biblemaximum.com/About/?VERSION=1.4.0 Commentary on John 16:8.

[36] John 16:11

[37] krisis. Strong's Greek Bible Dictionary. Electronic Source: The SWORD Project, v. 1.5.9. CrossWire Software & Bible Society. Tempe, AZ. Word reference number: 2920.

[38] See Genesis 3:15 and John 2:19–22.

39 regenerate. Dictionary.com. The American Heritage Dictionary of the English Language, Fourth Edition. Houghton Mifflin Company, 2004. http://dictionary.reference.com/browse/regenerate (accessed: April 03, 2009).

40 reform. Dictionary.com. The American Heritage Dictionary of the English Language, Fourth Edition. Houghton Mifflin Company, 2004. http://dictionary.reference.com/browse/reform (accessed: April 05, 2009).

41 John 3:1–5

42 gennao. Strong's Greek Bible Dictionary. Electronic Source: The SWORD Project, v. 1.5.9. CrossWire Software & Bible Society. Tempe, AZ. Word reference number: 1080.

43 eido. Strong's Greek Bible Dictionary. Electronic Source: The SWORD Project, v. 1.5.9. CrossWire Software & Bible Society. Tempe, AZ. Word reference number: 1492.

44 See Micah 1:7; 3:2, 3; 5:13, 14

45 See Micah 1:14

46 Micah 3:8

47 koach. Strong's Hebrew Bible Dictionary. Electronic Source: The SWORD Project, v. 1.5.9. CrossWire Software & Bible Society. Tempe, AZ. Word reference number: 3581

48 See Exodus 3:7

49 For great leaders, see Hebrews 11:8–10, 23–28; inspired prophets, see 1 Peter 1:10–12; oracles, see Romans 3:2; the priesthood, see Romans 9:3–5; the Law, see Galatians 3:16–25; Messianic promises, see Acts 3:18–26; the Temple, see Hebrews 9:1–10; and His covenants, see Jeremiah 31:31–33.

50 For idolatry, see Hosea 13:1–4; for hypocrisy, see Isaiah 1:11–14; for disobedience, see Jeremiah 7:22–28; for externalism, see Matthew 23:1–33; for unbelief, see Romans 11:1–31. The outlines appearing in this section were adopted from the Biblical Cyclopedic Index of The Open Bible, Expanded Edition. Thomas Nelson, Nashville, TN. 1985. p. 170.

51 See John 4:23, 24

52 See James 4:8

53 Leviticus 11:44. Also see 1 Peter 1:15, 16.

54 For God, see Romans 12:1–2; society, see Romans 12:3–21; government, see Romans 13:1–7; and neighbors, see Romans 13:8–14.

55 Romans 14:1–3

56 See Romans 14:5

57 See Leviticus 26:1

58 Romans 14:6–8, 13–16

59 law. Smith's Bible Dictionary. Thomas Nelson Publishers, Nashville, TN. 2002. p. 349.

60 Ibid.

61 See Matthew 5:17 and Galatians 2:16; 3:24

62 Disciplines of abstinence involve: solitude, silence, fasting, frugality, chastity, secrecy, and sacrifice. Disciplines of engagement involve: study, worship, celebration, service, prayer, fellowship, confession, and submission. An excellent study on these disciplines can be found in Dallas Willard's work, The Spirit of the Disciplines: Understanding How God Changes Lives. HarperSanFrancisco. 1991.

63 Romans 14:17

64 eirene. Strong's Greek Bible Dictionary. Electronic Source: The SWORD Project, v. 1.5.9. CrossWire Software & Bible Society. Tempe, AZ. Word reference number: 1515.

65 Coffman, J. Commentary of the New Testament. Electronic source: http://biblemaximum.com/About/?VERSION=1.4.0 Commentary on Romans 14:17.

Chapter Ten

1 John 8:34–36

2 See Philippians 4:13

3 pathological. Dictionary.com. The American Heritage Dictionary of the English Language, Fourth Edition. Houghton Mifflin Company, 2004. http://dictionary.reference.com/browse/pathological (accessed: July 15, 2009).

4 Carter, L. and Minirth, F. The Anger Workbook. Nelson Impact. Nashville, Tenn. See chapter one for these points on self-preservation.

5 See 1 Peter 5:8

6 2 Peter 3:9

7 contrite. Dictionary.com. The American Heritage Dictionary of the English Language, Fourth Edition. Houghton Mifflin Company, 2004. http://dictionary.reference.com/browse/contrite (accessed: July 17, 2009).

8 See John 21:1–6

9 See John 21:7–10

10 See John 21:12, 13

11 John 21:15–17

12 See Matthew 16:18

13 See Mark 14:29–31

14 See Matthew 16:13–18

CPSIA information can be obtained at www.ICGtesting.com
Printed in the USA
LVOW04s1439040315

429260LV00017B/181/P